W9-CYT-191

Praise for *Dust Bowl Girls*

"A compelling, heartwarming story of a group of college students determined to accomplish the impossible. This is a book you can't put down."
—*The Denver Post*

"Like other good sports histories, this one allows us to sit in the stands and watch a forgotten era when times were tough, odds were long, and underdogs rose to the occasion."   —*Minneapolis Star Tribune*

"A hidden gem of a story. Equal parts social history and sports legend come to life, Reeder's meticulous research and play-by-play game accounts are a fitting tribute to Coach Babb and the trailblazing athletes he inspired."
—*Library Journal*, starred review

"If you are a sports fan . . . do yourself a favor and pick up the new book *Dust Bowl Girls*."   —*The Oklahoman*

"A vivid, compelling story."   —*The Wichita Eagle*

"Lydia Reeder has crafted a thrilling, cinematic story that seems destined for the big screen."
—Karen Abbott, *New York Times* bestselling author
of *Liar, Temptress, Soldier, Spy*

"This is a multilayered history and a compelling story as the women who played basketball for OPC reveal much about their time and place."
—*New York Journal of Books*

"Destined to become a classic of sports literature."
—Patrick B. McGuigan, CapitolBeatOK.com

"Fun. Heartwarming. The story of a little-known but important moment in the history of basketball and women's sports in general."

—Erica Westly, author of *Fastpitch*

"Fascinating." —*Garden & Gun*

"Based on extensive research and told with the talented storytelling ability of the author, *Dust Bowl Girls* is an important and enjoyable story."

—Virginia Peters, former women's basketball coach
and Director of Women's Intercollegiate Athletics
at the University of Central Oklahoma

"*Dust Bowl Girls* reads like something pulled from the imagination of a Hollywood dreamer. However, it is a true story of a group of Oklahoma Dust Bowl farm girls melded together by a one-legged coach into the finest basketball team of the Depression era. This epic sports story is the stuff of which legends are made."

—W. Lynne Draper, former president and CEO of the
Jim Thorpe Association and the Oklahoma Sports Hall of Fame

"Reeder unearths the story a ragtag group of women—some of them teenagers—who took the first steps to proving women could be athletes, too. It's an inspiring story." —Jen A. Miller, author of *Running: A Love Story*

"Engaging storytelling. Equal parts personal homage to Babb (the author's great-uncle) and surprising underdog story." —*Publishers Weekly*

"Worthwhile and entertaining. As she tells the amazing story of Babb and his underdog women's basketball team, Reeder also reveals the challenges facing serious female athletes during the 1920s and '30s, including the perceived risk of 'destroying their feminine image by invading a man's world.' A heartwarmingly inspirational tale." —*Kirkus Reviews*

DUST BOWL GIRLS

★ ★ ★ ★ ★ ★ ★ ★ ★ ★ ★ ★ ★

The Inspiring Story of the Team That Barnstormed Its Way to Basketball Glory

Lydia Reeder

ALGONQUIN BOOKS
OF CHAPEL HILL
2017

Published by
ALGONQUIN BOOKS OF CHAPEL HILL
Post Office Box 2225
Chapel Hill, North Carolina 27515-2225

a division of
WORKMAN PUBLISHING
225 Varick Street
New York, New York 10014

© 2017 by Lydia Reeder. All rights reserved.
First paperback edition, Algonquin Books of Chapel Hill, December 2017. Originally published in hardcover by Algonquin Books of Chapel Hill in January 2017.
Printed in the United States of America.
Published simultaneously in Canada by Thomas Allen & Son Limited.
Design by Steve Godwin.

From the author's personal collection: pages 19, 148, 171, 259, 261; courtesy Thelma Worley Smith: page 28; courtesy Truby Studio, Durant, Oklahoma: pages 31, 52, 75, 76, 93, 96, 98, 114, 203; courtesy Cindy Berry: pages 29, 40; courtesy Curt Teich and Company, No 0A4230: page 46; courtesy the Library of Congress: page 158; courtesy of Tyrrell Historical Library, Beaumont Public Library System, Beaumont, Texas: page 165; courtesy John Gasquet / *The Shreveport Times*: page 245; courtesy Irene Williams' family: page 249; courtesy Virginia Hamilton Childers: page 257; photo courtesy Margaret Seaton: page 258. Best efforts were made to seek permission to reprint all photos in the book.

Library of Congress Cataloging-in-Publication Data
Names: Reeder, Lydia, author.
Title: Dust bowl girls : the inspiring story of the team that barnstormed its way to basketball glory / Lydia Reeder.
Description: First edition. | Chapel Hill, North Carolina : Algonquin Books of Chapel Hill, 2017. | "Published simultaneously in Canada by Thomas Allen & Son Limited." | Includes bibliographical references.
Identifiers: LCCN 2016016234 | ISBN 9781616204662 (hardcover)
Subjects: LCSH: Babb, Sam, 1891–1937. | Harris, Doll, 1913–2001. | Oklahoma Presbyterian College—Basketball—History. | Basketball coaches—Oklahoma—Biography. | Women basketball players—Oklahoma—Biography. | Basketball for women—Oklahoma—History.
Classification: LCC GV885.43 .O46 2017 | DDC 796.323/630976662—dc23
LC record available at https://lccn.loc.gov/2016016234

ISBN 978-1-61620-740-3 (paperback)

10 9 8 7 6 5 4 3 2 1
First Paperback Edition

For my grandmother,
Lydia May Babb Thomas,
and her big brother—
Sam Babb

There are some things you learn best in calm, and some in storm.

—WILLA CATHER, *The Song of the Lark*

★ Contents ★

★ CHAPTER 1 ★

New Recruit

February 1930

Doll Harris crouched in ready position, took a deep breath, and focused on the basketball now in enemy territory. More than anything, she wanted the ball back. Doll's high school team, the Cement Lady Bulldogs, was battling its archrival, the Fletcher Lady Wildcats, for the Southwest Oklahoma district championship and the right to play in the regional tournament. Doll was a senior and the Bulldogs' star forward. The game, in its final seconds, was tied, 28–28. The hometown crowd of 350 leaped to their feet when the Bulldog guards fought hard for the ball, the rubber soles of their Converse high-tops rendering sharp chirps with every move. The referee, expecting the tangle of players to commit a foul at any minute, held his whistle ready.

"Get the ball to Doll, you all," the pep squad chanted.

"Ball to Doll!" the crowd joined in.

Members of the boys' basketball team, scheduled to play directly after this game, were on their feet stomping against the bleachers, the racket thundering against the gym's redbrick walls. Rumor had it they were all in love with Doll. Part Irish and part Cherokee, she was petite—not much over five feet tall—with an athletic figure and thick shoulder-length black hair. For such a small girl, she had large hands. This strange attribute, the boys whispered among themselves, helped her to guide shots magically over the rim and into the basket. Doll made almost half of the field goals she attempted and nearly all of the free throws.

With twelve seconds left in the game, Doll and her teammates did the drill that would set up the final shot. The Cement forwards passed the ball to each other, keeping it in play to run down the clock. The frustrated Wildcat guards couldn't get their hands back on the ball. Finally, with three seconds left, Doll jumped to catch a wild pass from her teammate. With one second left, she made the shot. As if answering a magnetic call from the basket, the ball whooshed cleanly through the net. Cement had won, 30–28.

Cheers shook the gymnasium's rafter bolts. Farmers, ranchers, oil-rig workers, and their families who attended all the games leaped skyward. Schoolkids hugged each other, and the heroic Lady Bulldogs, still feeling the effects of the adrenaline rush, danced in circles while holding hands. A unifying spirit took hold, driving away thoughts about the plummeting crop prices, rising foreclosures, and growing food scarcity. These worries evaporated in the warmth spread by the delight in winning.

After more than fifteen minutes, the jubilant shouts dwindled to buzzing murmurs, and the boys began warming up on court for the next game. The crowd settled in to root for their team one more time.

Doll was on her way back to the locker room when she heard someone call her name. She glanced back to see her coach, Mr. Daily, motioning her over to where he was standing with a broad-shouldered man wearing a black suit and a silk tie. He stuck out like a sore thumb in the midst of all the people milling about in work overalls and cotton dresses. As she walked back toward them, the stranger fixed his collar and smoothed a hand down the front of his jacket. Mr. Daily introduced the well-dressed man as Sam Babb, coach of the Cardinals at the Oklahoma Presbyterian College for Girls in Durant, 150 miles east of Cement. Doll lifted her eyebrows and stared at Mr. Babb. His thick black hair was cut in a flattop above a high forehead and bushy eyebrows. He had a broad, stern face; a straight nose; and a prominent chin that turned double when he stared down at her. She never would have guessed he was a basketball coach. He looked more like a banker from the city. And she knew all she needed to know about bankers—her father, a sharecropper, hated them because they were always raising interest rates. As Babb took a couple of steps toward her, she noticed that he had a pronounced limp.

Babb greeted Doll in a smooth baritone voice. When he reached out to shake her hand, his solemn face lit up with a smile. He said he'd like to tell her about the basketball program at OPC, that he was looking for a talented forward to add to the Cardinals' offense. "I need players willing to work hard. Are you willing to work, Miss Harris?"

"I'm a competitor."

"But are you a team player?"

"I can be a team player."

"Good girl. Then I am prepared to offer you financial aid."

"Financial aid? To play basketball?"

"Yes, it would pay for your education."

Doll's jaw dropped, and she looked at Babb in disbelief. Being offered the chance to attend college *and* play basketball was a dream come true. For the past couple of years, Doll could never stop thinking about being recruited by a women's industrial team like the Dr Pepper girls in Oklahoma City or, even better, the Dallas Sunoco Oilers, last year's national champions. These big companies hired the best coaches and players to work in the factory and play basketball at night and on weekends. Winning sports teams generated lots of good publicity. Thousands of screaming fans flocked to their games, and ever since she was a kid playing on a homemade dirt court with a peach-basket goal, Doll had dreamed of glory.

Her heart pounded so hard, she thought it might just launch itself right out of her chest. Maybe this wasn't playing for an industrial basketball team, but in a way, it was even better because she'd be able to go to college, too. She folded her arms, leaned back on her right leg, and began to tap her left toe out of sheer excitement.

"Doll, listen to Mr. Babb," said Mr. Daily, putting a hand on her shoulder to calm her fidgeting.

"Yes, sir." She inhaled a deep breath.

For several minutes, Babb continued telling her about OPC, a women's college, but housed on a campus where poor Indian children also went to elementary and high school, paid for by the Presbyterian Church, of course. "OPC is nationally accredited, one of the best in the region, known for its quality of higher education," he said. Then he told her he wanted to meet with her parents, the next day if possible.

"Meet my folks?" Doll's voice cracked when she spoke.

"Is something wrong?" Babb said.

Yes, there was something wrong. While Doll was listening to Mr. Babb, thoughts of home began to percolate at the back of her mind. She saw the pail she used to milk the cow every morning, sitting in its corner in the barn, made of galvanized metal so heavy she couldn't lift it and had to drag it along the ground when she was a little kid. Her sister Verdie's long auburn hair braided with wild honeysuckle. The desperate look on her father's lean, tanned face when he told his family last October that because of drought, the wheat crop had shriveled to dust. Her shock when she found out that her parents quit eating the eggs from their chickens, selling them instead so that Doll could have new basketball shoes. She and her sister sometimes went without eating meat and eggs, too. Sinking into these thoughts, she stopped breathing—she knew she could never leave Caddo County.

The Great Depression was under way, and poverty lived like a king in western Oklahoma. Months of dry weather had lifted the crops right out of the ground as if the hand of God (or the devil) had pulled up row upon row of every corn, wheat, or cotton plant, exposing the roots and killing them. Fields and pastures had turned dead brown and seemed to rise on the wind like spirits yearning toward heaven, filling the air, sometimes, with sand storms and suffocating grime. Money for food and clothing was scarce. Many families ate what they could grow and supplemented that with what little they could hunt for. Where drought was worst, they gathered weeds—dandelions, sheep sorrel, and lamb's quarters—and ate them steamed with canned beans and lard. Squirrel hunting became an art. The hunter would scope out a squirrel's nest high in a cottonwood. Then he, or she, would lie on the ground and face the sky with a .22 rifle pointing at the nest in its sights. Sometimes they'd wait an hour or more for the squirrel to show its eyes. Squirrel gravy on eggs was considered a delicacy.

But not all was tragic in these wide-open spaces. Country girls like Doll grew up surrounded by endless acres of crops; pasture; and wild, open plains. They ran footraces with coyotes and horses, crawled effortlessly across the wooden beams holding up barn roofs, and created secret tunnels with hay bales. They played alone and with brothers, sisters, cousins, and friends. At night, the stars glistened a brilliant, bleached white in an immense black sky. The only noises were crickets and wind.

Doll couldn't leave her life on the farm. Everyone depended on her. She'd marry a farmer or an oil-rig worker like her sister did and have children of her own. But she also couldn't disappoint Mr. Daily, who had arranged for Mr. Babb to watch her play. So she said, "No, nothing's wrong. Come by tomorrow morning, early." And then she gave Mr. Babb directions to her home.

CHAPTER 2

The Making of a Coach

When Sam Babb scouted players, he'd watch their moves on the court and knew in an instant whether or not they had the strength of character to play for his team. He could sum up people by the way they walked through a crowd, could spot the kind of person who would sell you a blind plow horse without an ounce of regret. Thirty-nine years old in 1931, he walked with purpose and precision, but also with a stiff-hipped swagger. Most people didn't realize at first that he was missing a leg and wore a prosthetic. By then, they were already caught up in his forceful charisma.

While scrutinizing Doll, Babb was struck by her ability to steadily play her heart out. She never exhibited any anger toward a teammate and only showed frustration when, in a rare moment, she missed a shot. Her focus stayed on the unfolding action. Except for a bright tilt of her chin upward after sinking the final basket, she never gloated or bragged after winning. Even when he asked her to come and play for the Cardinals, she hid her emotion, clasping her hands together until her fingers turned purple. He could tell she had reservations about leaving home, but so did most of the girls he interviewed.

When Babb came shopping for talent in his spiffy 1929 burgundy Ford roadster with the brown leather rumble seat, most thought a rich man had come to call. He drove without any special equipment for a one-legged man, operating the brake and gas pedals easily after years of practice. In addition to being the coach of the Cardinals' basketball team, he also taught psychology at OPC, located in southeastern Oklahoma twenty miles north of the Red River and the Texas border in the bustling town of Durant. Searching for the best players from the high school senior girls, he often traveled the road alone, rambling down Oklahoma highways and back roads, from the Arbuckle Mountains to the Wichitas, the Red River to the Arkansas, humming "Livin' in the Sunlight, Lovin' in the Moonlight" or "Big Rock Candy Mountain" in his tone-deaf way. He'd grown to appreciate the rugged landscape where Doll lived, part of the ancient Keechi Hills in southwestern Oklahoma that once harbored outlaws like Jesse James, Quantrill's Raiders, Belle Starr, and the Dalton Gang. Sometimes men could be seen on horseback weaving in and out of the granite boulders, still searching for the outlaws' gold rumored to be hidden deep beneath the furry sage grass.

Farming could be difficult here, especially since Doll's father didn't own his land. He sharecropped several acres, backbreaking work that resulted in most of the money for his crops being given back to the landowner. On this chilly morning as Babb pulled onto the hard-dirt road that led to the Harrises' home, frost glinted off the dried Buffalo grass next to the road. The sun was just rising, turning the horizon burnt orange like the tip of a recently extinguished match. Built from oak logs and topped with a sod roof, the Harrises' small home looked more like a cabin. Babb set the brake, stepped out of his car, and watched as the front door opened and Doll and her mother poured out, followed by a half-grown pink pig that skittered around the side of the house. Farmers often nursed orphaned farm animals until they were big enough to join the other livestock.

Mrs. Harris was even more petite than her daughter, and she politely escorted him through the front door. The deep caramel smell of burnt sugar syrup filled the room, making Babb's stomach growl since he hadn't yet eaten any breakfast. *The Song of the Lark*, a school library book, sat next to a kerosene lamp on a small homemade oak table covered with a doily skillfully woven from feed-sack cloth. Doll wore a dress made from the same sturdy cotton, covered with tiny, colorful daisies. In the 1920s, the feed industry had seized the opportunity to expand business by printing fabric feed bags with unique patterns specifically to attract farmers' wives.

A corner fireplace with smoldering wood heated the front room. Doll's Converse All-Stars sat next to the fireplace. Girls who played basketball never washed their basketball shoes but let them sit in a warm place to dry out after games.

Just then, Mr. Harris, wearing faded overalls and an old blue work shirt, ambled through the front door, nodded at Mrs. Harris, and seemed antsy about getting back to his chores. A man of few words, he motioned toward the fireplace where two homemade ladder-backed chairs and an old rocker were grouped together. Babb politely refused a chair, preferring to stand. He may not have become a minister like his father whose job it was to save souls, but he did make it his business to change lives. To prepare for this task, he always stood to speak and chose his words wisely.

He began by telling Mr. and Mrs. Harris what a smart and talented daughter they'd raised and that she deserved a chance to make something out of her life by attending college. It was a speech he gave to all the parents of the girls he recruited. Doll was blushing the whole time he spoke about her. But Mr. Harris couldn't seem to absorb the fact that his daughter's schooling would be paid for by OPC. And even after Babb had explained several times that Doll would be receiving financial aid for her education, her father kept asking how a girls' school could afford to be this generous. But when it finally sank in that his daughter had achieved something so special that it was nearly unheard of, an excitement arose, an aura that Babb had often felt coming from the parents of his new recruits.

"She'll be the first Harris to go to college," said Mrs. Harris, her voice ringing with pride.

"Welcome to OPC," Babb said to Doll.

Any reluctance she had been feeling appeared to have vanished. Her face shone up at him like the full moon, soft and bright, a well of happiness and maybe even hope, a look that always made Babb's heart a little sore when he saw it on a new recruit's face. He hoped she made the team, kept up her grades, and graduated from college. Many didn't, but Doll seemed tough and driven on the court. She was one of the best he'd ever seen.

Satisfied that Babb would treat Doll like his own daughter while away at school, Mr. Harris insisted on showing off a picture clipped from a catalog of the Farmall tractor he hoped to purchase. Most sharecroppers aspired to own their land someday by purchasing farm equipment that increased production. Some did realize their dreams of land ownership, but most wallowed in debt and found themselves stuck forever plowing up someone else's land. But if Babb hadn't been scheduled to meet with another player's family in Lawton that afternoon, he and Mr. Harris would have spent the entire morning discussing farm equipment, broomcorn seed, and proper fertilization techniques. Babb listened with sincere interest to Doll's father because he identified with Harris's deep connection to the land.

Born December 18, 1891, on a farm near Buffalo, Missouri, Sam Babb was the fifth out of twelve children, six boys and six girls. Rhoda Ellen, Babb's mother, raised the children and ran the eighty-acre homestead. A practicing midwife, she knew about the healing qualities of plants and gathered fresh echinacea, jewelweed, dandelion, burdock root, and many other herbs for tinctures and medicines. It was said that if the family member of a sick person called the county doctor, he would first ask, "Is Ellen Babb there?" If the person answered yes, the doctor would say, "Don't worry. You're in excellent hands. Just do exactly as she says."

Babb's father, Joseph, was a circuit preacher in charge of establishing new places of worship for the Christian Church, a perfect job for this scarecrow-like man who could never slow down and hated farmwork. Joseph spent more time with Ezekiel, his saddle horse, Bible secured in his saddlebags while riding the roads and trails of Missouri, than he did with his twelve children.

One Sunday, when Babb was nearly sixteen and the eldest son still living at home, his father was scheduled to preach a sermon at the Christian church in nearby Buffalo. When Reverend Babb sermonized near the homestead, either in a church or revival tent, his family would dress up in their finest clothes and pile into a wagon pulled by a team of work-horses to attend services together. This day, Babb joined the family along with the other younger children, including five-year-old Lydia May, who always sat nearest the aisle, her short legs swinging nearly a foot off the ground. She was given the important job of timing her father's sermon with his gold pocket watch. When fifty-five minutes had passed, she was supposed to signal him and he would bring his sermon to a close. Babb, along with his other little sisters, Dolly, baby Pauline, and his two littlest brothers, Clay and Ray, ages seven and nine, were lined along the pew beside her.

At 10 a.m., the hour of worship began. Reverend Babb walked to the pulpit and took his place behind the podium. Every available space in the church was filled. Then he took a mighty breath and shouted, "Silence!"

Lydia May focused on her watch.

"The good Lord demands his silence."

The reverend bowed his head and didn't speak for a full minute, as Lydia May indicated by holding up one tiny finger well-hidden in the folds of her dress. After he received the signal, he resumed his forceful words.

"We are now in the presence of the Enemy, and only the sure recognition of your continued obedience to God holds these black gates of hell at bay. Your eternal lives are surely at risk. They are always at risk. That is why I am here before you, to speak God's words and help save your souls."

As he continued his sermon, drops of salty sweat trickled down his forehead and stung his eyes. He'd get so caught up in forceful delivery of God's message, warning his congregation against arrogance, pride, and lust, promising them that unless they curbed their human desires and gave themselves unto the Lord, upon death, they would be cast out from heaven, that he'd forget to wipe the sweat from his eyes. Babb's father cared about his showmanship because it was the only way he knew how to bring souls to God.

His sermons were sixty minutes on the dot. At five minutes before the hour, Lydia May held up five tiny shaking fingers. She kept them there until her father noticed the signal. He then closed his eyes in order to gather energy for his final plea for the salvation of every soul present. When he opened his eyes, the electricity in the room caused short arm hair to stand on end and dress hems to fasten to their owner's stockings. When the reverend finished, a hundred people came forward to receive salvation.

After church, Reverend Babb was asked to dinner by upstanding families from four different communities. The day had been a success, and he was glowing. He knew he had given a good sermon, possibly a great sermon. His fingers and toes were numb, and so was the end of his nose. He couldn't feel the top of his head, and his eyes were as dry as dirt because he had stopped blinking. The fact was, he had left his body. Often, during his most intense words, he'd hover above himself and watch the rail-thin man below, dressed all in black, waving his fists and shouting his warnings. Then he'd follow himself home or to his next appearance. It would take two days, sometimes three, for his awareness to return to his body. He thought this happened to all devout men of God.

Babb drove the wagon home with Lydia May sitting beside him. The rest of his family was in the back, gossiping and laughing. Except his father, of course, who was always solemn-faced after giving a sermon. Babb enjoyed his father's tirades against the devil the way some people enjoyed standing on the edge of a high cliff. They were an adrenaline rush. Still, he wouldn't like to hear them every Sunday. Meanwhile, Lydia May had grown completely silent, which was unusual for her.

Babb nudged her with his elbow. "I can tell something is vexing you," he said.

She looked up at him, her dark eyes tearful. "I'm afraid of going to hell," she whispered so that her father couldn't hear.

"Don't be afraid," he whispered back. "You're an angel."

"But father said God judges us and knows what we think, all the time. And I'm not really an angel," she said, sniffling.

Babb thought a minute. "I don't believe God knows, or cares, what we think. The constant jabber would drive him crazy."

Lydia May burst out laughing. "Then why do you want to become a minister, too, if you think God is always holding his ears?"

"Ask me after I get out of divinity school."

When the family arrived home, Babb decided to replace a rotting fence post. Being the eldest child still living at home, he did most of the crop planting and repairs. His three older brothers and older sister were all long gone by now. As each had turned eighteen, Babb's father handed him or her one hundred dollars, asked them to leave, and told them, "That's the last money you'll ever see from me." In less than a couple of years, Babb would be sent on his own way, too. It wasn't that they were poor. In fact, his mother came from one of the richest families in town and would have welcomed the help from her grown children. But what his father believed almost always became the house rules. His father also forbade smoking, drinking, and card playing, and he never let his daughters cut their hair. The first thing every one of Babb's sisters did upon receiving the hundred dollars was to get their hip-length tresses trimmed to their ears in a fashionable bob.

While Babb made fence repairs, the younger children played hide-and-seek in the front yard beneath the towering Siberian elms and weeping willows. Their father had a prayer meeting the next county over, so he asked his wife to shine his shoes and press his newest suit, while he went to the barn to curry-comb Ezekiel. He'd spent a good amount of hard-earned cash on a hand-made saddle and bridle to highlight the appearance of his chestnut-roan gelding with four high stockings and a lightning blaze down its face. But when he opened the walk-in tack closet to inspect them, anger surged from his forehead to his toes.

A few days earlier, he'd ridden home from a revival meeting through the pouring rain. Mud had splashed onto the saddle and caked across the bridle and girth strap. He'd given the chore of cleaning them to his two youngest sons, Clay and Ray. Now he found his prized saddle still covered with mud, dried and cracked, the expensive leather ruined.

He shot out of the barn like a disturbed hornet and combed the yard for the two boys, knocking over a butter churn to see if one was curled up inside. Of course, the boys, aged nine and seven, were too large to fit inside a butter churn. Finally, he heard young voices on the other side of the house and rushed there to find his children in the middle of an all-out corncob war. Dried cobs were flying everywhere; a tiny missile sailed past their father's ear. Dolly saw him first and through nonstop giggling explained that the girls were winning. The reverend ignored her.

"Clay and Ray," he bellowed, "come here, you heathen boys."

At the sound of their father's thunderous voice, the children paused in midthrow. It took a few seconds for the two boys, who had their hands full of corncobs, to realize that they were the focus of their father's rage. When that knowledge sank in, they ran. He strode after them. But when they actually had time to think about their doom, they decided to face it sooner rather than later and stopped dead. The reverend, his long legs churning, nearly ran them down.

"Come with me," he growled, and pinched the ears of both boys, dragging them across the yard and into the barn. He flung open the closet doors to reveal their crime.

The two boys stared at their father's riding tack. Recognition gleamed in their eyes.

"We forgot," said Ray.

"We'll clean it now," said Clay.

"Now is too late," said their father.

As the reverend inched closer, he towered over them and began to wring his hands. His voice took on the resonating, slow vibrato of his sermons, outlining the nature of their sins and the punishment the boys were about to receive. It carried clear to the mailbox at the county road where Babb happened to be finishing up his fence repair. His father's voice sounded so near that he jumped and dropped his hammer. Wondering what on earth had provoked such a tirade, Babb sprinted the full quarter mile toward the homestead until he registered that the commotion was coming from the barn. What he found there brought stinging tears to his eyes. His father was gripping a trace chain, part of the harness used to hook mules to a plow. The two boys had backed into a corner where the shadows had swallowed them up.

"Father," Babb shouted, "what are you doing?"

"This is none of your business, boy."

"It is my business if you don't put that trace chain down."

"Samuel. Remove yourself or suffer the consequences."

Knowing that he had just been threatened, Babb stepped between his father and his brothers. The chain lit out like a frightened snake. Babb dodged to the left, and the chain scraped a rock in the dirt floor and shot sparks. Joseph reeled in the chain and whipped it out once more, but Babb wasn't quick enough this time. The chain wrapped itself around his shin, the iron links cutting through his thin summer trousers and deep into his flesh. To Babb's utter horror, his father then tried to drag him across the floor.

"Joseph, stop. You're pulling his leg off!" Babb's mother's voice pierced through the crying voices of her youngest sons, who were nearly hysterical.

Who knew why the reverend let go of the chain? Perhaps his adrenal glands were finally spent and his uncanny energy had left him. His anger still remained, however, and he continued to stand over Babb.

"Get your brother and bring him inside," Babb's mother said to the younger boys, indicating that they move quickly.

Ray and Clay scurried from the barn's shadows, unwrapped the trace chain from around Babb's leg and supported him as best they could, helping him away from their father toward the house. Reverend Babb left home that evening and didn't come back for many weeks.

One month later, Babb lost his leg. His father's strength had fractured the bone, and despite his mother's skilled care, an infection grew. When the doctor came, he saw that gangrene had set in. There was no time to get Babb to the Springfield hospital. The doctor had to amputate the leg several inches above the knee. Babb had little time to prepare, but he trusted his mother to take care of him. She made a place to perform the surgery on the huge oak dining table in the middle of the kitchen. She put Dolly, the oldest girl, in charge of boiling water to sterilize the surgical instruments and sent the rest of her children outside. Babb lay on the table and breathed in the ether anesthesia to make him unconscious. He didn't feel any pain when the doctor removed the limb.

During the first weeks of his recovery, his mother changed bandages, applied antiseptic to prevent infection, and made nourishing meals such as bone soups from simmered whole chickens and root vegetables to provide vitamins and minerals. In addition, she gave him white willow and valerian herbs to calm him and help him sleep. To make sure her teenage son kept his senses and didn't turn to bitterness, she worked on healing his heart, especially when Babb experienced a fiery pain directly below his thigh, where his leg used to be. It felt like someone was pulling off his toenails one by one and then twisting his phantom foot round and round. The pain would corkscrew up his absent lower leg and end at the knee that was no longer there. He thought he was going mad. His mother assured him that he wasn't crazy. She called it a ghost pain. She'd seen it before in other patients. Sometimes it's harder for your mind to accept the loss of a limb than it is your body, she explained.

"Remember, Sam, you are the same person inside now as you were before the accident," she told him. "What happened to you is life changing, not life ending."

During this time, his "bed time" he would call it years later, he learned to calm the initial pain by focusing his attention deep inside himself. Concentrating on the thump, thump of his heart or the in-and-out of his breath minimized the pain by keeping it at the back of his awareness. After the wound healed, he performed exercises to strengthen his body so that he could learn to walk with a prosthetic. He refused to use crutches and never touched a walking cane. His mother obtained books and other resources for him to read that would help him finish his schooling and enroll in college. She believed that a good, strong education was the most valuable asset any child could have. Ten of her twelve children would eventually graduate from college.

Some evenings, when his eyes had tired of reading in the dim light of a kerosene lamp, he'd teach his brothers and sisters the fine art of debate, dividing them into teams and showing them how to argue either side of an issue. Instructing children ages four to twelve how to find the argument for or against a topic like doing the dishes or, more important, letting women vote, took patience. Clay and Ray often solved disagreements by starting a shoving match. But Babb's enthusiasm for the topic and precise ability to engage his siblings in a serious debate of issues helped them learn deductive reasoning and the art of rhetoric according to Aristotle's text. It remained with them for the rest of their lives.

After he finished with his schoolbooks, Babb read the Bible start to finish for the second time in his life. When his eldest brother, Everett, another Christian Church minister, came to visit, they'd discuss biblical meaning and even argued a few points. Everett kept in touch with the family and got to know his younger brothers and sisters even though he was old enough to be their father. In fact, Everett was very much like a loving father to them. His sermons were the opposite of his father's. With his quick smile and serene manner, Everett lured his congregation to God with the gentleness of his spirit.

Babb saw this difference between Everett and his father and experienced a flash of insight: the God that people imagined inside themselves, whether judgmental and punishing, or loving and compassionate, must reflect the emotions they lived with every day. Some of his father's past actions made sense now, like the time he sold a pair of plow horses, blinded by disease, to an unwitting buyer. When Babb had asked his father about the cruel deception, the older man, who seemed almost gleeful, had told him that God favors those who help themselves. The person who bought the horses didn't have the gumption to inspect the product correctly, and he paid a just price. Babb's father considered weakness a sin. Seeing this, Babb also reasoned that his father's sermons came from the vengeful God inside, one who could rise up in anger and maim his own son for life. It helped him to understand, and to forgive.

WHEN HE REACHED the age of eighteen, and it was time for him to leave, Babb felt he had all the attributes of a Christian minister. He decided to apply to divinity school at Everett's alma mater, Oklahoma Christian University. He quoted Romans 10:15 to his mother, "How beautiful are the feet of them that preach the gospel of peace and bring glad tidings of good things!"

His mother laughed at his reference to "beautiful feet." For nearly a year, she had watched him struggle for hours every day, at first learning to walk with a prosthetic and not lose his balance, until he had perfected his ability to balance and walk again. And now she was watching him work all day and night on his college application. When he finally finished his sermon, according to Everett, it was a beautiful song to God's ears.

Several weeks passed after Babb mailed his application to the university. Then came the reply. The gist of the letter from the seminary school read:

> We are acquainted with your father Joseph and your brother Everett, both fine servants of God. There is no question about your excellent and finely written words to God, and we congratulate you on your exceptional writing ability. However, the potential minister of the Gospel may have a great ability to sermonize, to place Godly thoughts in fine phrases on the solid page, but he must also be able to forcefully and powerfully deliver them to the listener's heart. You must understand that only a *whole man* can deliver God's words under the anointing of the Holy Spirit. Only a *whole man* can give the sermon life in the hearts of his listeners.
>
> We read your account of your farming accident and the loss of

your limb. And we ask you, sir, even though this question may be painful, but you must face it—how can your crippled body handle the rigors of study and preaching? God's work is the most strenuous on earth.

We are most sorrowful at the loss you have experienced. Nevertheless, with great dismay and regret, we must reject your application.

No one had ever called him a cripple, or even insinuated it, until now. And this insult came from an organization that he'd admired throughout his life. After the initial shock wore off, Babb's anger made him want to lash out. How could they do this to him? He grabbed a pen and paper and started writing a detailed letter about how un-Christly it was to deny any human being the chance to serve God. He imagined the committee members reading his letter, recognizing the error they'd made, and sending him an apology that begged him to catch the next train to Enid. But after he started writing, it occurred to him that he was putting time and energy into a task that didn't make sense. Why should he want to attend a school that didn't want him? He wasn't the type of person to sit and stew over anything, especially when it began to feel like self-pity. Instead, he started thinking about other careers that would still allow him the opportunity to change lives. A few weeks later, he applied to the nearby teacher's college in Springfield and was immediately accepted.

While in school, Babb fell in love with Mata Gorton, a schoolteacher known for treating all her children—grades first through third—as if they were angels; even the mischievous ones would turn sweet in her presence. She loved to paint watercolor portraits in muted reds, greens, and blues. When her students were injured or distraught or wanted to cry, Mata would fold them into her arms and they would emerge magically fortified. She had the same effect on Babb. Soon after they were married, Mata asked if she could help him with his prosthetic leg. He laughed at the idea, but then he rose and pulled on his top-of-the-line A. A. Marks prosthetic

Sam Babb

with a spring mattress rubber foot and cushioned knee flexor device and let Mata's long fingers gently lace the Comfort-Fit corset snug around his upper thigh. She then helped him secure the leather suspender-like straps, now softened with wear, over his shoulders. After that, Babb always let Mata help.

A year after Babb graduated, he and Mata left Missouri for Oklahoma. Babb earned a master's degree in education from the University of Oklahoma and quickly worked his way up to school superintendent. Mata followed him across the state, from small farming communities to the bigger towns, wherever the state board of education needed him. Though her gentle nature preferred gardening and reading to lively parties and gossipy quilting bees, she withstood the small-town politics necessary to being a school superintendent's wife. They finally settled in Arapaho, the county seat for Custer County and a fork-in-the-road trade center for the surrounding farms that raised wheat, alfalfa, and livestock.

As superintendent, Babb gained full authority over the entire consolidated school district because he felt that the local school board couldn't be trusted with hiring teachers or purchasing supplies. The district needed to conserve money, too, so he taught three high school classes each day. He knew all 302 students by first and last name, and knew whether they could write a complete sentence or were good at mathematics. Because sunlight shone through windows in the schoolrooms from two sides of the building, the cross light sometimes threw shadows on the pupils' desks during class. Babb instructed the teachers to take great care in adjusting the shades throughout the day. He often monitored the school halls and would menace the supplies salesmen that would sneak in without notice and pester the teachers even during class.

More than anything, Babb wanted a gymnasium. Young athletes playing basketball on an outdoor court had to battle the fierce wind that gusted across the Oklahoma prairie. So he rented a store building and used it as a basketball court. That year, 1922, he hired a coach and sponsored both boys' and girls' basketball.

The next year, Babb decided to promote a bond issue for a new basketball gymnasium that could also be used as an auditorium equipped with six hundred opera chairs, a moving picture machine, and a radio phone to make the school the town's social center used by the Farmers Union, Community Club, and the County Teachers Association. He and Mata campaigned for the vote by attending women's luncheons, knocking on doors, handing out pamphlets, and even gathering all the irritable farmers and ranchers together for a meeting. He convinced the local school board to support him and hired a new high school basketball coach named Roy Deal.

Town folks warmed to Babb's charm and promised to think about building the gym. The farmers and ranchers were not so easily persuaded though. They would have to contribute a substantial amount in taxes if the bond issue passed. Buster McElhaney, editor of the *Arapaho Bee*, the town's biweekly newspaper, began referring to Samuel Foster Babb as Sunflower Babb, a fitting metaphor for Babb's attempt to bring the community into the twentieth century. The sunflower sprouted tall and bright, but to farmers and ranchers, it was a weed tougher and more profuse than dandelions; they killed it as soon as it started to grow.

But then, just before the election, Coach Deal spoiled all of Babb's plans.

"Some girl has led our . . . basketball fiend astray," wrote McElhaney on the front page of the *Arapaho Bee*. "He has a wife and three children, but she got him."

Coach Deal, distressed by the public's discovery of his inappropriate actions toward a student, snuck out of town with his family in the middle of the night, leaving most of their possessions behind. Now the farmers and ranchers had the perfect excuse to vote against building the gymnasium. There was no telling about men coaching young girls, they thought. Some just couldn't control themselves.

Babb gave up his campaigning. Instead, he focused on coaching basketball himself. With Coach Deal gone midway through the season and no assistant coach to take his place, Babb took charge of both the high school boys' and girls' basketball teams. He knew the basic rules for boys' basketball, since he had attended all the men's games during college. But girls' basketball rules were another matter entirely.

Shortly after James Naismith invented the game of basketball in 1891, school girls hitched up their long skirts, stuffed them into their bloomers, and took to the court with boisterous enthusiasm. Young women were emerging from the severe restrictions of the Victorian era with gusto, shedding their bustles, hoops, and corsets along with the outdated beliefs that they were too delicate for any sport. Still, the ghost of the Victorian lady—someone who was obedient, graceful, passive, separate from men and in her own feminine world—would not go away. After watching the first official women's basketball game played on March 23, 1893, between freshmen and sophomore women at Smith College, various shocked newspaper reporters filed stories containing horrific descriptions of young girls flailing about in a desperate fight and nearly fainting from overexertion.

In response to this public reproach, female physical educators acted quickly to restore feminine dignity to their sport. Senda Berenson, the physical educator at Smith College who had coached the women to play by men's rules, now restricted players' movements up and down the court by dividing it into three equal parts for centers, guards, and forwards. A single player could hold the ball for no more than three seconds. No one could leave the part of the court she was assigned to, and the rules also outlawed dribbling. Since they couldn't travel on court, they learned to pass with precision. Anywhere from five to ten girls played on each team. The games were divided into fifteen-minute halves.

Berenson helped establish the Committee on Women's Basketball (the CWB) that started publishing the yearly *Official Basketball Guide* in 1901. Players referred to these guidelines for women as "girls' rules." In 1917, the CWB became a subcommittee of the Committee on Women's Athletics, a part of the powerful American Physical Education Association.

As more girls began playing basketball, the rules slowly changed to accommodate their growing skill. In 1922, the Amateur Athletic Union (AAU) began accepting qualified women's teams into its organization, giving them a formal means of competition. This development infuriated the conservative women physical educators who oversaw girls' and women's sports. Lou Henry Hoover, the wife of President Herbert Hoover, helped them form their own organization in 1923, the Women's Division of the National Amateur Athletic Federation (Women's Division). Using the power of the first lady, the organization began attacking competitive athletics for women, especially basketball, as being unhealthy and unladylike. Concerned that women's high school and college sports would become as corrupt as the men's, with quasi-professional rules that resulted in gambling, the Women's Division endorsed sports for health purposes and outlined a plan for the more gentle intramural "play days" that barred all spectators.

But in the rural schools and in the Midwest, girls kept playing competitive basketball under the guidance of the AAU. Most country girls loved basketball. At school, friends and teachers didn't give a second thought to girls picking cotton or running the buck rakes in the Johnson grass hay fields, so no one ever bothered to consider if it was unfeminine for them to play basketball. They practiced on dirt patches behind barns or on playgrounds, in small schoolrooms, or in large converted warehouses. Their hands became filthy with the jumble of sweat and dust from handling the ball. They'd wipe their hands on their shirts, just like the boys, so they could get a true feel of the basketball. At home, they practiced free throws in peach buckets nailed to trees, their hands stuffed in wool gloves during cold winter days, tossing and tossing the ball until the sun disappeared.

Babb came to understand these special rules for girls by finding out how they differed from the boys:

- As played under current AAU guidelines for women, the size of the court was the same, and so were the ball, baskets, and backboards. The girls' game was shorter—four eight-minute quarters instead of two twenty-minute halves.

- The girls' teams contained six players instead of five. The additional player was a guard. During a game, girls did less scoring, not because they were less aggressive or poorer shots than boys, but because their extra player made their guarding tighter.

- The court was divided in half, the offense on one side, defense on the other. Only one below-the-knee dribble was allowed.

- For boys, the team scored against took the ball out of bounds and then immediately started working it down the court. For girls, a team scored against got the ball from the referee at the opposing team's foul line, allowing them a few seconds of rest after each score.

• Coaching girls from the sidelines was prohibited except during halftime.

Watching his young students fall in love with the game heartened Babb in a way that he didn't expect. Coaching young women to be precise, skilled, and strong became Babb's calling. And his first-ever coaching job ended with a winning season.

Not long afterward, Babb accepted superintendent and coaching positions at nearby Thomas and then Pryor school districts, 230 miles to the northeast. But in the midst of the Oklahoma oil boom, Babb resigned his position as Pryor's school superintendent, Mata gave up teaching, and they moved to Chickasha to live with Babb's older brother, John, and his family. They bought a gas station and began investing in other oil and gas ventures. But just as they were getting started, oil prices plunged. Oklahoma produced too much oil for its own good. And when it became more and more likely that Babb's income from the gas station would not be enough, he embarked on a statewide search for another teaching position. That's when he discovered that the coach of the women's basketball team at Oklahoma Presbyterian College was leaving at the end of the 1929 summer semester. He interviewed with Dr. Ebenezer Hotchkin, the president of OPC and a Presbyterian minister, and the two men became immediate friends. Babb's tenure as school superintendent for the State of Oklahoma had left him with many friends and contacts within the school system, and they sent excellent recommendations to Dr. Hotchkin. Very soon after his interview, OPC offered Babb the position.

During Babb's interview process with OPC, he was out of town for several days, during which time Mata caught the flu. Within two weeks, it turned into pneumonia. She suffered for six weeks before she died. On February 6, 1929, eight months before the stock market crashed and weary ex-millionaires skydived from office windows, Babb and his family buried Mata in Rose Hill Cemetery in Chickasha. His brother, Everett, officiated, and his father even showed up. Over the years since Babb had lost his leg, he never held a grudge against his father, but he also never pursued a close relationship. The two tolerated each other. That day, though, he was glad to have most of his family there. Mata had been thirty-six years old, two years younger than Babb. He wept over his loss in private but maintained a stoic demeanor among friends and family. He never referred to himself as a "widower." But Babb would miss Mata for as long as he lived.

THE FALL OF 1930, eighteen-year-old Doll Harris settled in at OPC. She received a letter nearly every day from her family that first year. She studied algebra, American history, English and psychology, maintaining nearly straight A's while becoming Coach Babb's star shot maker and making a name for herself in the local newspapers who nicknamed her "Baby" Doll. For the first time, the OPC Cardinals were invited to the 1931 AAU national tournament, where they won the sportsmanship trophy for outstanding fair play on the court. Dr. Hotchkin stated that there was more honor in having received this trophy than in being the national champions. Doll even earned a spot on the All-American team. The Dallas Golden Cyclones won the championship.

That same year, another eighteen-year-old country girl was hired as a secretary at Employers Casualty Insurance Company in Dallas. She also had the nickname Baby, but soon the newspapers were calling her Babe. She led the Dallas Golden Cyclones, sponsored by Employers Casualty, to a victory at the 1931 AAU national tournament. That summer, Mildred "Babe" Didrikson rose to national prominence, winning eight track-and-field events at the AAU national women's track meet. She would be back as star forward for the Golden Cyclones in the fall.

In the late winter and early spring of 1931, Babb traveled from Tulsa to the Red River watching talented girls play basketball at hometown games in little gymnasiums as well as at the state tournament and then afterward approaching their parents about their daughters attending OPC. His constant search resembled the hunting technique of one of those black-crowned night herons that sat patiently for hours along streams and creeks, their hunched necks moving only when the perfect fish wiggled by. Babb searched and searched because, for him, possessing the sportsmanship trophy wasn't enough. He knew they could do better. And by the time he finished, thirty-five new recruits agreed to start at OPC the fall of 1931, all with big dreams and bright hopes for the future.

CHAPTER 3

The Field House, 4 a.m.

November 1931

Sixteen-year-old Lucille Thurman opened her eyes at 2:55 a.m., five minutes before her clock was set to jangle. In the dark, she reached over and pushed in the button to deactivate the alarm. For five delicious minutes, she lay in bed, closing her eyes and pulling the wool blanket up to her ears. She hated getting up when it was cold. Precisely at 3 a.m., other alarm clocks went off in a symphony that echoed through the fourth floor of Graham-Jackson Hall.

Time for basketball practice.

Climbing out of bed, Lucille pulled on a thick wool robe, and gave her roommate, Coral Worley, a nudge. When she still wouldn't open her eyes, Lucille flung the covers off of Coral, who moaned. "It's freezing."

But it wasn't *that* cold. Life in the dorms was luxurious compared to home. Both girls had grown up on farms in western Oklahoma. Coral was from Cache, near Lawton, and Lucille from a tiny dot on the map called Cookietown. Because there wasn't any indoor plumbing or electricity in rural Oklahoma, they burned wood in fireplaces for heat, used kerosene lamps, and tiptoed barefoot in the dark past the chicken run to use the

Sisters Coral and Thelma Worley

outhouse always hidden in a grove of trees several yards away. The most modern thing they owned was a radio that ran on batteries. If they wanted a hot bath, they had to cart in water from the well, boil it over the wood-burning cookstove, and dump it into a tub. Only the lucky few could pump cold water from inside the house.

To Lucille, a girl who had never stayed a single night away from her family before college or had used a proper flush toilet except at the basketball state tournament in Oklahoma City last spring, the steam heat from radiators and hot water from a faucet in the dormitory had seemed extravagant. And she was fortunate to have gotten Coral as a roommate. The second day after moving in, they were inseparable. The first day, though, they didn't like each other.

When her father left for home after helping her get situated in her bread-box-size dorm room, Lucille started crying and couldn't stop, even when Coral dragged in her suitcase and said, "Howdy." Lucille tried to hide her tearstained face and red nose behind a handkerchief while Coral introduced herself, and balked at shaking Coral's hand just because she was embarrassed. All Lucille noticed was Coral's shoulder-length golden-blonde hair held away from her face with numerous, evenly placed bobby pins, and the long legs that claimed almost half her body. At nineteen, Coral had three more years of life experience than Lucille, and it showed.

She had gotten herself to school, riding the bus from Lawton to Durant. Nothing seemed to distress her, not even Lucille's tears.

Next to Coral, Lucille, at five feet ten inches, had felt like an ungainly giant. Because she was in college, people often thought that she was older than sixteen. But she had worked hard in school and graduated early. That first day, they hardly looked at each other and never spoke while they organized their room. But the next morning, feeling less homesick and more curious about her new roommate, Lucille grabbed a basketball out of the utility closet and asked Coral if she wanted to find a court. They set off together searching the neighborhoods surrounding OPC and almost an hour later discovered an old rusty goal set up without a net

at an elementary school. At first, they took turns just tossing the ball through the hoop. But then Coral nonchalantly blocked Lucille's shot. When Lucille fought back, the game was on, and they didn't stop for two hours, barely making it back to the dorm cafeteria in time for supper.

Lucille Thurman

This morning, two months later, when Coral was finally up, the two girls washed their faces with the warm-running water, put on their thick cotton sweats, and headed downstairs. Their dorm mother, Aunt Lucy, gave them toast and hot tea to keep them fortified until they ate breakfast in the school cafeteria at 7 a.m. sharp.

Aunt Lucy took care of all the

students who lived in Graham-Jackson Hall, including the basketball players. The younger sister of Dr. Hotchkin, the president of OPC and senior pastor at the campus Presbyterian church, she was only as big as a minute, not even five feet tall, with slate-gray hair pulled back into a tight bun, a smooth complexion, and a smile that sprang from her face all at once. She always wore a corset even though they went out of style years ago. This morning, Lucy hadn't taken the time to put on her corset but was dressed in a warm woolen robe and offering the meager breakfast to all the early risers. Coral and Lucille sipped their tea and wolfed down the toast. As soon as they finished, they walked outside and watched their warm breaths dissipate into the cold air as they jogged toward the bus that would carry the players two miles to the Southeastern campus. Coach Babb had finagled use of the school's field house for basketball practice.

For the first three weeks of practice, before they had the field house, thirty-five girls had found limited space to learn passing drills and shoot free throws in OPC's small half-court gym on the fourth floor of the administration building. It had been nicknamed the Buzzard's Roost last year when the freshmen grew frustrated by the stale heat that lasted through October. They kept the windows open, and the stinky pigeons that roosted beneath the window eaves often hopped inside. The girls would chase them out, but the birds kept leaving heaps of droppings across the floor. Unlucky freshmen were appointed to sweep up. Knowing they needed a better place to practice, Babb sought the advice of O. L. "Runt" Ramsey, coach of the Savages, the boys' basketball team at nearby Southeastern State Teachers College. Ramsey offered the use of their field house when he was sure his boys wouldn't be using it—from 4 a.m. to 6 a.m. every morning.

"Long live the Buzzard's Roost," a deep-throated, saucy voice said from behind Lucille. Hazel Vickers, another freshman, better known as Vick, slammed her shoulder into the small of Lucille's back, knocking her off balance. Lucille grinned but didn't feel like roughhousing so early in the morning. Everyone seemed a little afraid of Vick, for good reason: her strength. From the time she was nine, she worked on her dad's farm,

Hazel Vickers

running a plow behind four work-horses. Those horses weighed at least a ton each. "That's how I got in shape for basketball," she joked. She had chestnut hair, green eyes, and a plain face, but her sturdy frame looked like it housed muscles of iron. She had played basketball in Cooperton, near Lawton, for seven years. By the time she was thirteen, she was good enough to practice with the high school players.

Soon about thirty other players were shivering along the sidewalk waiting for the bus. Long as a limousine, with three doors on each side, the ancient nine-seat crank-start bus shed oil in dark puddles. With its fading red paint and erratic engine, the OPC bus was a dubious form of transportation.

Juanita "Bo-Peep" Park, a sophomore guard and vice-president of her college class, helped the school out by driving the bus and even making the repairs. Her family lived on a farm a few miles east of Durant in an unincorporated community called Blue, named after the nearby Blue River. She had nicknamed herself at age five after the same Little Bo-Peep from the fairy tale because her family raised sheep and she had loved the girl in the story. Her father taught her to drive when she was eleven, mainly because she was tall for her age and could reach the pedals easily. After six years of driving a hay truck, Bo-Peep was an expert, but on this frigid morning the bus refused to start. The engine revved up as if it were about to turn over, then sputtered out with a nasty cough. The smell of gasoline leaked into the morning air. She was forced to hop out, crank the engine, hop back in, and push the starter.

"Looks like I'll need a push," Bo-Peep announced as Lucille and the other girls gathered around. "If you all could just get me a little ways across the lot, this old thing should start up."

Lucille, Coral, Vick, and the other players distributed themselves near the back of the bus. Each found a portion of metal to lean against, and heaved forward. Several girls had left their mittens in their rooms but gripped the frozen bus barehanded anyway. When the engine finally choked to life and Bo-Peep gave it some gas, every girl without gloves yelped as the cold metal unstuck from their fingers.

"Ready to go?" Bo-Peep yelled over the chugging engine. "Hop in. Hurry up. Ugh, it's cold. Feels like we might get some snow."

The players climbed into the bus, some rubbing their raw hands together, grabbed gray wool blankets from a pile on the front seat, and tossed them over their coats and around their shoulders. The old bus had no heat, and not wanting any of the players to get sick, Babb made sure that the school provided blankets. The Cardinal teammates scrunched together in chilled silence during the two-mile drive to Southeastern, staring out the windows at the prairie grass, barely visible in the darkness, that grew lush and thick along the roadside.

The twenty-three-acre OPC campus sat near bustling downtown Durant, just a few blocks north of Main Street. Southeastern, a state school built with public funds, was located on the east edge of town across from the muddy banks of Mineral Bayou, where fat channel catfish up to three feet long swam along the creek bottom scavenging for crawfish, algae, and other bits of food. School kids often waded into the creek and, using their thumbs and forefingers, snagged the slippery crawfish hiding under rocks or in shadows and made a few extra pennies selling them for bait. When the water ran high, Mineral Bayou became one of the best fishing holes that no one knew about. Many families without money for food sustained themselves by catching the bass and trout in the swift-running Blue River, a bit farther east of town. Fishing the Blue meant putting up with a noisy crowd sometimes. Even the hobos just passing through knew about the Blue River. But not Mineral Bayou.

Durant looked like a colorful paradise to those basketball players from western Oklahoma. Rain had kept the rivers and creeks full. Oak, maple, and locust trees grew in tight groves, and their leaves were just starting to turn the fall colors of red, yellow, and gold. Pecan groves sprang in clusters in and around Durant, providing thirty-six boxcar loads of pecans shipped in one month during 1928, but dwindling to five boxcar loads during the same month in 1930.

The drought had been much kinder here in the eastern part of the state. But last year's dry weather had devastated crops and killed livestock in the more arid parts of western Oklahoma where Coral, Vick, and Lucille were from. The usually green outcrops of post oaks and blackjacks were parched and stunted. Streams and lakes dried up. Even the dependable hairy grama and Indiangrass, which sustained the cattle and horses, grew inches instead of feet and quickly disappeared during the summer from overgrazing. Oklahoma had been the first state in the nation to get the federal drought money for loans to farmers in 1930. Hundreds of families in the southwest portion of the state received feed for the farm horses and cattle, wheat seed, and coal just to survive the winter.

Lucille, sitting next to Coral, wasn't thinking about any hardships back home. She was too busy looking down at her feet. She lifted them up off the floor and rotated them, flexing and warming up her ankles. Crack, crack, crack! Her misplaced ankle bones sounded like popping corn. She winced.

"Are you okay?" Coral asked.

Lucille shrugged. "It's my ankles again." She hadn't told anyone, but her ankles had started to turn during practice, causing her to land on the sides of her feet after a good, hard jump, bothering her afterward for days. Since competition for a spot on the first string was fierce, any injury could be devastating. She feared losing her scholarship, turning a successful attempt at college into failure. If that were to happen, she couldn't imagine facing her parents, who had been so excited by her good fortune. Her father loved basketball and had always wanted his tall daughter to be a basketball star.

The bus jolted to a halt in front of the field house. Bo-Peep pulled the emergency brake and turned off the headlights. Lucille, Coral, and the rest of the Cardinal players stepped out into the pitch-black morning with their woolen blankets still wrapped securely around them. Once inside, they clasped the blankets even tighter because it felt like an icehouse. The place looked like a big barn with long steel beams holding up the roof. Shadows engulfed every corner. The basketball floor had the best lighting, and the polished wood glistened. A few feet back from the court, rows of seats with chair backs followed by wooden bleachers were built on either side of the court and would hold over a thousand fans. Wandering toward the basketball court, they found Coach Babb sitting in the front row of the stands wearing his winter coat and thick, leather driving gloves, sipping coffee out of his Icy-Hot thermos, and going over his notes from the day before. Babb often claimed that coffee was his only vice. And sometimes vanilla-flavored milk shakes. He never took a drink of hard liquor, smoked a cigarette, or even played cards, this virtuosness hard-wired into his brain from growing up as a minister's son.

"Good morning, Mr. Babb," each player said as she discarded her blanket and began jogging up and down the court to warm up. Usually Babb made announcements about class changes or gave notes to certain players before starting practice. He never drew up a playbook. He didn't believe in having a system for basketball. He believed that the individual must make her own decisions and meet the move herself, with each player weaving her action into the common fabric of the game as it unfolds. Babb often said his goal was to develop expert players "who thought and acted instinctively with all but perfect eye, mind, and muscle coordination."

This morning, Babb had a different sort of announcement. "The heat for the field house won't be turned on until 5 a.m. every day when the caretaker arrives." They would have to put up with the cold for an hour.

Overriding the quiet moans, Babb continued. "Dr. Hotchkin has asked me to tell you about a new activity required of all basketball players on scholarship, which includes just about everyone. Starting on Monday, you will be assigned to a table during lunch with several of the younger Indian children. You will help them learn proper table manners. Aunt Lucy will assign the students and give a more extensive explanation of what's required of you. Please save your questions for her. Right now we need to get started."

Then Babb shouted for Lera and Vera Dunford to scrimmage with the first team. The two girls trotted onto the court. Before OPC, Lucille had never known any girls taller than she was. That all changed when she met the six-foot-tall redheaded Dunford twins. They looked exactly alike, from the blazing red hair that grazed their shoulders to their fair skin; broad, freckled faces; and prominent cheekbones.

"Toka Lee, I've decided to move you to defense permanently," Babb said. Toka Lee Fields was the smallest player next to Doll Harris. Both were sophomores and best friends. They never seemed to go anywhere without the other tagging along.

Positioning Toka Lee as a guard was a sly choice. At five four, she didn't look terribly intimidating, but she could jump as high as Vick or the six-foot Dunford twins, and she possessed the quick hands of a good shooter, which allowed her to steal the ball with great success. Her quiet demeanor off the court hid a startling ability to battle a player nose to nose, or nose to neck as was often the case with Toka Lee.

Toka Lee nodded to Babb and then sauntered on the court to join Lera and Vera.

Not everyone who had always played forward would have accepted changing to a guard without complaining like Toka Lee did. Even though guards must be skilled players, it was the forwards who received all the fanfare because they scored all the points. Under girls' half-court basketball rules, there were always three forwards and three guards for each team playing on opposite ends of the court. Except when a forward made illegal contact and fouled a guard, who then was allowed one or two free throws depending on the foul, guards only protected the goal; they never scored points during actual play. Babe Didrikson, the crack shot who played at forward for the Dallas Golden Cyclones, might have gone unnoticed if she had been a guard.

Babb then assigned Doll and Lucille at forward and center positions.

Just then, the field house's door clanked open and banged shut. Everyone's eyes turned to the player arriving late. As she made her way toward the court, the others looked at each other or down at their Converse high-tops. They knew what was coming. Their coach rarely raised his voice in anger—he believed that girls didn't respond well to that kind of instruction. They needed encouragement, understanding, and above all, deep support. Babb never raised his voice except when a girl didn't seem to appreciate the opportunity she'd been given or understand the fact that a depression was on and many people were suffering. In Durant, the Depression was just getting started and everyone kept thinking that things would get better. But during the period from 1931 to 1933, thousands of Oklahoma farmers would lose their land to foreclosure. By 1940, almost 8 percent of rural Oklahoma, better known as Okies, had relocated west to California and Arizona. So in comparison, getting up extra early for basketball practice in a cold field house should be treated as a privilege, not a hardship.

Babb waited until the late arrival was within hearing distance, and then he laid in. "Now listen to what I have to say because I have said it only a thousand times. All players contribute. All players will attend every practice. You're in college now and you live in my world. If you can't be here on time, you don't belong on this team. It's up to you."

"I don't know why I have to get up this early every morning," the girl said as she approached the group. "Why should I stay in such good physical condition? I'm just a substitute."

Every player on the court this morning understood how the girl was feeling: in her home town, she'd been a star, but on this team, she was second string.

"No team is better than its poorest substitute," he replied. Then he turned toward the other players and said, "Just remember, there's a depression on and we make do with what we have."

Lera Dunford snorted and turned to her sister and whispered, "Vera, honey, if he mentions the Depression one more time, I'll just lay back and die right here."

"It sounds like he'd rather scold us than coach us," Vera whispered back.

The Dunford twins would have kept on complaining and gotten into trouble themselves if Vick hadn't shushed them.

"You will *all* practice because you will all play," Babb continued. "That is my first rule. Maybe we should take the time to review the others."

Every girl who wanted to succeed knew Babb's rules by heart. Most of the girls had written them down:

MR. BABB'S RULES

- Everyone will play and support the team.

- Girls will maintain a proper diet. They will not skip meals. They will drink lots of water.

- Players will not eat any sweets during basketball season. No bananas.

- There is a 10 p.m. curfew during the week and 10:30 p.m. on weekends. If a player misses curfew, she will not be allowed to play in the next game.

- Girls will always confide in Aunt Lucy.

- In addition to a two-hour practice, girls must run one mile and shoot one hundred free throws in the Buzzard's Roost every day.

- Girls will study hard and maintain at least a B average. OPC is one of the few colleges in the nation to offer basketball scholarships to girls, so the school board requires them to perform.

- Players will not gloat, brag, exhibit meanness, or show off. OPC does not tolerate bad sportsmanship.

- Players will learn to win gracefully.

Babb continued to lecture about how crucial it was for them to come together as a team quickly. Their first exhibition game was in two weeks, and after that, they must be ready for the Christmas barnstorm tour—fifteen games played in three weeks throughout Texas, Louisiana, and Arkansas.

"Are you capable of winning?" he asked, and saw the doubtful looks in his players' eyes. "Don't worry. You will be."

They had no choice but to win. In the barnstorm style of play popular with the AAU, the better the team, the better its competition. Matchups not on the preseason schedule could be held at any time. If the Cardinals won most of their games early on, better teams would challenge them later in the season, and that could lead to an invitation to the AAU national tournament in March. The Cardinals would never get to play the Dallas Golden Cyclones, last year's national champions, if they didn't prove right up front that were a team to be reckoned with.

But it was more than just going to the national tournament. What Babb didn't include in any discourse, and what remained unspoken when he met with Dr. Hotchkin or the school board was that, in order to survive, the team had to make money. To make money, they had to win. During his previous two years as coach, OPC did not spend a penny to maintain its basketball team. The Cardinals paid for all of their equipment, meals, and hotel bills. They hadn't always been a self-sustaining team. Only after Babb arrived. Now, it's what was expected, especially since the economy crashed. Fewer paying students meant more responsibility for Babb and his players. Bringing the Golden Cyclones, the number one women's basketball team in the country, to play a game in Durant, along with their star forward, the now famous Babe Didrikson, would be a financial coup. They had to win.

Having finished his lecture, to the quiet relief of the players who had heard it all before and were anxious to get started, Babb turned back to the late arrival and told her that she would sit out this practice and to find a seat, making sure she had a blanket. Then he asked a second-string player to jump center with Lucille while Toka Lee and Vick started on defense. During most practice sessions, Babb had a sort of freestyle way of coaching that seemed almost like conducting music. It all came together like unexpected magic. He'd let them continue to play on their own and see what moves they came up with. Then he'd approve or criticize, tell them why, and move on to the next.

"I'll substitute as I see fit."

Holding the basketball, Babb walked to center court. Lucille stood facing her opponent in the jump circle. Babb heaved the ball into the air and

Lucille Thurman

they both jumped at once. Lucille felt shaky. Her stomach lurched. She knew everyone could see her legs wobble. She hated being nervous. But her nerves were quickly forgotten when her hand reached the ball first. Vick guarded Lucille. Without thinking, Lucille tipped the ball just over Vick's head, stepped past her teammate and caught it, then passed the ball to Doll who scored. Lucille felt joy at first, then dread. She knew Vick burned inside because of her misstep. She also knew that Vick, a superior guard, would adjust her play so that it didn't happen again. Vick was one of the best players on the team, not because of her athletic ability, but because she had an unrelenting self-confidence. Lucille watched as the other team worked the ball down the court. She stayed in a low, ready position. When the ball came back her way, she leaped for it and came down hard on a turned ankle. She fell to one knee, and Babb called a halt to play.

"Are you hurt?" Babb came to stand next to her.

"No, sir. It's just that my ankles won't stay put."

"Let's try taping them," he said, helping her up. They walked to the sideline where Babb opened his medical kit. Lucille sat on the bench while he spent several minutes wrapping thick white tape around both of her ankles. "You're playing well today, Lucille. If we can get your ankles fixed so they won't turn on you, you'll be good for the team at center position."

"Really?" she said. His words caught her by surprise.

"Really."

Mr. Babb had faith in her. Lucille suddenly felt lighter.

"Done." Babb stood up. Lucille stood next to him. At five ten, she was the same height as her coach. He gave her a short nod and then took a step toward the rest of the team.

"Mr. Babb . . ."

"Yes, Lucille," Babb said, turning back.

She moved closer to her coach and spoke in low tones. "I think you missed a button this morning."

Babb looked down at his shirt and found that he'd slipped the fourth button into the third buttonhole, causing his shirt to pucker outward an inch or two. Lucille thought she saw him blush. He quickly rebuttoned his starched white shirt and ran his hand over the front, smoothing it down. He looked up at Lucille and winked. Then he strode back out on court.

Toward the end of practice, after Doll faked out Toka Lee and sank an impossible shot like she always managed to do, Babb told them that defending a shot like that was almost impossible. But they'd have to learn how. Those Texas teams on the schedule wouldn't allow for any mistakes. Everyone here could play good basketball, he told them. But he wanted them to do more. He wanted them to learn how to play as if they were invincible.

CHAPTER 4

A Good Shot Maker
Believes in Herself

Doll Harris breezed out the side door of Graham-Jackson Hall, sped past the Oklahoma Presbyterian College campus church, and headed down Elm Street. She listened to her feet pound the blacktop—*clomp, clomp, clomp*—imagining tall oak, maple, and pecan trees bending in her wake as she shook the earth like a furious Goliath. Lengthening her stride, arms pumping hard, the muscles in her legs, arms, and stomach gradually acquiesced. Cool, humid air filled and escaped her lungs easily. The strenuous physical activity soon caused something like joy to spring from her heart and shoot through her body.

She hopped off the blacktop and cut across a wild and overgrown vacant lot. A rosebush with dried-up blooms and black thorns spread out thick and sudden from the shadows, threatening to halt her progress. Instead of slowing, Doll increased her speed and leaped, knees high and waist bent like a half-folded pocketknife. One small thorn caught a thread on the bottom of her sweatpants, but she made it and headed back onto the sidewalk. When she spied a piece of trash, a crushed paper cup caught in the breeze and skipping haphazardly down the street, she scooped it up, aimed for a nearby trash can, and made a clean shot.

In the crisp, fall afternoon air, Doll ran on, her shoulder-length black hair streaming behind her, sweat starting to soak through her T-shirt. She wore loose gray cotton warm-up pants made for boys and a matching sweatshirt. She refused to wear old-fashioned broadcloth bloomers or the stylish but impractical playsuits belted below the waist that looked like baby-girl dresses. A top athlete with any self-respect would never be seen working out in a pink or yellow baby-doll outfit. That's not to say that Doll didn't think about buying one if she ever had the money. She'd look cute on a picnic in a pink one. If she had her choice, she'd be working out in gym shorts, but only men ever wore gym shorts in public.

A young man driving a beige convertible Ford roadster that matched his blond hair passed Doll just as she turned down First Street. He gunned the engine, and Doll was caught by surprise. She stubbed her toe on the blacktop and nearly fell.

City folks, she thought as she ran on. Durant, with its population of about seventy-five hundred, was a bona fide city to Doll. Galloping over the red cobblestone used to construct the streets downtown, Doll wove in and out of both cars and pedestrians, holding her breath as she plunged by the pungent wagon yard near Market Square where farmers sold livestock and produce on Saturdays. More than a dozen sturdy workhorses and mules, some still wearing their leather harnesses attached to thick collars, waited for their owners to finish the day's business in town, hitch up the buggy or wagon, and head home. Buckboard wagons often mingled with the automobiles on the main roads, making traffic congestion and right-of-way concerns open to debate.

Picking up speed, Doll rounded the corner, dodged a wrought-iron streetlamp, and encountered the four-story shiny red brick of the Bryan Hotel that stretched for a half block at First and Main.

The town of Durant was in Bryan County, named in honor of William Jennings Bryan, the populist Democrat and common-man candidate for president who had attacked Darwinism at the Scopes trial in 1925, and then died of heart failure five days later. His rousing monologues about Christian morality as the foundation for peace and equality drew hundreds to the popular Chautauqua gatherings held in Durant during the early 1900s. Built in 1929, the Bryan Hotel became southeastern Oklahoma's center for social and political goings-on. Dignitaries, politicians—including Oklahoma governor, William "Alfalfa Bill" Murray—bankers, and other famous people just passing through would stay at the Bryan, attending dances and receptions in the ballroom. Rumors spread that Charles Arthur "Pretty Boy" Floyd, who grew up in the Cookson Hills three hours northeast of Durant, behaved himself when he frequented the hotel's coffee shop. Those rich enough to buy their way in laid their cards on the table in the nefarious poker game held on Saturday nights. Everyone thought that William Jennings Bryan had stayed there, too, since the hotel was his namesake. No one remembered that he had died four years before the hotel's grand opening. And surely if Bryan were still alive, having fought for temperance and the perfect understanding of God's will, he would have thrown out the Saturday-night cardsharps.

Traveling past the hotel at a full-out sprint, Doll liked to imagine these high-society folks glancing out the hotel lobby's street-level bay windows and admiring her fleet-footed performance. She felt at home when she had an audience.

This morning, parked automobiles lined the busiest two blocks of Main Street like books stuffed onto a shelf. She ran past storefront after storefront: Thacker's Department Store, the U.S. Post Office, a local gas station, the Building and Loan, the National Bank, the offices of the *Durant Daily Democrat*, Woolworth, Boyet-Long Drug Store, J. C. Penney's, Piggly Wiggly, and the Ritz Movie Theater, where the Cardinal team members had free passes. Once past the main part of town, she turned right and headed up Evergreen Street until she reached the county courthouse, a formidable building made of limestone with towering Greek columns built in 1917 by the same architect who designed the state capitol and the governor's mansion.

A few blocks later, Doll sometimes encountered a nanny pushing a baby carriage in front of the enormous Victorian homes owned by bank presidents, doctors, and lawyers. She had shaken hands with several of the men who owned these homes last year when Babb and other team members attended a Lions Club luncheon given in their honor after winning the sportsmanship trophy at the 1931 AAU national tournament. Since the OPC basketball team didn't have much school funding, Babb sought financial assistance from local businesses that, for a few dollars, could attach their names to game-day programs and receive good publicity in the newspapers. The businessmen, all dressed in wool suits with silk ties, had watched the girls while they sang the school song (in the same tune as Cornell's school song) over the microphone, with first-string-substitute Buena Harris's clear soprano leading. The daughter of a prominent Cherokee chief from Pryor, up near Tulsa in northeastern Oklahoma, Buena was also vice president of the campus Utopian Literary Society and had just been elected secretary-treasurer of the sophomore class. Every girl, including Doll, felt more confident when she sang with Buena.

The businessmen seemed quite impressed. Never in her wildest dreams had Doll imagined that she'd be charming bankers, store owners, and automobile dealers so that they might help fund a woman's basketball team.

Just two years ago, at the beginning of Babb's first coaching season, the Durant townspeople were introduced to the curious sight of the OPC Cardinals in training, including running in public. Almost all of the girls chose to exercise at the outdoor running track on Southeastern's campus. A few residents worried that the poor things might faint from overexertion. And yet, after months of training, followed by a respectable basketball season of seventeen wins and ten losses, even the most disapproving town members admitted that running didn't seem to present a danger to Babb's athletes.

But no Cardinal had ever run down Main Street. Doll was surprised, and then delighted, by the gossip she had elicited when she was a freshman last year. A few distraught citizens told Babb, sometimes when Doll was within earshot, that fast running was entirely inappropriate for young college girls. Doll thought that was the funniest thing she had ever heard.

Postcard of OPC's administration building. The top floor is the Buzzard's Roost half-court gym where the team first practiced. A few years after the Cardinals graduated, the top-floor Buzzard's Roost was blown off by a tornado and never rebuilt. Current photos of the building don't have the fourth floor.

If she could work the fields alongside her father, she could certainly run a mile. Babb would listen intently to the complaints, nodding his head with an appropriate frown. Then, after they'd gone, he'd smile at Doll and tell her not to worry. She'd stirred up excitement about the team without ever stepping onto a basketball court.

Doll kept a map of downtown stored in her mind along with a nearly accurate measure of one mile. When she passed her mile marker, she slowed to a walk and vowed to wear a hat the next time. Sweat stung her eyes so badly, she needed to rinse them with water. Fortunately, she always ended up at the Williams Public Library at Fourth and Beech, where there was a water fountain. After splashing her eyes and drying them with her sleeve, she sipped some water and then walked the six blocks back to OPC.

The school's small campus sat beneath several towering pecan trees at the west end of Durant. The property consisted of two four-story redbrick buildings with white stone trimming—the main administrative building, Graham-Jackson Hall, and the campus Presbyterian church. A sturdy brick corridor connected the dormitory and the administrative building, allowing students to commute between the two buildings in inclement weather. Besides the Buzzard's Roost gym that topped the administrative building, the two structures also housed the dorm rooms, offices, classrooms, cafeteria, library, auditorium, laundry, a swimming pool in the basement of Graham-Jackson Hall, a post office, and a supply shop. Doll entered Graham-Jackson Hall through the vast white-painted front door, six inches thick and fixed with two secure locks. She wondered if the locks were meant to keep unwanted visitors out or the dormitory's residents in. Doll's home in Cement didn't have any locks, just a hook latch on the inside of the screen door that kept it from banging in the wind. Inside the dormitory, the rooms were cool. Their polished wood floors and long halls provided a nice breezeway during the hot summer months. Residents always marveled at the ten-foot wood-beamed ceilings and the speckled sunlight filtering through the huge bay windows.

When Doll walked in, Toka Lee Fields was leaning against the front desk talking to Aunt Lucy, who had to stand on a sturdy, wooden box about a foot high so that she could converse with students. The two had their heads together, giggling. Doll asked them what was so funny, and Toka Lee handed her a copy of the school's student newsletter, the *Polished Pebbles*. There was an article about Dr. Hotchkin, the school's president (and Aunt Lucy's older brother), and his sweet sorghum syrup problem. Due to the economic depression and the conditions of the Southwest, the article stated that the people in the rural districts had been compelled to live solely on corn bread and sorghum. Because of this, there might be a sorghum shortage. Nobody could forecast just how great the shortage might be, but Dr. Hotchkin was quoted as saying, "Wholesome food will be provided! No girl will ever leave O.P.C. saying 'They denied me sorghum!'"

Doll finished reading and looked confused. It didn't seem very funny, especially when some people only had sorghum and corn bread to eat. When she mentioned that to Aunt Lucy and Toka Lee, they both burst out laughing. Perturbed, Doll waited for them to calm down, and then Toka Lee explained, with Aunt Lucy nodding along, that the Cardinals would never care about a sorghum syrup problem. In fact, if Mr. Babb ever saw any of his players touching the stuff, he'd suspend them from the team since one of his rules was the strict avoidance of all things sweet. Aunt Lucy commented that it was just like her brother to take a stand on something that contradicted Babb. She could just see them, an old man and his stubborn young protégé, getting into a pointless, heated argument—like Sisyphus from Greek mythology arguing with the boulder about the exact steepness of the incline as he rolled it up the mountain. Of course, the boulder was Mr. Babb. He could be as unmoving as concrete when it came to disciplining his players.

Doll finally cracked a smile. But she'd had enough gossip. She needed a shower, and she was just a little *perturbed* with Toka Lee. No matter how often she had asked, her best friend always gave excuses not to run with her: she hated the stink of the wagon yard; the rough, cobblestone streets gave her shin splints; she didn't want to be seen wearing her old sweats in public. Doll accepted her excuses but didn't really believe any of them except, maybe, for the last one. But much to her chagrin, she could never be angry with Toka Lee for very long. At the end of last year, after their first basketball season together, Toka Lee had written this in Doll's college yearbook:

May 14, 1931

Dearest Doll,

College days, or high school days, what does it matter? They're days that will forever be cherished and held close to my heart in remembrance of the sweetest friendship I have ever been a part of.

"When twilight pulls its Curtain,

And pins them with a star,
Remember that you'll
Have a friend,
Altho' she may be far."

Very truly,
Toka Lee Fields

Toka Lee was attractive, with light brown hair, high cheekbones, and full red lips. Boys were always asking her out on dates. She liked to experiment with makeup and usually wore some piece of jewelry. Doll didn't own any jewelry except for the bracelet that held the gold and bronze basketball charms awarded to her at last year's AAU regional tournament for placing third and being named an All-American. In fact, besides her basketball uniform, Doll owned only one dress for church, a pair of saddle oxfords, a wool skirt, work pants, two blouses, one wool sweater, two cotton undershirts, her sweats, and her Converse high-topped basketball shoes. She planned to purchase more clothes this year with the money she earned coaching basketball on weekends to some of Durant's high school girls. But as Toka Lee liked to point out, Doll didn't have to fix herself up. She had charisma.

"Oh, Doll, dear, I have a piece of mail for you," Aunt Lucy said in her girlish, high-pitched voice. "You get more than any girl at school."

"It's all my relatives," Doll explained, holding up one of the envelopes with the name on the return address listed as "Piss" Aunt Pauline. "I'm the first Harris to go to college." Then she put her other arm around Toka Lee's shoulders and guided her toward the stairs for the climb up to their room on the third floor. They couldn't be late for supper. And Doll would probably wager good money that sweet sorghum syrup would be on the menu.

DOLL HARRIS HAD always been tenaciously self-reliant. When she was younger, she studied hard to make straight A's even though her daily chores had her up before dawn milking the cow, feeding chickens, gathering eggs, and hauling water. She never resented her place in life, but she would seize opportunities to rise above it. In school, she learned to always wear shoes when she did her chores or visited the outhouse rather than going barefoot as was usual for farm children. Hookworm larvae thrived in polluted areas and entered a host through cuts or wounds in bare feet; lived on blood in the intestines; and caused loss of energy, weakness, stunted growth, and general anemia. Hookworm plagued rural areas without public sanitation, electricity, or indoor plumbing.

She honed her athletic skills on the hard-dirt, homemade courts built outdoors on driveways; in backyards; and on other good, flat surfaces. Even though in sixth grade she was only a head taller than the candy-store counter, she was always picked first in any after-school, get-up game and was the last to leave, staying so late that she missed the bus and had to walk the three miles home. As she grew older, despite the many demanding chores at home, she became the high school's star player. Other kids liked her. She had several best friends, and many more who wanted to be her best friend. "Here's hoping you have every bit of happiness and success in your future life for everyone knows Doll always gets what she goes after," wrote a friend in her senior yearbook.

But she had another side, one formed by growing up dirt poor with four older sisters: that of a fierce competitor vying for attention. Doll often felt insignificant, being the youngest. Her elder sisters seemed like heroes from a mythic drama, able to perform incredible tasks—driving a truck, baking bread, galloping a horse. These frailer parts of her, the parts that relied on other people to survive, she tried to keep hidden.

Meanwhile, she would find her own significance. She would make sure no one would dismiss her as ordinary. That's why she kept a secret: her real name wasn't Doll. She was christened Velma Bell Harris. God, she hated that name. It announced to the world that she was a hick. It wasn't a fitting name for a star athlete. The day she turned twenty-one and became an adult, her first act would be to file the official paperwork that would make Doll legal and send Velma Bell into permanent oblivion. Sometimes, though, she wished that she *could* let others know her name so that she could also reveal the origin story of how she came to be called Doll. When she was born, her sister Verdie, who was just two years old, scooped up tiny Velma Bell in her chubby arms and carried her around like a favorite toy. To anyone who would ask, and even if they didn't, Verdie would hold the baby up and proclaim that this was her brand-new baby doll. Verdie was so charming, and Doll so cute, that the name had stuck. Throughout her life, everyone called her Baby Doll. As she got older, she started going by just Doll. Only Aunt Lucy and Mr. Babb, who had both seen her birth certificate, knew her real name, and she was grateful that they had never asked her about it. They did her the courtesy of even listing her on the school roster sent to the teachers as Doll.

LUNCHTIME AT OPC was a noisy affair. Everyone ate together in the cafeteria, including the Indian children from the primary and secondary schools housed on campus. Since most of the freshman basketball players were required to sit at assigned tables with the younger students and help them learn table manners, the girls didn't have much time to chat until suppertime. All ninety of the young women attending OPC ate supper together, and it was then that the basketball players felt more like regular students. But the players always finished early. Most of them had a million other things to do before they could even start studying.

After supper every night, Doll and Toka Lee put on their warm-ups, walked up the four flights in the administrative building to the Buzzard's Roost, and spent an hour shooting the required hundred free throws. Other girls usually showed up, but there was no set time since all the players had to fit the routine into their tight schedules. To make sure every player met her daily goal, Babb asked them to partner up so that one could vouch for the other's performance. And now that the season's start was getting closer, Babb upped the ante by requiring that each girl make eighty out of the one hundred free throws.

Doll Harris

Some of the younger girls complained about the hard practice, and that irritated Doll to no end. Didn't they want to win? If they did, Babb expected them to train. She saw how the freshmen had acted during their first early morning at the field house—one poor girl even arriving late! Something like rage had boiled in Doll's heart when that happened. Didn't these girls know how to act when they'd been given the moon? To be a great player, you had to like to sweat. You had to like to train. You had to believe in yourself. There was a reason Babb made them run every day. If you can't run, you can't play basketball. Doll could tell that a few of the new girls grimaced a bit when they wiped sweat off their bodies, and she figured that they'd grown up sheltered. Well, that just wasn't going to work at OPC. It would take plenty of sweat, practice, and aches and pains on the part of any freshman before Doll would ever respect her.

Tonight Lucille, Coral, Vick, and Bo-Peep were already using two of the six goals that dotted the edges of the half-court gym. Soon after, Alice Hamilton arrived with her younger sister, Ginny. Alice and Ginny lived with their mother and two older sisters in a house near campus. Because they were half Chickasaw, they could attend OPC free of charge. Four years ago, their oldest sister, Gwen, played on the first basketball team at OPC under a different coach. Doll liked Alice, who was secretary of the dramatic club. Doll was vice president, and they were planning to perform two one-act plays this semester in the school's auditorium. Alice's mother, Mrs. Hamilton, was the team's expert seamstress. She was in charge of turning the dull-red bloomers they played in last year into up-to-date spiffy uniforms. The bloomers had to be taken in and shortened to make their uniforms look more like the men's shorts. OPC wasn't the only team still wearing bloomers that went past their knees, but to get attention from sportswriters and to look like a real basketball team, the uniforms had to at least meet the AAU standards. This year, if everything worked out, meaning that Durant citizens turned out and attended games, they might even get brand-new uniforms made from the shiny satin that all the top teams were now wearing.

Doll always shot her free throws from the chest, with a little twist. Her motto was: never shoot when in doubt. During a regular game, due to her height issues, she rarely tried a layup but would make goals from farther out, sometimes even near the half-court line. She had a sneaky weapon. To surprise the girl defending the goal, Doll, after receiving a good handoff or pass from her teammate, would suddenly catapult her arms skyward while she was still holding the ball. The quick motion distracted her guard. When the ball became even with her head, she would push it off in a soft, fluid release that sang past the guard. Much of the time, the guard would just stare at Doll, openmouthed. Sometimes she'd even laugh because Doll's form seemed so unusual. But the smirk would become a glower when the ball swished through the net.

Doll's shooting style might be eccentric, but she hardly ever missed.

That's why Babb had made her team captain. But he also had reservations about Doll. He was constantly berating her about cooperation, solidarity, and mutual understanding. He cautioned that her harsh feelings toward new teammates might keep her from being a team player. Getting ready for basketball season made Babb stay up nights worrying, so Doll had to remind him that she had led the Cardinals to a third-place trophy at the regional tournament last year and add reassurances that she was every bit as skilled a player as Babe Didrikson, the star forward for the champion Dallas Golden Cyclones. Babb valued her input and even began relying on her like he might an assistant coach. They sometimes held lengthy conversations about the business side of basketball. She was the only girl on the team who understood just how much work Babb had to do in addition to coaching—fund-raising, scheduling games, and making sure the freshmen learned discipline. They all had to stop seeing themselves as small-town high school athletes and start imagining victory.

Doll had learned about excellence from her junior high and high school coach, Mr. Daily. They had become close friends even though her team, the Cement Bulldogs, ended up losing at the regional tournament in Rush Springs during her senior year. She was glad that Babb didn't see her lose that game. As sportswriter Charles Saulsberry who penned a column in the *Oklahoma City Times* called In the Sports Spotlight wrote, "Cement's great season had a fatal ending." He had called Cement the home of the "highly efficient and pretty-girl basketball players." Doll, like most girls who played basketball, didn't see anything wrong with using her looks to build publicity for the sport she loved. She had pasted that newspaper column into the enormous scrapbook she'd started as a senior and now kept stowed in her dorm room. In that same book, she kept a farewell letter from Daily.

Dear "Doll Baby,"

It is just too bad that we have to graduate, check in our suit and commence life anew. It is bad enough for you—it is worse for me as for the next coach.

Many are the hard battles we have lived through during these four years. I have always appreciated your "Bull-dog tenacity" and was selfish enough to think a bit of it was to save "my" scalp. You have been worth a lot to the team and I am depending on you to make the all-star team in the game of life—Don't disappoint me.

Possibly many times you have grown tired of my supervision but now that the end is near I hope you can look back and see that it was for the best and will repay me and help some other little girl "make good."

Remember that your fight, team work and loyalty made you a friend who is and always will be interested in you—his "little, freckle-faced forward."

C. F. Daily
Coach '23–'30

Doll took Daily's words to heart. Despite her tendency to strive to prove her own worth, she thought she understood the dynamics of teamwork and team building: a good team always followed her lead, just like in high school. She decided that she would continue to stand out and set an example. Be the hero to them like her older sisters were for her when she was growing up. It wouldn't hurt if the freshmen hated her in the process. None of those girls would ever be as good as she was anyway. Her goal was to make them just half as good and still create the best women's team in existence!

It never crossed Doll's mind that by ignoring the younger players during practice and by showing off, her behavior might make team building worse. All she could think of was winning. And to Doll, winning meant "getting the ball to Doll" no matter what.

CHAPTER 5

Choctaw Town

Dressed in gray overalls, long underwear, and a plaid Woolrich shirt jacket, the president of OPC, Dr. Ebenezer Hotchkin, was taking advantage of the quiet few hours before Sunday church service by raking fertilizer and straw mulch into the soil of his backyard garden. He removed his wire-framed glasses to clean perspiration off the lenses and then turned his face into the beginning sunrise. A lazy hawk circled overhead searching for the rabbits and mice attracted to the homemade fertilizer that smelled like cow manure and rotten eggs. The orderly rows would sprout sweet potatoes, beets, green beans, turnips, mustard greens, onions, and garlic in the spring. After church, his wife, Maria, would finish planting spring flowers like pansies and snap dragons with the help of one or two OPC professors who rented out the bedrooms previously occupied by the Hotchkins' children who were now grown.

At sixty-two years, Dr. Hotchkin felt more feeble than he should for a man his age. Just raking the garden caused a dull ache in the arm he'd injured last March when a freight train making a routine switch had backed into Hotchkin's automobile, parked too close to a crossing near the rail yard. Dr. Hotchkin and his car skidded into a drainage ditch and the car overturned. When the train conductor and an assistant scrambled to assist Dr. Hotchkin, they found him shaken but uninjured. The three men decided to right the car, and in the struggle, Dr. Hotchkin slipped on the wet grass and flung his left arm into a shattered car window, nearly severing an artery. A policeman who had arrived on the scene just minutes before, staunched the bleeding as best he could, drove Dr. Hotchkin the two miles to Durant Hospital, and then telephoned Mrs. Hotchkin. Weakened by the loss of blood and the splintering pain, he spent several days in the hospital.

Even though his arm had healed completely, it felt sore, and he still took great care when putting on his shirt in the morning. This frailty didn't sit well with a man who was born in the middle of Indian Territory at Living Land, Choctaw Nation, not long after the Civil War. His paternal grandfather, Rev. Ebenezer Hotchkin Sr., was renowned as the only missionary, along with his wife, Philena, to travel with fourteen thousand Choctaw when the U.S. government, after the Treaty of Dancing Rabbit Creek in 1830, forced them to move from their homes in Mississippi to the Indian Territory, part of present-day eastern Oklahoma. Hotchkin Sr. liked to go by Lapis Hanta, his Choctaw name, which meant "Peace Trumpet." It was said that he spoke Choctaw better than English and even translated the Bible into Choctaw. During the removal, Philena, known as Mother Hotchkin, rode a tough little Indian pony and carried her baby daughter in her lap. More than two thousand Choctaw died along the way from exposure, fatigue, cholera, or other diseases. The desperate journey became known as the Trail of Tears. After long days of suffering and hardship, when they finally arrived at their destination north of the Red River, there was nothing but cold winter, empty wilderness, no provisions, and no shelter. The farming equipment promised by the government, including plows and hoes, didn't show up until the spring of 1832. A few buffalo still roamed the prairies in Indian Territory, but the Choctaw along with the other removed Indians known as the Five Civilized Tribes—Cherokee,

Choctaw, Chickasaw, Creek, and Seminole—had abandoned hunting while in Mississippi to become skilled farmers, growing cotton, corn, potatoes, peas, beans, pumpkins, and melons. Some of the wealthier Choctaw owned slaves who had joined them on the journey. They developed languages, lived in large orderly towns situated in what became the southeastern United States. Now forced out of their well-established home, they started over in what was known as the Wild West. Ultimately, it took the government two years to supply all the tools necessary for survival, and during those first months, they built houses out of blackjack logs with mud-cemented walls and tree-bark shingles. The hard-dirt floors were covered with blankets or animal skins. Flour hauled from Little Rock, Arkansas, cost fifty dollars a barrel. Pumpkin and other squash became a food staple, the staff of life.

Both of Hotchkin's parents followed in his paternal grandfather's footsteps, working as Presbyterian missionary schoolteachers in the Indian Territory. Young Hotchkin attended early grades in his mother's classroom with the Indian kids and later left his family for high school at the Haskell Institute, a government Indian school in Lawrence, Kansas. Hotchkin could attend without charge because he was the son of missionaries living in Indian Territory. But Haskell was a rude awakening. It was regimented like a military school, designed to strip away the "savage" Indian and assimilate students into civilized European culture. Eventually, at age seventeen, Hotchkin decided to leave school and work as a cowhand on the Bar-Z Ranch near Pauls Valley, Oklahoma. The treacherous job had him always on the lookout for cattle rustlers and outlaws like the notorious Killer Miller, Bill Doolin, and the Dalton brothers. Some of his fellow cowboys who didn't have any luck were shot and killed.

The cowboy life could easily lead to wild living and hard ways, so cowmen and ranchers had established a code of ethics that was strictly enforced. The code included honesty, pride in your work, taking care of the land, and speaking clean language around the camp house. Anyone violating these rules received twenty lashes with a wet rope. Young Hotchkin never drank alcohol or played cards because of his religious upbringing, but he did have a loose tongue when it came to four-letter words. He broke the code, received his twenty lashes, and afterward, wasn't able to sit in his saddle for a week. A few weeks later, he gave up the rough life and resumed his education, eventually obtaining his doctorate of divinity at Austin College in Sherman, Texas. He still swore every now and then but only under his breath.

Just then the screen door slammed shut, and Dr. Hotchkin looked up to see Babb, who rented a room from the Hotchkins. The coach was stepping off the back porch and plodding over the fresh mulch that stuck to his shoes. Babb wrinkled his nose in disgust when the fertilizer stench caught up with him. Dr. Hotchkin barely noticed Babb's limp these days. Sometimes he wondered what could have happened to cause such an injury, but Babb never talked about it and Dr. Hotchkin never asked.

It was just like Babb to be up before sunrise and working on Sunday morning. His face always gave away his thoughts, and Dr. Hotchkin knew the younger man well enough now to see that something needed to be taken care of, a bill signed, a check endorsed. Since Hotchkin was the president of OPC, he was also Babb's employer. Sure enough, Babb wanted to discuss his additions to the quarterly report about the basketball team to the Presbyterian Board. When Babb had a problem brewing, nothing, not even lack of sleep, would keep him from finding an immediate and proper solution.

Dr. Hotchkin had developed a deep respect for Babb, who, with his love of politics and public speaking, had quickly undertaken the task of raising funds from Durant's local businesses. Everyone liked Babb and no one had ever complained about his dogged persistence. The fact was, Dr. Hotchkin and Babb's personalities complemented each other. Unlike Babb, Dr. Hotchkin took things at face value. He didn't try to comprehend motives or cipher out hidden agendas. He mainly listened to what a person had to say. When he first met Babb back in 1929 at his interview for the OPC coaching position, Dr. Hotchkin had decided to give Babb the job because he liked his ideas about coaching young women. They needed approval more than boys. Their motivation often came from wanting to please, and so they tended to underestimate themselves. Stressing teamwork and cooperation often helped shy girls gain confidence and self-respect and sometimes revealed an inner toughness necessary to play good basketball.

This morning, while the two men were talking about Babb's report, Dr. Hotchkin caught sight of Alice Hamilton and her sister Ginny carrying a sturdy woven basket. Along with three other freshmen, Lucille, Coral, and Vick, the girls were sneaking through the narrow alley behind his home. The Hamiltons lived with their mother across the street from OPC. The basket was part of the gear that included a stiff bristle brush and a sharp knife used to gather wild mushrooms. Alice must have found something special in the tag-along freshmen because she and her sister rarely took strangers mushroom hunting. Dr. Hotchkin had asked Ginny once where she'd unearthed the beautiful golden chanterelles she was carrying in her basket, and she just winked at him and kept on walking. But her cotton dress had been covered in sticky grass seeds, so he knew she'd passed through town and waded through the waist-high prairie grass a half mile away. On the other side of that field was a thick post oak forest, and he imagined the two girls following a ghost of a trail that only Indian eyes could find. Having spent his childhood going to school with Choctaw kids, Dr. Hotchkin once told a friend, "I am about half Indian in heart and mind."

Before the girls disappeared from view, he called out and reminded them not to miss his special sermon at church later on. They turned and waved back reassuringly.

IN ADDITION TO Bible studies during the week, every student was also required to attend services on Sunday. Most of them didn't mind. Dr. Hotchkin related stories so vividly that when he finished, listeners were startled to find themselves still sitting in a pew.

Over two hundred OPC students filled the old wooden pews of the redbrick church. The mushroom hunters, Alice, Lucille, Coral, Vick, and Ginny, were now dressed up and seated with the rest of the basketball players including Doll, Toka Lee, La Homa Lassiter, Teny Lampson, and Bo-Peep. Babb sat in the back with the other instructors, next to Aunt Lucy.

Today Dr. Hotchkin intended to be inspirational, not preachy, to open hearts by speaking the entire hour about a courageous woman who began her journey into Indian Territory when she was the age of these college girls. It was a personal story that included bits from his own life. But he'd decided that these young women now looking up at him needed to understand that if this story had never happened, they would not be at OPC receiving such a fine education. In fact, OPC would not exist.

The story of the founding of OPC is much like the story of the West. Ministers, educators, Indians, outlaws, pioneers, and visionaries flocked to Indian Territory, and some of those same groups came together to build OPC; it was a community effort.

Lands ceded to the Indians once covered vast swaths of the western United States, but by the 1850s treaties and other maneuvers by the U.S. government had reduced Indian lands to approximately the modern-day Oklahoma borders except for the panhandle, which was called No Man's Land. These lands became known as Indian Territory because it's where many tribes ended up after the Indian Removal Act of 1830. In the early days of Indian Territory, just before and right after the Civil War, most of those living there had either been forced to move by the U.S. government, like the Choctaw, or they were called by God, like the teachers and ministers who helped the poor. Included among those called by God was Mary Jane Semple, Dr. Hotchkin's mother.

Semple grew up in Steubenville, Ohio. Her father practiced dentistry and she was afforded all of the luxuries of upper-middle-class girls—pretty dresses, delightful parties, a society of chattering friends. Inquisitive by nature, she became a top student but with a strong Presbyterian upbringing that kept her feet on the ground. At age ten or twelve, in Sunday school one day, a famous medical missionary to India, Dr. John Scudder, lectured the children about his travels and upon closing told his audience to write in their Bibles, "Mr. Scudder asked me to be a missionary." The minute Semple wrote down those words, she felt bound to them. In the coming years, when other girls started talking about wedding rings and handsome young men, Semple dreamed about far-flung destinations. One day, when she had just turned nineteen, she sang a solo part in her church choir that read, "There comes a call and I must go." As she sang, tears coursed down her cheeks. A shining epiphany had warmed her heart. She was singing her own call to mission; it was time for her to leave home.

Becoming a missionary could lead to injury, illness, starvation, and even death. But Semple, in such a euphoric state, didn't care. Her only desire was to find out where she was going. At that time, the famous Presbyterian missionary Rev. Cyrus Kingsbury sought teachers and other workers for missions in Indian Territory. At first, the federal government wanted to train Indians in vocational tasks—horseshoeing, flour milling, telegraphy—creating a class of servants and technicians. The missionaries admitted that learning these jobs would be very practical, but they saw a greater future for the Five Civilized Tribes. Their curriculum also included classical education—grammar, physics, geometry, Greek, and Latin.

Semple traveled to meet Kingsbury in Kentucky with another woman who seemed like an ideal missionary. She was older and more experienced with a rather stoic demeanor. She could cook, sew, and raise vegetables. On the other hand, Semple wore fashionable hoop skirts and impractical shoes. She carried a guitar because she loved to sing. Together they attended the General Assembly where Kingsbury would be recruiting mission workers for his stations among the Chickasaw and Choctaw. Kingsbury immediately accepted the older woman but took one look at the teenage Semple and in his best fatherly voice began listing all of the hardships she would have to endure: poor food, strange people, a difficult language, and long years of work in questionable living conditions. She would be leaving behind a future as a doctor or lawyer's wife for hard work and very little rest or reward. Still, she insisted she would not be turned from her calling. As a last resort, Kingsbury brought in the shock troop—a young friend of Semple's family who had spent time in Texas and the Indian Territory. He spoke of drunk Indians, vile customs, and strange superstitions that had created a depraved people. He complimented her mother's generosity, the fine food she served when his family visited, and the soft beds they stayed in overnight. But Semple insisted that she wasn't the soft, spoiled, and naive girl they took her for. They couldn't keep her from her path.

So, after convincing Kingsbury to sanction her trip, she left behind everything and never looked back. On her journey to Choctaw country, Semple traveled with one or two other missionaries by boat down the Ohio and Mississippi Rivers to Arkansas. They journeyed over land in a wagon pulled by sluggish oxen until they reached the swamps filled with nearly impassable underbrush. The sun's incessant heat sent snakes underground and grasshoppers singing. Mosquitoes followed in swarms by day and fed on their tired bodies by night. They crossed streams and rivers, wading through rough waters. At one point, they spent the night in a large plantation filled with slaves and their thirty or forty children. The overseer begged them to stay and teach the children, an unusual request in the slave-owning south, offering them three hundred dollars each per year plus room and board, with time off every summer. Although their mission work paid only one hundred dollars per year plus room and board, with time off every eight years, Semple and the others refused the offer and journeyed on until they reached Indian Territory.

Semple's first school had been founded in 1832 for Indian orphans, mostly Choctaw. The Wheelock Mission and Academy (named after Eleazer Wheelock, the first president of Dartmouth College) was located in southern Indian Territory, about ten miles north of the Red River and the Texas border. Upon her arrival at the mission in 1856, Semple's youth and quiet ways caused concern. Why had Dr. Kingsbury chosen such a delicate teenager—who spoke no Choctaw—as a missionary? How could he allow such a butterfly to come to this bleak place? But Semple surprised her critics when she brandished a willow switch to discipline the wayward in her classroom. By the end of the year, all her students knew English, and she spoke Choctaw perfectly.

As a teacher for the Presbyterian mission, Semple went where she was needed. The next year, she taught at Bennington Mission Station, located about twenty miles east of what would later become Durant, near the Boggy River. The food was scant—only corn bread, sorghum, and bacon—and poorly prepared. Never any milk, much less butter or cream. She thought of returning home, but then she transferred to nearby Living Land in 1860, the mission established by Ebenezer Hotchkin Sr. There she met his son Henry, and thoughts of home evaporated. The two were soon married. Soon after, though, he left his bride and joined the Confederate Army in Texas, serving as Second Lieutenant in the Commissary Department and supplying the troops with horses. Semple was shocked, but didn't complain. He was, however, the only Hotchkin known to be on the Confederate side of the Civil War.

A few years after Henry returned home, they transferred to Caddo, a new mission situated in Indian Territory thirty miles north of Denison, Texas, on a broad prairie named after a tribe of blanks—Indians annihilated by another tribe. Semple moved with her by then five children into a two-room house near the brand-new Missouri-Kansas-Texas Railroad, nicknamed the Katy. Eventually, Semple would give birth to twelve children, including Ebenezer, a middle child, and Lucy, born eight years later and one of her youngest girls. Three would die of pneumonia or other illnesses before the age of ten. Oftimes, she taught with a baby in her lap.

The school grew, and a new building was soon filled with Choctaw children. But soon after, her husband moved them again, this time to a wilderness called Chikiki about one hundred miles northwest of Caddo. With her husband already in Chikiki finding a place to live, Semple gathered her now eight children and traveled as the only adult in a covered wagon over rough roads and through swift streams. At night, they camped on the roadside and were entertained by the howling wolves and hooting owls kept at bay by their burning campfire. Three days later, dusty and tired, they arrived at Chikiki, joining her husband who had purchased a log cabin on twenty acres just south of the school building. The cabin had homemade doors, boards for the roof, one small window in each room, and rough-hewn wood floors. The school was not much better: only one room with log benches, no desks, and poor lighting. Semple's husband traveled back and forth from Living Land to Chikiki several times to bring lumber for new buildings. After a year, the new school was finished, with six more rooms filled this time with Chickasaw children.

They stayed in Chikiki for several years, teaching, expanding the school, and raising their children. But in 1888, Henry, who had left teaching by then and gone back to farming, came down with pneumonia and passed away. A few months later, Semple was driving a buggy hitched to a team of young mules when they became frightened. The runaway team's quick movements threw Semple from the buggy, and the hard landing broke her hip. She was left in the woods alone and in great pain until a search party found her. The hip never healed properly, and she walked with crutches.

BY 1870, THE U.S. government, in its increasing pursuit of westward expansion, promised land grants to the first railroad that reached the entrance to Kansas via the southeast border. The Katy railroad swallowed up smaller rail companies including the Union Pacific, St. Louis & Santa Fe, and the Hannibal & Central Missouri, eliminating the competition and forming the foundation of its far-reaching railway. With the grant funding won, Katy pushed its way from the Kansas border into Indian Territory, passing through Caddo in 1872, about the same time that Semple was moving her family to the two-room cabin that her husband had built.

Sixteen miles southeast of Caddo, Katy officials plopped down an old, rusted boxcar on the east side of the main tracks and used it as a makeshift depot. They ran a line from Mineral Bayou Creek and used mule power to pump water into a tank across the tracks from the boxcar depot. The railroad called this rustic stopover Durant Station. The arrival of the railroad brought paying jobs to the area, but it also attracted entrepreneurs, white men who set up gambling tables and sold liquor in a previously dry territory. The older, more conservative Choctaw leaders resisted the advancement of white culture that threatened its customs and land. Others saw a chance to improve living conditions and develop a thriving community. Whenever a pioneer family or profiteer came looking for land and a place to build a home, they were directed to the home of Dixon Durant.

In the 1830s, Durant came with his family from Mississippi over the Trail of Tears, on foot and in wagons to Chickasaw Bluff, down the Mississippi River to the mouth of the Arkansas River, and up the Arkansas to Little Rock. From there, they traveled on foot and in wagons to the Choctaw Nation, a land that spread east to Arkansas Territory, a few hundred miles west to the Chickasaw Nation, north to the South Canadian River, and south to the Red River. The Choctaw held their lands in common. Citizens could homestead anywhere and fence surrounding lands as long as they weren't closer than a hog call (about one-quarter mile) to another homestead. Any citizen could make improvements—build barns and houses—and sell the improvements but not the land. Non-Choctaws could rent land from the tribe by purchasing a permit from the Choctaw government as long as they were endorsed, or sponsored, by Choctaw citizens.

The Durants settled down and built cabins on the black-soiled bottomland found just north of the Red River. They fenced the land and raised cattle, branding each of the herd with a *D* on either side of the hip. A small herd of buffalo grazed the prairie, along with wild turkeys, deer, prairie chickens, quail, rabbits, and squirrels. Pecan and walnut groves thrived in the numerous river and creek bottoms. Ten years later, the federal government built Fort Washita near the Washita River and eighteen miles north of the Red River to protect the Chickasaw and Choctaw from angry Plains Indian tribes who had been uprooted from their lands.

Dixon Durant, a Presbyterian minister, was one-fourth French Canadian and three-fourths Choctaw. Anyone who wasn't Choctaw and who wanted to secure a permit for a home and/or business in and around Durant Station had to gain sponsorship from Durant and then pay him rent.

Hundreds of whites had entered the territory since the introduction of the Katy, but Durant, a righteous Presbyterian who would cancel contracts at the whiff of anything illegal, like drinking alcohol, kept the town's growth to a minimum. Noncitizens could not vote or participate in lawmaking, and the deputy U.S. marshals helped the Indian police keep the peace. Unfortunately for those like Durant who wanted slow growth, Durant Station was not only on the Katy's route but also just a few miles west of the Texas Road. Travelers would purchase a ticket on Colbert's Ferry, a few miles south of Durant Station, to cross the Red River and then head to Texas.

At some point, Durant Station, in the heart of the Choctaw Nation and a throughway to the Red River crossing into Texas, became known simply as Durant.

When the Five Civilized Tribes walked the Trail of Tears, Indian Territory was wilderness, and most white people didn't have much interest in traveling anywhere west of the Mississippi. That all changed as the U.S. population exploded. Passed in 1890, the Oklahoma Organic Act drew a rough, jagged divide through the middle of Indian Territory, and the western half, including No Man's Land, became known as Oklahoma Territory. *Oklahoma* is a Choctaw word meaning "red people." First-come-first-served land runs opened the western half to whites and other non-Indians.

Then the creation of the Dawes Commission in 1893 further aggravated life for the Durant Choctaws. The commission sent government representatives to negotiate agreements with the Five Civilized Tribes that would extinguish tribal governments and give each tribe member ownership of a portion of tribal lands: 180 acres of farm land or 320 acres of grazing land. Tribal leaders didn't see the point of land ownership and balked at making any pacts with the commission. But the changes kept coming. Between 1894 and 1895, over a hundred thousand non-Indians poured into Indian Territory. By 1895, the Indian Territory's total population stood at 350,000, with whites outnumbering Indians four to one.

Also in 1895, electricity came to Durant, and the population surged to twenty-five hundred. Hotels sprung up—mostly populated by the land appraisers—an ice plant, a cotton gin, the First National Bank of Durant, a flour mill, and the construction of waterworks. At one point, amid the frenzied hustle and bustle, a man undertook to build a house in the middle of the public square near Main Street. Irate townsfolk got out their Winchesters and forced the workmen to stop. Then the owner of the building gathered together some of his friends, and they with their guns in turn put the builders to work again. The other side tossed a dynamite bomb near the building. The explosion solved the problem. All the workers quit. Needless to say, tombstones and monuments, prepared on short notice, became a thriving occupation in Durant.

In 1897, seeing continued resistance as futile, the Chickasaw and Choctaw Nations came to terms with the Dawes Commission and signed the Atoka Agreement, making all tribal members U.S. citizens. Those non-Indians who had rented property from Dixon Durant, along with his son William, now had the option to buy the land outright. The town of Durant thrived, but it was missing something of growing importance: schools.

DURANT HAD ONE school for all grade levels, Halsell Hall, established in 1892 by a man from Texas who had named the school after himself. He had rented property from Dixon Durant at South Second Avenue and West Arkansas Street, a little over a block away from the hustle and bustle of Main Street. Arguments over curriculum and failure to attract enough patrons kept the school from thriving.

A man named C. J. Ralston, then superintendent of the Armstrong Academy, a nearby boarding school owned and operated by the Choctaw Nation, was in the middle of speaking to the Choctaw Council, located in Tuskahoma, the capital of the Choctaw Nation, when he received a telegram informing him of a family tragedy. His four-year-old son, Calvin, had drowned in a pond in eastern Bryan County. Ralston returned home to Durant to bury his son. To take his mind off his grief, friends persuaded him to attend a meeting about the inefficiencies and lack of funds for Halsell Hall. Sharp, piercing disagreements echoed off walls during the meeting. If the school kept its doors open, Halsell would have to listen to his patrons and compromise on policies and curriculum. But Halsell stubbornly refused. Mediator Ralston could not find any common ground between the two factions and finally saw only one way to solve the problem.

Calvin's grandmother had set aside two hundred dollars for the boy's education. Seeing that young children often failed to survive childhood due to disease and life in the rough Indian Territory, the practical woman had also stipulated that in the event of Calvin's death the money must be used for education purposes. Ralston offered to purchase the building from Halsell and open another school within twenty days. The Indian Presbytery eventually approved the purchase, giving Ralston the full support of the national Executive Committee of Home Missions of the Presbyterian Church, which promised monetary support each year of up to one thousand dollars.

The Calvin Institute opened in the spring of 1894 and soon hosted a student body of 140 Choctaw and non-Choctaw, ranging in age from six to eighteen years. But school administrators still couldn't agree on a curriculum or how funds should be distributed, and the school found itself mired in turmoil without progress. At this point, Ralston decided to call on an expert, offering her the management position. She accepted.

Mary Semple Hotchkin, now sixty years old, was teaching at a Chickasaw academy near Wynnewood, Oklahoma, about ninety miles northeast of Durant. Before she set out on another journey, the secretary of the Executive Committee of Home Missions sent her an urgent letter, advising, "See and hear, but don't talk!" Semple understood the warning. After all, she had experienced much worse than a gaggle of irate townsfolk who liked to hear themselves yammer. But right before she could leave, one of her children came down with pneumonia. She nursed her patient through the worst but couldn't yet leave Wynnewood. So she asked her son Ebenezer to go in her place, telling him that she would join him two weeks later. Young Hotchkin had inherited his mother's love for teaching, her ability to accept Indians as people, and her talent at finding order in chaos. But he took it a step further. He had become a champion fund-raiser. September 1, 1896, the first day of school, found both Semple and her son in charge of the Calvin Institute.

Over the next two years, Semple and Dr. Hotchkin got to work. Dr. Hotchkin made friends among the much needed prospective patronage, including William Durant, son of Dixon, a prominent attorney who one day would become chief of the Choctaws. Semple and Dr. Hotchkin made some policy adjustments so that more non-Indian students could attend, and by 1899, attendance soared to three hundred. To meet the needs of the increased student body, Semple hired her daughter, Lucy, along with two other faculty members.

In addition to primary and secondary schools, the Calvin Institute also included a collegiate studies department with curriculum that included higher algebra, Latin, Greek, higher English, geometry, physics, general history, and Bible studies. The Calvin Institute's fast growth triggered a visit by the president of Austin College and the reverend from the First Presbyterian Church of Dallas. These two men were in charge of the Presbyterian Synod of Texas that oversaw the Indian Presbytery and Calvin Institute. After careful inspection, they gave their blessing for a larger building and added equipment. But Semple and Dr. Hotchkin had bigger ideas for their school. They persuaded the representatives from the Presbyterian Synod to stay a few more days and attend a meeting Dr. Hotchkin had arranged with prominent Durant businessmen.

The meeting took place at the Methodist church, and Semple was the only woman present. She and Dr. Hotchkin sat in church pews with such well-known men as Lewis Paullin, editor of the *Durant Eagle*; R. L. Williams who, after statehood, would be elected as governor of Oklahoma; William Durant, Dixon's cousin, lawyer, and future Choctaw chief; Green Thompson, a pioneer banker; and Judge G. T. Ralls, an attorney who handled Indian land claims. Representing her students, Semple stood up and opened the meeting by saying that the best heritage you can leave your children is trained hearts and minds. Then she turned the proceedings over to Paullin, who spoke about the Calvin Institute, describing its students and the funds that would be needed to enlarge and continue the school's operation. He proposed that Durant businessmen raise five thousand dollars toward a new school, that the Synod of Texas raise two thousand, the Executive Committee of Home Missions raise another two thousand, and that one thousand dollars come from donations at large in Durant.

Breaking the silence after Paullin finished speaking, future state governor Williams talked about the spirit of idealism that drew pioneers out west, knowing that no matter what obstructions arose, the school would succeed. "Men who act move the world," he said, and urged those fortunate men present at this meeting to act in behalf of the Calvin Institute. Then Durant rose, and as he spoke a vision for the new school began to take shape. He saw a momentous future for the southeastern section of Oklahoma. He professed his eagerness to provide a means to train young people for leadership. "Shall we follow or shall we lead?" he said.

Durant's stirring speech sealed the deal. Days later, the institute had secured ownership of a block of city property in northwest Durant. A few months later, at the turn of the century, 1900, the Calvin Institute signed a contract with the Choctaw Nation for the education of Indian children. Dr. Hotchkin called a meeting between the town of Durant and the Choctaw leadership, who agreed to cooperate with the school's board of trustees in sharing building costs of not more than eleven thousand dollars. Construction began of a two-story brick building for classrooms and an auditorium. Builders uprooted the old Calvin Institute structures and moved them to the new site, remodeling them into dormitories. Finally, during the summer of 1901, the trustees decided to change the school's name to Durant Presbyterian College. The young city then celebrated the opening of its first official college. In 1910, the school began operating under a new name: the Oklahoma Presbyterian College for Girls.

Semple chose that moment to end her work with the Choctaw and Chickasaw. But because she loved working with children, she didn't stop teaching. She journeyed to Utah and then Oregon to work with other poverty-stricken tribes. Sixteen years later, she joined one of her daughters in Stigler, Oklahoma, where she passed away.

DR. HOTCHKIN WAS suddenly silent. All eyes focused on him. He often told stories about his mother, and always by the end he could feel her deep strength like she was right there with him again. To keep from going past the hour, he quickly drew his sermon to a close, saying that his mother lived a simple life devoted to her desire to lift children out of poverty and that her story represented the Christly ideals of persistence and hard work without expecting any reward. His mother had taught him to be both preacher and teacher, and he encouraged all those present to spread the Word, and to do everything in their power to help lift spirits during these hard times.

Afterward, he stood outside the church entrance to greet his parishioners. When the mushroom hunters appeared, they grinned sheepishly, and Alice handed Dr. Hotchkin a linen sack. He peeked inside and saw not the yellow spring chanterelles but the milky brown and hairless gills of an oyster mushroom the size of a mule's ear. Perfect sautéed with butter. Lucille and Coral gave him firm handshakes. Vick asked him if his mother would have approved of girls playing basketball. The directness of her question caught him by surprise, but an instant later he responded that he himself very much approved of their basketball playing, that it was his favorite sport, and if playing the game achieved the exceptional goals of lifting spirits and educating deserving young women, then yes, his mother would have been cheering in the stands along with the rest of Durant.

CHAPTER 6

A Man's Sport

Itching to get started at practice after the Thanksgiving holidays, Lucille caught herself whistling as she warmed up on court with Lera and Vera in the cold field house just before Babb arrived at 4:30 a.m. Nineteen girls remained on the team. The number had dwindled from the original thirty-five new recruits because some freshmen had fled due to homesickness, and some didn't want to make the effort and had walked away out of sheer discouragement. Every day brought hard work, and every day the Cardinals' ranks seemed to dwindle.

The six-foot Dunford twins teased Lucille, calling her Shorty. Lucille teased them back by calling them Reds, and soon everyone was referring to the twins as the Reds.

When Bo-Peep joined in, they decided to break up into teams, Vera playing at guard position and Lucille at forward, against Lera at forward and Bo-Peep as a guard. Lera tossed a coin to see who got possession first, and when she won, Vera grumbled, "We'll crush you next time."

Lera took the shot, missed, and Vera snagged the rebound, dribbled once, and passed off to Lucille down court.

Fighting against Bo-Peep, Lucille grabbed the ball and cheated by drib-bling more than once along the hard ground, feeling a thrill because girls' basketball rules allowed only *one* dribble, below the knee, during official games.

Soon others arrived and joined, including Doll, Toka Lee, Coral, Vick, Teny, and La Homa. Doll stuck her hand in Teny's face and then tossed a wild pass to La Homa, who bent her knees and leaped to catch it. Bo-Peep managed to block La Homa's pass without causing a foul, but the ball bounced out of her hands and onto the floor. Doll yelled at La Homa to keep her eyes on the ball, and La Homa beat Vick and Teny to the escaped basketball. Glancing sideways to make sure Doll was watching, La Homa held the ball low on her hip, faked left, and then scored from ten feet out. Everyone cheered.

When Babb arrived, he halted play long enough to announce that he was retiring their old wool uniforms. The top AAU teams had started wearing shorts, just like the men. Alice and Ginny's mother, Mrs. Hamil-ton, would be taking measurements for new uniforms, made out of satin, after classes today in the dormitory lounge. There was enough money for nine uniforms.

Then Babb rolled up his sleeves, tossed out several balls, and they prac-ticed passing drills for a full half hour before he halted the drill, removed all but one basketball, and told them to listen carefully because he would only give instructions once. Making large gestures, he instructed that ev-eryone who played guard would now be a forward, and all the forwards would act as guards. Someone huffed in exasperation, but no one com-plained. Vick was the first on court. Even though she was their toughest guard, she was also a crack shot maker.

Babb often told his players he believed that basketball was a laboratory for life. Six-on-six basketball—a nickname for the girls' rules authorized by the AAU—where the offense stayed on one side of the court and the defense on the other, meant that every Cardinal was highly specialized in her position. They hardly ever switched from offense to defense, like the

Some OPC Cardinals from the 1932–33 season. From left to right: *Doll Harris, La Homa Lassiter, Irene Williams, Vera Dunford, Lucille Thurman, Coral Worley.*

men did when they played the full length of the court. Specialization under girls' rules could dull a player's ability to anticipate the opposition's moves. Babb wanted the defensive guard to learn what it felt like to play offense, to execute the fast break or develop the pivot play by feeding the ball to cutting teammates, shooting, and rebounding. Likewise, the offensive player should know how to put her full focus on the ball, not the *player* with the ball, to always be alert for interceptions, shift quickly to offense after an interception, and move the ball into her team's scoring zone.

Babb recognized that with so many girls dropping out, players might be called to play a different position. Babb believed in making the best of the moment at hand, as the situation arose. To accomplish this feat, the team had to cultivate its second nature along with the desire to win, steady nerves, and excellent stamina. Part of the Cardinals' training included learning to anticipate the opposition's next move.

Ernestine "Teny" Lampson

The two guards Vick and Lera jumped center to start the game. Doll tried to bat the ball away from Teny, and Babb called a foul. Teny nailed her free throw. They jumped center again, and Vick got the ball to Bo-Peep, who passed back to Vick, now in scoring position. Lucille, her arms in motion, kept after Vick to block a shot or dislodge the ball. But no one could steal the ball from Vick. Or from Toka Lee, who had played forward all her life until this year when Babb put her at guard. Those two could anticipate everybody's move.

After ten minutes, the Cardinals seemed to have settled into their new positions. That's when Babb told them to switch positions after the next score without halting play. The girls raised their eyebrows, blinked repeatedly, and then concentrated on their task. Bo-Peep finally freed herself up to make the next goal, and then, in what looked like goofy footage from a silent movie where the movement and facial expressions were exaggerated for dramatic effect, everyone managed to switch again. Doll, back in her normal forward position, grabbed the rebound. Lucille got herself open to receive her pass, and Toka Lee, taking advantage of the awkward moment just after everyone switched, stole the ball.

After ten minutes, Babb called out to shift positions again. They continued this back and forth for an hour. When Babb halted practice, everyone was dripping with sweat and needed a few minutes to cool off before they headed outside to the bus. On the way home, they couldn't stop talking about how much fun they'd had playing in another person's shoes, figuratively speaking.

IN ADDITION TO coaching, Babb taught Psychology 101. In 1931, the science of psychology had intertwined itself with popular culture. In towns and cities throughout the country, the YMCA, churches, and libraries, among other organizations, drew paying adults to continuing education classes to study how to better their lives through developing the powers of the mind, and improving self-direction and self-organization. Horror movies *Dr. Jekyll and Mr. Hyde* and *Dracula* sold millions of tickets and depicted the terrifying results of improper use of mind control and manipulation. When they first arrived at class, most of Babb's freshmen thought they had "used psychology" on their parents whenever they wanted out of doing chores. They had interpreted *psychology* to mean some form of manipulation or control. Some of his basketball players who took his class—La Homa, the Dunford twins, Vick, Lucille, and Coral—initially thought that Babb would teach them how to control their opponent's behavior.

Babb had a different idea. Reminding his students that the only thing they had control over was themselves, he defined psychology as the science of mind and behavior. Learning about psychology would teach them how to look at things.

This afternoon, he asked his students if they'd ever paid much attention to who made up the population of OPC campus. He gestured toward the window, and every girl turned her head. In the fall of 1931, nearly two hundred young women were enrolled in Oklahoma Presbyterian College for Girls. Eighty-four had Indian blood, one was Spanish, five were from Mexico, and the remaining were white. Besides the college girls, there were maybe seventy-five lower-grade children. How many were boys? Could they all speak English?

Did they remember the color of Aunt Lucy's eyes or, better yet, what they had for breakfast two days ago? Lucille, sitting in between La Homa and Vick, along with the Dunford twins, all looked at each other and shrugged.

Vick said that she knew she had bacon because she always had bacon, and Babb suggested that she raise her hand so that he could call on her to answer. Vick nodded.

La Homa's hand shot up, and Babb called on her.

What does it matter if they remembered these little things, she asked.

Babb explained that what a person paid attention to helped shape who they were. He said that most people these days weren't taught how to properly look at things. In order to make tough decisions, they must learn to ask questions and search out the best answers. Questioning personal assumptions was the first step in thinking critically.

"Learning how to question and think is essential because we are all completely different from one another, inside and out," Babb continued. "Take Vick and La Homa, for instance."

Everyone turned to look at the two girls who exchanged glances with raised eyebrows.

They were both excellent basketball players, Babb said. Both young ladies. But that's where their similarities ended. They had different styles, different motivations. "Vick relies on her strength."

Vick flexed her arm muscle and everyone burst out laughing.

"La Homa may not be as strong, but she can charm bees away from honey."

La Homa smiled sweetly.

"Here's my point," Babb continued. "Vick grew up as the only girl in a family of boys. Playing with her brothers helped build her strength. La Homa, on the other hand, was raised with all girls."

"Does that mean I'm more ladylike?" La Homa said. Remembering to raise her hand, after Babb called on her, she continued, "Can you promise me that playing with the Cardinals won't destroy my ability to be a lady?"

At those words, the whole class grew silent in anticipation of Babb's answer. Though they never said anything out loud, several players were concerned about how playing basketball might reflect on their reputations. Sports like tennis, golf, and swimming were considered appropriate pastimes for women. Even field hockey, played mostly by young women attending colleges and universities, garnered approval as a properly feminine sport that would help to improve what was considered to be a girl's best assets—her grace, charm, and lasting cheerfulness.

But what if a middle-class girl on her way to a prestigious university decided she liked the smooth-leather feel of a softball, enjoyed tossing it around, and got herself a horse-hide mitt and joined a league? Or maybe she was used to outdistancing her brothers when they raced down the block to school as kids, and her favorite shoes became the sneakers she wore when she sprinted around the high school track. The sight of girls expertly running the bases or clearing a hurdle was not met with such approval. Besides developing the more masculine qualities of strength, daring, and endurance, these sports attracted the coarse beer-drinking working-class crowd who populated the industrial teams, and God forbid a cherished daughter would practice softball or track-and-field over dancing the foxtrot. Maintaining a sweet smile in the midst of an intense battle on the ball field was rare to impossible.

But the worst game a girl could ever get good at was basketball.

In 1899, the Conference on Physical Training, organized by the YMCA, decided on the official set of women's basketball rules and created the Women's Basketball Committee to oversee such rules, which were to be published every year by the Spalding Athletic Library. The women's rules restricted players to one of at least three sections of the court. Dribbling was a problem since it allowed women to move across court, so the committee eliminated dribbling in 1910 and then brought back a single below-the-knee dribble in 1913. That dribbling rule was still in effect in 1931.

From the very start after the sport's invention by James Naismith in 1891 (the same year Sam Babb was born), girls and women formed teams and competed against each other. They found ways to make the game more fun by making it more competitive. Some kept playing by men's rules. Even the games played under girls' rules become rough and tumble. To help women develop more expertise at the game, male school supervisors and coaches began to support women's basketball and didn't care if they formed their own teams and played like the boys. Even in the colleges and universities, women formed varsity teams sometimes before the men did, and by 1919, hundreds of women were showing up to play basketball.

A new spirit infused seemingly proper young ladies with the desire to train hard, excel, and win. This newfound aggressive nature exhibited during women's basketball games that entertained so many caused grave concerns in others. One prominent physical educator warned that a respectable woman should "never be seen by the opposite sex when she is likely to forget herself." Another said that women were like plants, closely attached to the soil, and men were more animal-like. When these critics watched women playing basketball, they didn't see people enjoying themselves playing a sport they loved. They saw young faces malformed with grimaces and sweat, legs yawned wide in a crouch, eyes shifting like an animal's, mouths half open, gasping for breath, soft bodies crashing together in desperate combat. A slaughter of innocents.

The fact was, women who played basketball acted more like men. Many women's leagues continued to play by men's rules. Even worse, women competing in basketball games would sooner or later cause the downfall of modern culture.

Common wisdom held that because women gave birth, they were in a unique position to be the guardians of culture and morality. Motherhood and marriage gave women a feminine uniqueness that was thought to make them morally superior to men, who were aggressive, competitive, dominant, and violent. If that were true, then women had to be cooperative, maternal, selfless, and passive in order to provide a balance in the community. Otherwise, all would be lost and civilization would dissolve into chaos. Childbearing was women's most important function, and the male doctors who advised female patients and brought their children into the world held the highest authority over women's bodies.

In the 1920s, most of these doctors still believed that women by nature were physically underprivileged, weak, and needful of care and rest because that's what the medical textbooks said. Mainstream medicine considered the uterus to be the most vulnerable and fragile part of the female body. With every vigorous jump a woman made, her uterus pulled at its sinews. Too much jumping might even cause the organ to tilt backward. It was as if women had little fluffy pillows secured only by tenuous and silky cobwebs instead of organs, fascia, tendons, and muscle.

Another theory held that too much training of the muscles, especially in the abdomen and pelvis, would make the muscle fibers too taut and childbirth difficult if not impossible. Women should have slack pelvic muscles that could expand easily, like a balloon. A physical educator named Ernst Hermann Arnold performed a study where his female students who exercised heavily reported the date and length of when they menstruated. After several months, he discovered that athletics lessened the flow of menstruation. Shocked and bewildered, Arnold proclaimed that his worst fears had been confirmed. Girls who played hard at any game, but especially basketball, had fewer periods, and if the hard play continued, their pelvises would eventually wither and shrink. Even worse than not being able to have babies was the unspoken possibility that the uterus would completely disappear, turning her into a man.

Even when medical doctors conducted systematic research in the early 1930s that showed athletics didn't hurt women's reproductive capabilities and, in fact, improved health, educators didn't change their minds about competitive sports for girls. The tidal wave of anxiety that basketball would make young women more masculine had shaped the nation's understanding of women's athletic potential. Those who should have been on the front lines advocating for female athletes instead preached against the immoral seductions of fierce competition, especially in basketball. Their focus switched from the body to the mind. Everyone knew that girls' minds were more malleable than those of boys, more open to suggestion, less able to control their emotions. Girls were always at the mercy of bad moods and prone to hysteria. They did not have the capacity to withstand the intensity of high-spirited competition and would collapse under nervous strain. Those who thought they knew best needed to take control of the situation. They needed to organize.

The first to bring physical educators together to form a coalition against women's competitive sports on a national scale was Blanche Trilling. Newly appointed as the University of Wisconsin's athletic director in 1917, Trilling ferociously campaigned against the evils of competition. A true believer, she infused her words about women's physical education with a patriotic and almost spiritual tone: "A sound constitution, a good understanding, a benevolent heart, an honest and upright personality, these are the characteristics which physical education, if wisely administered, may develop in an individual . . . . May we never fail to maintain them, while working always for an increased and more efficient activity which, if it comes to perfection, can never perish, but will instead go on upbuilding the physical and moral fiber of a great people!"

Previously the director of physical education at Chicago Normal School, Trilling had advocated that young women's good health depended on highly controlled exercise developed specifically to meet their needs as future wives and mothers. She forged new territory by establishing undergraduate degrees for women in physical education and dance and a master's degree in physical education. She organized a more egalitarian sports system designed to thwart the corruption, commercialism, and win-at-any-cost attitude rampant in men's sports. Naming her campaign Athletics for All, Trilling eliminated varsity women's sports, along with the idea of elite, superstar athletes, and replaced it with club and intramural sports. Even in the dance recitals her students gave, Trilling held to her belief about the evils of competition. She kept the names of dancers off the program because the publicity might ruin the dancers' joy in the activity itself by infusing them with performance anxiety.

She was so confident that students and fans would lose interest in varsity

and other competitive sports for women *and* men, she believed that in ten
or twenty years sports stadiums would cease to exist.

In 1917, Trilling organized a symposium held in Wisconsin between
students and physical education faculty from twenty-three universities
across the Midwest. After several heady days of meetings, luncheons, and
speeches, a new institutional governing body for the controlled development of women's college athletics was born, the Athletic Conference
of American College Women (ACACW). In accordance with Trilling's
principles, the ACACW fostered student participation in the organization
aligned with the Department of Physical Education and officially discouraged intercollegiate play. Participants hoped that other schools and institu-
tions would incorporate their recommendations, along with those from the
Committee on Women's Athletics (CWA)—part of the American Physical
Education Association (APEA)—who made the rules for women's sports
including basketball. They believed that a new day would arise where the
evils of competitive sports had disappeared.

But something unexpected happened. By eliminating varsity sports
for women, the ACACW forced competitive basketball underground.
Girls and women who loved the game found another place to play, giving
strength to a force that encompassed all things despicable when it came to
women's sports, at least according to Trilling and other physical educators.
The Amateur Athletic Union.

College sports developed "ladies." Community sports entertained the
masses. Men in the AAU encouraged and fostered the expansion of competition for women when the AAU, in 1922, decided to send a track-and-
field contingent of top athletes drawn from the secondary schools and the
industrial sports league, to the Women's World Games in Paris. The team
finished second overall to Great Britain and came home to a champion's
welcome. The widely positive press coverage included a quote from AAU
president William Prout: "The girls have become athletes. We can't stop
them. We must simply standardize their games."

Prout lived up to his words when the AAU, in 1923, assumed control over all of women's competitive sports. And it was then that all hell broke loose.

The CWA claimed that the AAU didn't have any women in charge of women's sports, which was true. But the CWA, formed and populated by women, didn't have any power within the APEA, which was led by men. The CWA was afraid that if given APEA voting rights the women would take over. The only solution to upending the AAU's announcement was for the women's organization to make an even bigger announcement of its own.

Both the secretary of war and the secretary of the navy from President Warren Harding's cabinet contacted Lou Henry Hoover, wife of Herbert Hoover, the current secretary of commerce, and asked if she would lead a new women's unit within the National Amateur Athletic Federation. The NAAF was formed by the U.S. government after World War I to improve levels of fitness in the nation's youth. Hoover demanded a separate group altogether for women, and she called it the Women's Division of the National Amateur Athletic Federation, or just Women's Division. It might as well have been called the CWAACACWWDNAAF because its membership also included physical education leaders from all the other previous organizations. Its directive: to combat the bad tendencies of competitive women's athletics and promote a national interest in the right kind of sports and games for girls.

With the famous Hoover as leader, the battle to prevent exploitation by the AAU and save the feminine souls of American girls had begun.

Hoover had become well known when her husband ran for president in 1920. People liked the straightforward woman who had attended Stanford University as the only female geology major in 1894; it is here where she met her husband. She often rode her bicycle in public, looked slim and athletic, and was a world traveler who spoke five languages, including Chinese. In 1922, she became president of the Girl Scouts, and was still at its helm when she established the Women's Division. Hoover warned against the exploitation of girls and women participating in sports without proper supervision. She labeled the general tendency to copy boys' athletics with an emphasis on setting records and having championships "a cancer that must be killed."

After two days of discussions among a group of affable, agreeable people (not one representative from the AAU or other community organizations who sponsored women's sports was included), a committee adopted sixteen resolutions, modified to eleven by 1931, which became the platform of the Women's Division. Only those organizations and individuals who subscribed to these principles and ideas could pay the membership fee and join the organization.

The resolutions called for girls to learn to enjoy playing sports over winning, supported athletics for all versus training for the few, and established the role of the female physical educator as protector of girls from physical and mental exploitation.

They advocated against male coaches. Only women would be able to understand the psychological, motivational, and bodily needs of other women. Of course, the resolutions also mandated proper medical supervision, and almost all of the doctors overseeing the girls were men.

Further rules forbade girls playing any sport during the first three days of menstruation, declared that any awards for sporting accomplishment would have no intrinsic value, and emphasized a well-balanced sports program so that girls wouldn't overdevelop skills in one particular sport.

Educators established a regimented series of medical examinations and follow-ups that led to special classes for the overly thin and overly heavy girls, nude posture photos, and the posting of weekly weight gain or loss. Girls forced to enroll in these classes often didn't attend. Women physical educators interpreted this lack of enthusiasm as laziness and complained that too many girls and women were preoccupied with the radio, motion pictures, and the automobile, losing any mental ability to find their own sane outlets for energy. One physical educator, while making a public speech, was quoted in newspapers as saying, "When we have nothing to do, what shall we do? The answer indicates the standards of a nation."

The Women's Division also resolved that the proper motivation for all competition be play for the sake of play that incorporated the utmost qualities of sportsmanship. The division would protect athletic activities for girls and women from the evils of commercialization and the win-at-any-cost ethos by abolishing travel to other cities, gate receipts, and finally, the leering fans who lost themselves while cheering for their favorite teams. Young women should not be forced to sacrifice themselves for a winning team and would never again play in front of a crowd.

The Women's Division further resolved to replace competitive sports with programs of inclusion geared to the average girl. The philosophy of this movement became their slogan: *A sport for every girl and every girl in a sport.*

In her slim-fitting dresses with practical hems for walking and bicycling, Hoover embodied the ideal active woman. Her very presence solidified funding and recognition for the government-sponsored Women's Division. She kept every member on task and her division in the news, celebrating the impact each resolution would have on girls' lives. She opened a main office in New York and then elected an executive committee to oversee the division. Soon branches opened up in Southern California, Cincinnati, Kansas City, New Jersey, and Boston, and the executive committee selected representatives from every state. Oklahoma's chairwoman was Flora May Ellis, the women's physical education director at Oklahoma A & M College in Stillwater.

These ground soldiers organized state conventions and meetings and published articles in periodicals. Some articles included "Girls Athletics at the Crossroads" in the *Catholic Educational Review*, March 1925; "Competitive Sports Too Strenuous for Girls" in the *Philadelphia Ledger*, June 1929; and, "The Playtime of a Million Girls or an Olympic Victory—Which?" in the *Nation's Schools*, August 1929.

They interviewed for newspaper articles and magazines and sent out press releases about upcoming public speaking events. They gave radio broadcasts and personal interviews and acted as a clearinghouse for all kinds of questions relating to girls' and women's athletics.

But the most quoted member of the Women's Division wasn't Hoover.

A persuasive public speaker, Trilling aggressively rallied her cause, and newspapers across the nation printed and reprinted her authoritative words about safeguarding girls' athletics. As a member of the Women's Division Executive Committee, she received letters from superintendents, principals, physical directors, physicians, and mothers asking for help and advice. Quite often, these letters concerned the game of basketball, and Trilling labeled the sport the "chief offender" when it came to spreading the evils of spirited competition.

To make her point and also provide chilling real-life examples for her audiences, she would read these letters aloud during her frequent public appearances. In an address given before the annual meeting of the National Association of Deans of Women in Dallas, Texas, in February 1927, Trilling spent several minutes reading the first letter from a physical educator and coach of a small-town basketball team:

> To get to the basket ball court, one had to wind his way among the spectators down a series of ill-constructed steps, finally gaining access through a pseudo dressing room, a little two by four containing a shower and three lavatories, which were out of order, and a sink. . . . The gymnasium itself was a box; fenced in on three sides by walls and on the fourth by a howling, yelling, yapping, uncouth, for the most part disrespectful audience whose principal object seemed to be to get amusement from the girls' game, and toward which they encouraged the players in such a manner as to arouse all the fighting blood and animal instincts of antagonism they possessed. Our opponents were coached by a man. . . . It was all a gladiatorial combat, witnessed by a primitive people yelling they knew not what.

To prove this letter was not an isolated case, Trilling recounted a few condensed quotations from the 1926 annual report of the General Secretary of the Women's Division:

> Basketball is the major problem in girls' athletics in the United States, and narrowed down it is confined very largely to three types of organization [sic]—industrial groups, Church or Sunday school leagues, and secondary schools. We have reports of girls . . . fainting in games from heart attacks or overstrain, and being put back into the games if they could be revived. . . . In practically every city and every community, however large or small, there are groups of girls to whom athletics mean only basketball. It is the most popular game for girls, the game which all girls want to play, and they are often allowed to go into it regardless of whether they are strong enough. . . .
>
> The type of competition involved in basketball tournaments and championship contests is (another) big part of our girls' problem. The nervous strain and excitement, the tendency to put all of the emphasis on "the team," to the neglect of all of the other girls and all other athletic activities . . . to play during menstrual periods and to play beyond the effort a girl ought to make, for the sake of a championship . . . the travel involved (not only the elements of distance and time, but the fact that girls' teams so often reach their destinations after long trips and have to begin playing immediately) . . . the type of audience often involved (mixed groups whose attitude and comments are anything but constructive) . . . the number of games played during a week during the basket ball season; and in all too many instances, the fight rather than a game.

Such speeches by Trilling, Hoover, and other members of the Women's Division spurred many listeners into action. Eventually, most women's varsity teams disappeared from college campuses, replaced by intramural sports. High school administrations across the country got rid of state basketball tournaments and installed play days where school girls got together, had some fun playing all sorts of sports, and to instill goodwill afterward, shared cookies and milk. Play days were a democratic form of athletics not intended for the expert athlete. In fact, the Women's Division actively campaigned against even the possibility of women being top athletes. According to Hoover, girls should strive to become not stars but first-class all-round players because they were not "pioneers enough to discover their own possibilities." In other words, a girl shouldn't work too hard to get good at anything because by her very nature she didn't have, and would never develop, the courage, power, and self-knowledge to succeed.

This dark philosophy grew from the deep-seeded belief that women were God's rejects. Men, and men's bodies, were the ideal. Those who bought into this view never even considered that women shared the dreams, capabilities, and weaknesses of all human beings. No girl or woman ever could be a great athlete on her own because she just wasn't built that way. She had to have been forced into it by the men exploiting her. That's why the Women's Division saw the AAU, and any male coach, as the greatest evil. The AAU wasn't simply giving a platform to girls and women who loved competitive basketball—it was imposing its will on the silly, unwitting but athletically inclined girls and forcing them to play in front of crowds for money. These sporting events, in the eyes of the Women's Division, were acts of violence.

The AAU responded to the Women's Division by ignoring it. The AAU held the first women's national basketball championship in 1926 and welcomed women to its national track meet, where in the summer of 1931 Babe Didrikson came to national prominence by taking first place in eight events. Along with the International Olympics Committee, the AAU was planning to increase the competitive opportunities for women in the upcoming Olympics to be held in Los Angeles in 1932.

The Women's Division fought back with an onslaught of publicity that took on a life of its own after the election of Herbert Hoover as president. Now everything the organization instigated had the backing of the first lady. Across the nation, articles in newspapers, public presentations, and speeches over the radio increased fourfold. This time, though, the publicity didn't share the positive aspects of sports for all girls. It described the horrors of competitive women's sports, especially basketball. Headlines read, "Basketball Tourneys for Girls Condemned," "Woman Runner Falls Senseless During Race," "Experts Say Interschool Games of Basketball Menace Girls' Health." In the national newspaper column called "Your Boy and Your Girl" by Arthur Dean, a girl wrote, "I want so much to join the girls' basketball team at school but mother says it won't be good for me as it's too strenuous and rough for girls. Do you think she's right?" And the response: "You know that bruises, strains, and displacements are more serious with girls than with boys. . . . A good school allows a pupil to play a strenuous game only when the individual is carefully examined beforehand and watched for after effects."

The July 1, 1929, issue of *Harper's Magazine* published a nine-page article titled "Women and the Sport Business" by John Tunis. A prolific freelance writer and sportscaster from Boston, Tunis's articles had appeared in the *Atlantic Monthly, Colliers*, and the *Saturday Evening Post* to name a few. Tunis had got his first writing job at the *Boston Globe* because he had played against the famous French tennis star Suzanne Lenglen in a mixed doubles match and the *Globe* editor had demanded a story. His first novel, *American Girl*, appeared in 1930 not long after he wrote the article for *Harper's. American Girl* was fiction, but everyone knew it was about tennis prodigy Helen Wills and how she secretly hated competition because her parents made her do it for the money and in the end regretted everything because she wasn't married. The book was optioned by Hollywood and later made into the 1951 movie called *Hard, Fast, and Beautiful*, directed by Ida Lupino and staring Claire Trevor. The movie poster featured a picture of Lupino wearing a bra-like bathing top and short shorts while carrying her tennis racket and trying to get away from a man holding her arm. The tag line read: "The price of fame in the big-time sports racket!"

Tunis despised the commercialization of amateur sports and lamented the fact that a highly organized class of men—athletes, newsmen, coaches, and trainers—made their living off of sports. He argued that these men devoted time to sports for the sake of their own careers and not the good of the game. "Women and the Sports Business" then described the lightning-fast advancement of women in sports and how they were catching up with men, invading their territory by forming teams and competing in every known sport, from polo to track, and squash to basketball. He described the innocent working-class women forced to compete for the industrial teams sponsored by men who were only interested in making money and exploiting young women through physical contact and injury, inevitable exhaustion, the immorality of men looking on, and the emotional over-excitement caused by competition.

"And it is the great mass of American girls, the thousands and thousands of girls in industry—not the comparatively few who attend college—who are most likely to be injured," he wrote.

And how should women, according to the article, save themselves from the men's athletic perdition? Not by taking a more altruistic attitude, creating new rules, and instigating proper oversight. Women should give up athletic competition altogether. Why? Because the dangers of exploitation and injury greatly outweighed the thrill of winning. Women who participated in the wrong kind of sports risked destroying their feminine image by invading a man's world. Tunis brought this point home by reporting some of Trilling's horror stories about girls' basketball, warning that "soon we shall begin to have Vassar-Smith basket ball games, with the scramble for seats, the vast sums coming in at the box office, the eligibility rulings, the amateur-professional tangle, and all other absurdities."

The rest of the article vividly recounted the Women's Division and their heroic mission to uplift society by abolishing elite competition and instituting democracy in women's sports—a girl for every sport and a sport for every girl. Tunis gave the organization created by Hoover four pages of accolades.

"Women in the Sports Business" put the case against competitive sports for girls and women in a nutshell, and that issue of *Harper's* remained on coffee tables in physical educators' offices for many months.

But despite all this hullabaloo, when the Women's Division came to Oklahoma and other rural states, except in the colleges where women's varsity competition had already been replaced by intramurals and play days, nobody paid much attention to them. Their pamphlets, articles, and speeches told middle-class and even wealthy girls and women how to adequately enjoy the ever increasing leisure time. Rarely did they speak about the Great Depression and the growing millions of people who didn't have enough to live on. What's the best way to tell a girl living in a ramshackle house with one pair of shoes, a coat that's too big, and parents who worried every night because their children's stomachs were always growling that she needed more time for gentle play that would preserve her dignity? If she decided that high school basketball was her game, that making a jump shot at top speed or blocking a shot and winning the game gave her a shred of hope in these unimaginable times, then let her play and let the whole town watch.

Most of the OPC Cardinals didn't know that the Women's Division existed. Babb and Dr. Hotchkin quietly took care of the inner workings of running a girls' school basketball team. On the other hand, since he had recently been appointed to the AAU women's basketball Rules Committee, Babb would be in the middle of the battle heating up between the AAU and the Women's Division. The AAU planned to make use of his skills at debating, mediating, and figuring people out.

BACK IN HIS psychology class, when La Homa had asked Babb about her ability to remain a lady even while playing basketball, Babb had an answer for her.

"Yes, I can make you that promise. Basketball encourages all ladylike abilities, especially critical thinking and good judgment. You came here a lady, and I want you to leave here a better lady."

At his answer, La Homa sighed with relief. She loved playing basketball.

Besides being the most beautiful girl on the team, she was also the fastest. Her older sister was a basketball coach in Mangum, where Babb's brother Ray and his wife lived. That's how Babb had discovered La Homa. Her dad raised cotton on their farm near town where, during the summer, she and her sisters would help out by chopping cotton. They wore wide-brimmed hats because otherwise the sun would burn their skin to a crisp. After sharpening the hoe if the edges were dulled, they would walk through the field along the endless rows and chop out the musty-smelling

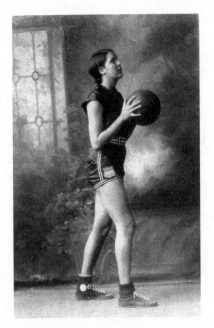

La Homa Lassiter

weeds taking root between the cotton plants. Most kids on their parents' farms often worked barefooted in the summertime, saving their one pair of shoes for the winter. They always hoped for rain, even a sprinkle, the night before because the moistened soil more easily released the weeds and made the task a little easier. Cotton had to be chopped throughout the spring, and everyone helped out. No one thought to question La Homa's femininity while she took part in a chore that required an effort similar to digging ditches. Everyone just did what was required to survive.

The summer before her senior year of high school, La Homa told her dad that she wanted more than anything to go to college. She had good grades and knew she would be a top student. He told her that if the cotton crop was a good one, he'd be able to pay for her school. Sure enough, sun and moisture performed their magic. It was the prettiest crop they'd seen in a while. La Homa hid her excitement but just barely. Then, one late-summer night, she awoke to pounding on the roof so loud that it sounded like gunfire. Hail the size of golf balls was crushing the beautiful cotton field, and the entire crop was lost.

Like almost every Cardinal team member, La Homa never would have gone to college if it hadn't been for the opportunity offered by Babb and her own skill at playing basketball.

CHAPTER 7

Weak Ankles
and Weaker Nerves

The jam-packed Buzzard's Roost smelled like lye soap and old socks even with the windows open. Doll barked orders at the freshmen to clean up the pigeon excrement that spotted the floor near the windows as well as the feathers that kept blowing across the little half-court.

Lucille grabbed a broom and took full advantage of the chilly early-December breeze that helped calm her growing anxiety about shooting free throws later that night. Most of the time, she practiced in the afternoon right after classes or just before supper. Maybe four or five other girls were on court with her, and they always just took turns. Somehow on this night, the stars had aligned and all sixteen of her teammates had skipped study hall and showed up after supper.

Unspoken among them was the fact that more than a dozen players had quit the team and some had left school completely—great athletes recruited by Babb who either didn't have the heart to stick it out or were needed back home: Katherine Mathis, a player who hailed from prairie country where she had been a team captain for two years and played on several district all-star teams; Lena Japp of Lawton, the all-state jump center; Zeta Pickens, a high school all-star; Alma Mayberry, who had played forward for Terrell High School and who had the reputation of having a "dead eye" for the basket. Considering the renowned abilities of these players, Lucille couldn't believe that she was still in the running.

Babb required his team to shoot a hundred free throws every day because during a game free-throw accuracy was an offensive weapon. Since space was limited in the half-court gym, Doll organized a goal-shooting contest. That way, all seventeen players would have their turns and have some fun, too.

Lucille was petrified at the thought of these star athletes watching her while she tried to sink the ball. Every move she made needed to be either survived or won. Practicing free throws alone or with just a couple of other girls in the stifling little gym helped because she

Lucille Thurman

could flub a shot and then make a correction. But these were the best athletes she'd ever known. Of course they would be using her mistakes to beat her out of a starting spot. Besides fixing her wobbly ankles, failing to win a starting position worried her the most.

Doll's contest rules were simple: (1) Girls would take turns shooting one shot each. (2) If a girl missed, she was done. (3) The last person standing would win. Just as she tossed the ball to Bo-Peep, first in line to shoot, lightning brightened the gym and thunder shook the white-painted brick walls. Excited to get started with the contest, no one had noticed the storm outside. Seconds later, icy-cold rain started falling like bullets, blowing in through the open windows, and Lucille raced to close them before giant puddles formed on the polished wood floor.

Now she stood dead last in line, but she didn't have to wait long for her turn. Every girl made her shot and then jogged to the back of the line. No one missed the first time. When she finally grasped the ball, it almost fell from her hands because her palms had become oil slicks. Her stage fright acting up again. She put the ball down and held it steady between her feet while she wiped her hands on her shirt, pretending they were still wet from the rain. Next she swooped up the leather ball, brushed her fingers past the laces, found the familiar grooves, took her stance, raised her arms, and made the shot. When the ball sank through the net, her heart started beating again, nerves ebbing.

Outside, the wind picked up and the rain sounded like pebbles being tossed against the windowpanes. Throughout the storm, the players kept taking turns, five, six times, and no one missed. Doll had a pleased expression, and Lucille counted to forty before Toka Lee made a poor shot and the ball bounced off the rim. She went and stood near the exit, and soon after a few other girls, including Lucille, joined her. The last two standing were Coral and Doll. Since Doll had made up the rules, she went first. She glared at Coral, bounced the ball at least six times, and then exaggerated the time it took to aim at the basket. When she took the shot, it flew through the basket and everyone watching let out her breath. Doll knew how to raise the tension in a room. But it didn't rattle the notoriously calm Coral. Six shots later, Doll missed, and Coral won, giving her the new reputation as the Cardinals' best free-throw shooter.

Because the team had done so well, Doll excused them from completing the rest of their hundred throws. Vick mumbled that Doll was embarrassed that she lost and wanted to leave early. Everyone started to leave, except for Lucille, who congratulated Coral, and then told her roommate that she needed to study and not to worry if she wasn't back in the room until late.

After everyone was gone, Lucille opened a window and breathed in the sweet-smelling air. The rain had stopped. She removed her shoes and socks and stood barefoot on the wood floor, which felt warm against the soles of her feet. Balancing herself with her right-hand palm flat against

Coral Worley

the cold north wall, she rose high onto her toes and began a tiptoe prance around the small gym's perimeter. She'd been performing this exercise to strengthen her ankles three times a week for almost two months. With slow deliberation, she moved one foot in front of the other, determined to keep getting stronger.

Because Lucille had realized long ago that her greatest weakness was not her ankles but her performance anxiety, she always appreciated this time to herself, moving around the room, working up a little sweat, thinking about nothing but the way her muscles felt beneath her skin. Sometimes, after she started getting tired and extra adrenaline kicked in, her mind would wander, and tonight that extra energy sparked an idea. She would organize a "picture-show day" for the Cardinals since they all had received free passes from generous theater owners. They could meet Sundays after church and attend a matinee together. The Durant City Council had just repealed an ordinance that forbade showing movies on Sundays, and now the two theaters on Main Street, the Colonial and the Ritz, were packed. Lucille went to the picture show twice a week during the summer, sometimes more if she could afford it. But now, with school and basketball practice, she hardly had any time for fun. This way, she could bring along her teammates, and they could talk about the show afterward. Her favorite so far this year was *Dishonored*, starring Marlene Dietrich who played a secret agent during the European war. *I vill make zat Cardinal team*, she kept repeating in her deep Marlene voice as she tiptoed around the Buzzard's Roost. Later that night, when she finally returned to her dorm room, Lucille stayed up into the wee hours doing schoolwork.

The following morning on the bus ride over to the field house, the players were buzzing about a rumor started by Toka Lee, who couldn't keep a secret even if her roommate Doll made her swear on the Bible. Now everyone knew that Babb had scheduled their first scrimmage game for this Saturday. When he arrived, Babb confirmed that on Saturday at 2 p.m., they would play against an Ardmore high school girls' basketball team. Ardmore, about sixty miles west and south, was two times bigger than Durant, and their girls' team was tough. High school and college girls' teams would often scrimmage because of the few nearby college teams. Doll said to be thankful that they weren't playing her old high school because Cement had won state last year even without her on the team.

Lucille started to worry about the game anyway and wondered if she'd be the starting center. Probably not. Who was she but just one among a whole team of great freshmen players: Allene West of Celeste, Texas, who was considered the best high school guard in Texas; Vick, who was also a track star; Buena Harris, who at five feet eight inches had scored 251 points her senior year. Teny Lampson, whose first name was Ernestine, from Welch who had lost only two conference games in two years (she wasn't a show stealer, but she played good basketball); La Homa, an experienced forward with a star basketball player for an older sister; and finally, Coral, five foot six, 115 pounds, a versatile athlete who could jump center or play at forward, and one of Lucille's fiercest competitors for a starting position (also her good friend).

After practice, she showered and hurried to breakfast at 7 a.m. and almost fell asleep during chapel at 8 a.m. That's why, by late morning, she was dreading algebra class.

Math was not her favorite subject. The professor's name was Scroggs, a burly man with a booming voice, graying hair and a hawkish nose. He owned a black fur coat that he would wear in class everyday while teaching during the wintertime. Scribbling math exercises on the blackboard, he looked like a big black bear, earning the nickname "Old Bear" Scroggs. He'd pop his knuckles, too, and over the years they'd grown to the size of cherry tomatoes. Scroggs was the only other male professor at OPC besides Babb.

Lucille found herself drifting from Scroggs's lecture, no longer focusing on the linear equations and polynomials on the chalkboard. The scrimmage this weekend signaled a do-or-die situation—she had to perform. But some little voice inside had started questioning her abilities. She had always been shy and insecure, unlike her younger sister, Dink, who never seemed to be afraid of anything. The sisters, only two years apart, did almost everything together before Lucille went away to school.

Lucille fell into a fit of nostalgia thinking about home. Suddenly she longed to be back doing chores with her sister. First thing in the morning, they'd pull on their work clothes, old overalls or denim trousers. After trudging outside in the dark, Lucille would scold Dink until she slid back the heavy barn door, and the sweet odor of fresh-cut hay would rush out to greet them along with hungry animal sounds, which always reminded Lucille of an orchestra tuning up before a concert. The sharps were a bit flat—the goats. The string section was always in a panic—the chickens. And the percussion, their old milk cow, was having a hard time waking up. But before she or Dink even touched a feed pail, Lucille would light the kerosene lamp and then pick up the basketball always in its place next to the barn door. She'd crouch in ready position, take a dribble against the musty wood floor, and shoot the ball up toward an *X* painted on a crossbeam. After hitting the spot, she'd hand off the ball to Dink, who played basketball, too.

Once they finished their chores, they'd get ready for school. The smell of her mother's biscuits rising in the oven, prepared from soured dough and fresh butter, always made Lucille's mouth water. Knowing all six of her children—two girls and four boys—were in a hurry, Mrs. Thurman would often hand them a biscuit cut in half lengthwise with two pieces of bacon inside like a sandwich, and they would walk the one mile to Union Valley consolidated while nibbling on their breakfast. Lucille missed her mother, Dink, her brothers, and her dad. Even though they didn't have much, they were luckier than most. Her family owned their property outright. Her father, a farmer and rancher known to his neighbors as Jim J. Thurman, had bought their land years ago from a wealthy Indian. He loved basketball and had always encouraged her to play.

The Union Valley Consolidated Schools where she attended junior high and high school was so small, the basketball team practiced on an outdoor court where students played during recess and after school every day, even when the wind gusted to fifty miles an hour. They always had to correct for wind drift. That's where she was when the girls' and boys' basketball coach, who was also the school superintendent, came up to her one noon hour and said, "Haven't I seen you shooting the ball through the basket out there pretty regular today?"

Lucille turned pink all over and grinned sheepishly. She realized later that he had picked her because she was one of the tallest kids in school.

"Why don't you come out and practice with the girls? I have an idea you might make us a good forward."

Shaking off her shyness, Lucille had turned out for practice, making her father very happy. He'd taught all his kids to play when they were barely out of diapers, scraping together a homemade court in the front yard that had a peach basket with its bottom sawed off for a goal. Their front yard became a gathering place for neighboring kids on Sunday evenings to practice. During all the training sessions after school, she played as if every one of them would be her last because she didn't have much hope of making the team. But when the coach told her that he was assigning her to one of the forward positions, she walked on air the one mile to her home and informed her mother and father that they had a basketball-playing daughter. Her dad learned to drive and bought an old Model T just so he could bring Lucille and a few of her teammates, along with her mother if there was room, to every game that Union Valley played. Lucille built good muscles pushing that truck out of mud holes.

During her senior year, they'd had a good enough team to win the Cotton County tournament followed by the district and regional play-offs. By that time, Dink was a second-string forward for the high school team, so both girls traveled to Oklahoma City to play in the state tournament. Lucille went into the tournament with the realization that she would be playing her last basketball game. Even though she loved basketball, her mind was set on attending Southeastern State Teachers College after graduating—if her dad could find the money. Her mother was taking in other people's laundry, washing them on a rub board, to earn extra cash for her schooling.

Union Valley was crushed by a stronger team at the state tournament. Lucille was only thinking about getting home when a stranger who introduced himself as Mr. Babb asked her if she had a minute to talk. Other friends who played basketball had told her about Babb and the Cardinals, and there had been an article or two in the newspaper her parents read. With her mother standing nearby, Lucille listened while Babb gave his best arguments as to why she should play basketball for him, including financial aid to OPC. Still hurting from her team's big loss, she said, "I've just played my last basketball game, Mr. Babb."

She said that her future was as a teacher, not a basketball player. He told her she could play basketball and become a teacher, too. She didn't believe him and cut the conversation short, telling him that she just wasn't interested. Then she got in the car with her mother and Dink and on the drive home dismissed the whole encounter.

The next morning, Lucille was helping clean up the kitchen while she and her mother discussed the tournament. During the course of their conversation, her mother gently steered the topic to Babb and the possibility of attending OPC. Lucille shrugged and said she'd put the whole thing out of her mind because playing basketball didn't interest her. A few years from now, she would be teaching school.

"Maybe it wouldn't hurt to go to Durant and look the situation over," said her mother.

Before Lucille could say no for the millionth time, her dad, who had mighty big ears and had been listening in, decided the matter once and for all. He had made up his mind. She was going to be a college basketball star.

Now she had to live up to his expectations.

FINALLY, THE TWELVE thirty lunch bell clanged. Lucille escaped algebra class and made her way to the dining hall. Each day, Aunt Lucy would guide a dozen or more young children, almost all attending the first through third grades, through the line to get their food trays. Some were noisy, but most stood quietly by, waited their turn, and obediently carried their tray and silverware to their seats with Lucille, Lera and Vera, Coral, La Homa, and Teny, who were all helping the Indian children learn table manners.

Before eating, Lucille always bowed her head and said a blessing. All four kids at her table would look at his or her lap while she thanked God for their food. Then she would unwrap the silverware from inside the cloth napkin, put the napkin in her lap, the fork on the left side of her lunch tray, and the knife and spoon on the right. The first day she had her charges, she walked around the table and put napkins in laps. Now they all knew what to do. She also figured that mimicking her would be the best way for them to learn, so after showing them the proper way to hold their silverware, she just sat down and started eating.

But after several weeks, she found the job to be more difficult than she had first thought. Some of the younger kids didn't even know that the plate in front of them contained food. When she had shown them how to eat, they looked terrified. She explained that eating it wouldn't hurt them and then proved it by taking a bite from her plate. When she told Aunt Lucy what had happened, the dorm mother revealed that most of the children had been raised on corn bread and molasses. Right then, Lucille was determined not to feel sorry for them. Pity never helped put food on anyone's table. Hard work along with a good education did, and she was determined to help these kids live better lives.

Most of the children at her table were Seminoles. They talked in their native tongue and joked about her, often looking her way and laughing. Lucille would always smile, no matter what. Finally, she asked them to teach her the Seminole names of common things, and they did.

Then one day Barney was assigned to her table. He was the smallest child at the school, quick and quiet like a mouse. Barney fidgeted while sitting with the three other kids for his first meal. After saying grace, Lucille started passing around the butter, salt and pepper, giving instructions along the way on how and why to use the condiments. She showed everyone how to spread butter on their dinner roll, and then she demonstrated the proper way to hold the silverware while scooping up some food and putting it in her mouth. She always chewed with her mouth closed.

Barney ignored her instructions and began shoveling food in his mouth with his tiny hands. Food was ending up on his face, the table, and even the kid next to him.

She told him that he must eat with his fork and asked one of the other kids to show him how. Still, he refused. Lucille considered her options and then took the hardest but most direct route. She told him that it was just fine if he didn't eat at all. Barney sat there with his little face hung down. When his eyes teared up, the pity Lucille felt made her sick. She knew that he was so hungry he couldn't help himself. Many of these children were orphans or from families who couldn't afford to take care of them. They were lucky to be at OPC. Some of her neighbors back home were worse off. She had heard about a little boy whose parents sent him away to work on a wealthier neighbor's farm for money they pocketed. He hadn't even learned to read. That's why she knew that in the long run, it was beneficial for her charges to learn table manners. She had a job to do.

The other kids at the table kept on eating with their forks. After every bite, they sneaked a look at Lucille and then at Barney, waiting to see which one would give in first. In a minute or so, Barney glanced around to make sure no one was looking, picked up his fork, and started to eat, awkwardly at first but then with greater ease. He ate everything on his plate. But the next day the same thing happened, and the next day, too. In fact, Barney's refusing to eat and then reluctantly giving in became a daily ritual. Lucille kept waiting for that day when he would forget to eat with his hands and automatically pick up his fork.

AT NIGHT AFTER study hall, right before she and Coral said good night, Lucille had started sitting up in bed and writing down a sentence or two in a notebook about her day or any thought that seemed important. She was only about five pages into the notebook because she wrote on the fronts and backs of pages. Her first entry read, "I Glena Lucille Thurman, shall try to be kinder to everyone, especially my sister Dink." Another entry described how Aunt Lucy could tell which girl was walking through the foyer just by the sound of her shoes.

Lucille sometimes jotted down her delight with Barney's progress or frustrations with "Old Bear" Scroggs, but tonight she closed her eyes and thought about this Saturday and their first scrimmage. Babb would be scheduling a few more before they left on their Christmas barnstorm after the semester ended, three weeks away. But he would also be deciding who the starting lineup would be. A genuine team was taking shape: Doll and Coral starting at forward position, with La Homa as a first-string substitute. Everything was coming together.

On defense, Vick was certain to start, plus Bo-Peep, Toka Lee, and Teny, a sweet but deadly powerhouse, with Lera as a strong substitute. The team was almost set. But thinking about where she fit in caused that fluttery sensation in her stomach. The next few days at basketball practice would reveal her destiny.

But Babb just kept working out the Cardinals in his usual manner, scrimmaging against each other while he refereed, switching girls in and out of positions. But Lucille always started at center. This weekend's game against Ardmore would feel like a practice session with a few extra players. Lucille would be about the same age as the senior Ardmore girls. That should have been reassuring, but she never took anything for granted. Once during practice, Babb had told her not to chew on her mistakes. Make the correction and let it go. That was her problem. She liked to worry about everything.

Over the next two days before the official scrimmage game, the *Durant Daily Democrat* started running one-paragraph fillers in the sports section announcing the Cardinals' upcoming scrimmage. Doll, a familiar face from last year who was also an All-American, was featured. The scrimmage would be at Southeastern's field house. Free to the public, everyone was invited to stop by.

The night before the game, Lucille wrote down a few things in her notebook and then fell asleep. In her dream, she was trying to shoot a free throw, but her arms felt like lead. The ball shot up about a foot and then dropped to the ground like a bullet. Everyone watching her howled with laughter: Dink, her mother, Babb, and even her dad.

When she woke up, her tears were pooling beneath her chin because she was sleeping on her stomach. Her nose was running, too, making her pillow a wet mess. Keeping her eyes closed, she turned over on her back and tried to recover from her bad dream when funny sounds penetrated her thoughts, scraping, whooshing, and even bumping against the floor. Rolling over a little and opening both eyes, she couldn't see anything at first except remnants of her terrible nightmare. Then, little by little, the scene came into focus. A barefooted girl with blonde shoulder-length hair, wearing a brown cotton jumper that hung loosely on her lean frame, was running a broom covered with a cloth along the upper edge of the walls. *Thump, thump, swish, thump.* Coral was really working hard.

When Lucille asked, in her scratchy morning voice, what in the world she was doing, Coral said that she was getting rid of the dust and cobwebs. Lucille had no idea that their room had cobwebs, but nonetheless she got up, found another broom, and started cleaning up the dust under her bed. Soon they were showered and ready for breakfast, with time to study before game time.

That afternoon, Babb started Buena at center position, keeping Lucille on the sidelines.

Ardmore came out of the gate fast and won the jump. Their offense passed quickly down court but was stopped dead by guards Vick and Toka Lee. When Toka Lee, with her quick hands, stole the ball, the Cardinals were greeted by a storm of booing that startled them. From the sidelines, a crowd from Ardmore had gathered along with others from Durant. Lucille recognized the postmaster, Milus C. Mhoon, sitting next to Dr. Hotchkin, his wife Maria, and Aunt Lucy. The dorm mother would be their locker-room chaperone after home games. All the OPC girls who weren't basketball players had shown up, and they shouted for their team in an effort to drown out the racket coming from the Ardmore fans.

Ardmore stole back the ball to stay in the game. Eventually, though, Doll scored the first two points by sneaking through the unsuspecting defense. Then an Ardmore guard fouled her and Doll sank a free throw. The Cardinals were ahead by three.

Lucille was itching to play and couldn't sit still. When Coral made her first basket, she yelled louder than the crowd. Slowly, more OPC fans trickled in, and soon a shouting match erupted between Cardinal fans, mostly other OPC students, including a couple of the older Seminole children that Lucille ate lunch with. At halftime, the Cardinals were ahead by eight. Babb told Buena to sit out the rest of the game and motioned for Lucille to start the third quarter. She was about five inches taller than Ardmore's center. She got to the jump ball first and directed it to Doll, who scored a nice shot that just floated over the heads of the taller guards and into the basket.

Ardmore came back strong and sliced the lead to four. Babb removed Doll, sent in La Homa, and that's when things started to happen. La Homa's quickness seemed to confuse the Ardmore guards. The Cardinals got their second wind. By the fourth quarter, Babb had taken out all the sophomore players to give the freshmen more time on court: La Homa, Ginny Hamilton, and Lucille on offense; Vick, Lera, and Teny on defense. When he said that everyone would contribute, he meant it.

Lucille scored her first two points, and she didn't even notice. This was just a scrimmage after all and didn't count as an official game. When the final whistle sounded, OPC was ahead by eight points. Not a blowout but still satisfying to the new freshmen.

Babb and the Ardmore coach shook hands. The Ardmore team members were all good sports. But when the Cardinals were heading to the locker rooms, Babb didn't want to let them go just yet. He asked them to take just a minute and tell him how they thought the game went.

Terrific, someone said.

Others, all freshmen including Lucille, said that they had had fun. She even considered that not being a starter might be the best thing for her. She hadn't gotten her usual stage fright.

Babb then turned to Doll and asked her what she thought.

Doll folded her arms in front of her and looked very concerned. She eyeballed every girl before asking them if they realized that the teams the Cardinals would be playing weren't youthful high school girls, but semi-professional athletes who had been together for years. Did Babe Didrikson ring a bell? These industrial teams like the Golden Cyclones had well-paid coaches and strategic game plans. The players worked for a living and were on the teams because they had talent. After playing today, Doll told her teammates that they were not ready to go up against even the weakest industrial team.

By the time Doll was finished, all the joy of winning was gone. Even the more understanding sophomores like Bo-Peep had looks on their faces that told Lucille that they thought Doll was right. Lucille felt drained, like a sweaty rag doll.

But when Babb spoke, his upbeat voice sounded like an oasis. Players were looking to him for guidance and confidence, and he framed everything in terms of success. He smiled at Doll, and then said that her opinion mattered, but he'd thought everyone had played a good game. Yes, they could do better, but that's what the days ahead would bring. He told them that he was proud of the way they handled themselves and that they should get cleaned up and enjoy the rest of their weekend.

THAT NIGHT, LUCILLE and Coral were in their pajamas getting ready for bead when La Homa stuck her head in and asked if they'd like to come over and try some of her mother's homemade fudge. Lucille's mouth started to water, but she and Coral didn't move. They would be breaking one of Babb's rules. Seeing their hesitation, La Homa said to come anyway because other girls were there celebrating their first win even if it was against a high school team.

Lucille and Coral grudgingly followed La Homa to her room a couple of doors down from theirs. Vick, Lera, Vera, and Teny Lampson were all disobeying Babb and eating fudge. Everyone was whispering because it was supposed to be lights-out. Smiling gently, Teny offered the sweets to Coral, who gave Lucille the side eye, and then took some. Thinking that it could be her last sweet indulgence of the whole season, Lucille finally gave in. Teny giggled when Lucille took her first bite, shaking the soft, brown curls that brushed her forehead and cheek. Teny was quick to greet everyone with a smile, but she was a strong guard on court. Like most of the other

Cardinals, she had grown up on a ranch her dad owned and never gave a second thought to early-morning workouts. In fact, after much thought about the issue of so many girls quitting the team and going home, Lucille had decided that the poorer the girl, the harder she worked. All the poorest girls were still there.

The next piece of fudge melted in her mouth, just like the first. While she was still enjoying it, La Homa opened her top drawer and pulled out a Mars bar, a half-dozen licorice strings, and a bunch of caramel pieces. Eat these, too, she pleaded. And then she explained that she would probably die a slow and painful death trying to follow Babb's rule because she had a sweet tooth the size of Texas. Everyone wanted to know how she could eat so much candy and stay so thin. She shrugged and said she'd always been thin because she played hard and worked harder picking cotton and doing other chores.

The other girls nodded. They were all alike in that way. Then they started talking about boyfriends. The sugar had entered their bloodstreams and loosened their tongues. La Homa, being so pretty, had one, of course. Teny asked if she missed him.

La Homa shook her head. "He's not husband material."

Coral said she understood completely, and even Vick mentioned her high school beau.

On and on, they kept talking late into the night about boys—the ones who frightened them, the ones who ignored them, the ones who made them laugh, or the ones whom their fathers chased away. A heaviness came from the girls' yearning. They ate more fudge to get rid of it.

Coral decided to change the topic and said that she thought Doll had been right to tell them they weren't good enough yet.

"Doll thinks too much of herself," said Vick.

Lera agreed with Vick, then pointed out, "She has to make the shot from across court. She's too short to ever make a proper layup."

Vera wondered if Doll was in love with Babb since she spent so much time with him. That comment caused everyone to stop talking. Lucille finally giggled and said that she was having a hard enough time dealing with her nerves to imagine Doll and Babb having an affair. That would just be wrong.

"I wonder how Mr. Babb lost his leg," said Vera.

Every girl scrunched her eyebrows together. Babb's missing leg was the topic everyone wanted to discuss, and no one ever did.

"Farm accident," said Vick.

But Lucille shook her head. "Fighting in the Great War," she said. Thousands and thousands of young men had lost at least one limb during that momentous battle.

When Vick asked Lucille what she had meant by "nerves," Lucille realized all eyes were on her and that she had to explain.

Her problem was that she wanted to win more than anything. Vick said that wasn't a problem, and Coral pointed out that everyone who played good basketball wanted to win. It was more than that, Lucille said. The feeling built up inside of her like a Red River flood until her nerves couldn't stand it. Sometimes she threw up. But right after she made the first jump of the game and started to play, she was fine.

"Like stage fright," said Coral.

The others started nodding because they knew that basketball was a game of nerves—whichever team stayed focused and played their best could beat a better team that got easily rattled.

Then they started offering advice.

"Every night before I go to sleep, I picture new ways to guard a forward and keep her from scoring a goal," said Vick. She'd always done that, ever since she started playing basketball, and it might work for Lucille, too.

Teny and Coral discussed how great players always rose to the occasion and met the competition head on. They sounded just like Babb. And then every girl began offering her another remedy, and Lucille realized that—right at this moment—she was making true friends for life.

True friends who were also her fiercest rivals. Lucille studied their faces. How good were they when it counted? Better than she was? What if Coral made first string and not Lucille? Her dad would be so disappointed. That nauseating thought began to hound her. She couldn't sit there any longer because she might start to cry. So she said that she was tired and needed to go to bed. Everyone agreed that it was getting late, and soon they were tiptoeing back to their rooms.

When Lucille rested her head on her pillow, the painful doubts from earlier settled in like fire ants. She had always been the best in her class at schoolwork and playing basketball. But now she was wide awake at 1:30 a.m. because the thought of making a fool out of herself repeated over and over in her brain like a horror show. She wished that her dad were there. Maybe he could drive Dink out to Durant next weekend. She decided she would spend some of the money she earned at her part time job to call home tomorrow.

But even after she pulled her covers up to her chin, she couldn't stop thinking about being a kid and throwing baskets for hours at a time on an outdoor court. Falling down on that hard-dirt court had stained her knees an orangish brown throughout basketball season. If she hadn't been crazy enough to keep up her game, even in the fierce Oklahoma wind, this would not be happening to her. She'd be a normal girl who always thought about getting married and having kids. She wanted those things, too, but they weren't the be-all and end-all like they were for normal girls. She couldn't help it: she had far grander dreams.

CHAPTER 8

Barnstorm

CARDINAL SQUAD ROSTER, 1931–32

Lera Dunford . . . . Forward

Vera Dunford . . . . Guard

Toka Lee Fields . . . . Guard (*starter*)

Alice Hamilton . . . . Forward

Virginia Hamilton (Ginny) . . . . Forward

Buena Harris . . . . Center

Doll Harris . . . . Forward (*starter*)

Ernestine Lampson (Teny) . . . . Guard (*starter*)

La Homa Lassiter . . . . Forward

Susie Lorance . . . . Guard

Monk Mitchell . . . . Guard

Juanita Park (Bo-Peep) . . . . Guard

Lucille Thurman . . . . Center (*starter*)

Hazel Vickers (Vick) . . . . Guard (*starter*)

Allene West . . . . Guard/Forward

Coral Worley . . . . Forward (*starter*)

OPC Cardinals, 1932–33 season. Back row left to right: *Ernestine Lampson, Hazel Vickers, La Homa Lassiter, Buena Harris;* middle row left to right: *Irene Williams, Vera Dunford, Lera Dunford, Lucille Thurman;* front row left to right: *Doll Harris, Juanita Park, Coral Worley, Toka Lee Fields.*

Lucille picked up her suitcase and followed Coral down the sidewalk to the bus parked next to the curb. Their home on the road for the next three weeks practically sparkled. Under Babb's scrutiny, the auto mechanic had spent his Saturday making repairs and checking the tires. A wooden ladder was leaning against the side of the bus, and Bo-Peep was balanced at the top stacking luggage onto a large oak rack. Lucille lifted hers to Bo-Peep and then held the ladder steady.

Each girl could bring one suitcase on the journey.

It was Monday, December 21, the day the Cardinals began their barnstorm through Texas, Louisiana, and Arkansas, sacrificing their holiday for the good of the school, according to the semester's final edition of *Polished Pebbles*. They had taken their last final exam on Friday and spent the weekend packing while other girls had wished them Merry Christmas and hurried home to their families. In less than three hours, the team would be on the court playing their first official game against Celeste, Texas. Doll kept shouting for everyone to hurry up as each basketball player handed up her bag to Bo-Peep. They had to be on the road by 3 p.m.

But for eleven of the sixteen girls traveling today, this would be their first Christmas away from home. Most had spent Thanksgiving break finding Christmas presents for their families while nurturing the eager anticipation of being on the road and playing basketball. The freshmen were all teenagers, not much older than Lucille, at sixteen. Since returning from break, Lera and Vera had started irritating Aunt Lucy by calling their mother several times a week and tying up the only telephone in the dorm. Even now, they wanted to say good-bye to their mother one more time. Aunt Lucy pointed out that since the closest telephone to their farmhouse was at a Piggly Wiggly five miles away, by the time a store attendant notified her parents and they were able to find a telephone and call them back, the girls would be on the road. Still, the twins wouldn't give up until La Homa informed them that they could do what she was planning on doing—sending a telegram to arrive on Christmas Day. Lera and Vera started jumping up and down with excitement. No one in their family had ever gotten a telegram on Christmas. They began saving money right away so that they could afford the expense, even though it was cheaper to send a telegram than make a long-distance phone call.

Promptly at two thirty Babb arrived with Maria Hotchkin, who would be the chaperone. The wife of the OPC president was a kind, sturdy woman in her fifties. Wire-rimmed glasses emphasized large eyes that were usually crinkled in a smile. She had a broad face and graying brown hair cut short in a wavy, modern style. Asking a few girls to help her, she lifted boxes of food and stored water out of the trunk of Babb's car and stowed them on the bus. Babb dug out two maps from his glove compartment, both with the trip route highlighted in red marker. He handed one to Bo-Peep and then carefully outlined the schedule: tonight they would play at Celeste, Texas, only sixty miles south of Durant. Then they would drive to Houston where they would play a double header against the Houston Green Devils and a game against a Galveston team on Christmas Eve. They would have Christmas Day off and then travel east, playing at Port Arthur, Dalisetta, and Jasper in Texas; Collinston, Bastrop (two games), Shreveport (two games), Castor, Athens, and Harris in Louisiana; and two games in Eureka Springs, Arkansas. On January 9, they would finally head home.

Lucille stood next to Bo-Peep and stared at the map. Babb had scheduled seventeen games in three weeks. None of the freshmen, including Lucille, had ever barnstormed, but it was a popular way for athletic teams to earn money in a short period of time. Many of these teams weren't members of a league and some didn't even have a home court.

Glancing back at the dorm, Lucille realized that for a few weeks, home would be the camp courts and auto courts that had sprung up along roadsides during the past few years, primitive motels or court residences named after a local attraction or the comfort they provided. Dew Drop Inn, Cottage Courts, or Crystal River Tourist Camp, some costing less than a dollar a night. The thought of staying at these little villages made her smile. Traveling these miles, at least a thousand by the time they were done, would be the biggest adventure of her life thus far.

Ever since the Cardinals' first scrimmage almost three weeks ago, Lucille had been working on her mental game, a term she had learned from Babb in his psychology class. She had started doing what Vick suggested, picturing moves on the court. A few days later, Babb put her at starting center, and that's where she intended to remain. Her nightmares had disappeared because she now understood how much Babb believed in her abilities. More than ever, she felt strong and ready for this road trip. But then she glanced at the old crank-start bus, remembered that it could be as cold as an icebox, and her mouth suddenly felt parched.

"Lucille," a familiar voice called out, and she shook off the sudden anxiety when Babb asked if she was ready to win her first game on the road tonight. "Yes, sir," she said automatically. But then she watched him check with every girl, and that old reassurance kicked back in. None of them would be here if he didn't think that they could win. Still, when she boarded the little bus and found a seat next to Coral, she closed her eyes and said a quiet prayer for good weather, excellent road conditions, and no mechanical problems.

Doll, adapting well to her duties as team captain, asked each girl boarding the bus if she'd remembered to use the bathroom. Only one scooted back inside the dorm.

As soon as everyone was seated, Babb asked for their attention. He reminded them that their parents expected Babb and Mrs. Hotchkin to be their constant guardians. In return, he expected the players to take care of each other because this wouldn't be an easy trip. They would be traveling hard and playing hard.

"Remember why you're here—to learn discipline and sportsmanship, and play good basketball."

They shouldn't hesitate to confide in Mrs. Hotchkin about any problems. They would eat properly and behave like young ladies.

Babb patted Bo-Peep on the shoulder and thanked her for driving the bus. They weren't a wealthy industrial team and couldn't afford to bring along a professional bus driver. He trusted Bo-Peep to drive safely *and* play good basketball.

"I won't hesitate to discipline anyone if it becomes necessary," Babb continued. "But most of all, I want all of you to have a good time."

As soon as he left, each girl stopped holding her breath.

If Babb were traveling with them, by the end of the trip they'd all be suffocated, Vera said in her loud, joking voice. Several nervous giggles erupted. Doll told Vera that if she said anything else about their coach that she didn't like, she'd tell Babb.

"You don't think he's awfully strict?" Vick asked.

Doll ignored her and took the seat next to Toka Lee, just behind Bo-Peep.

Lucille hated it when they derided her coach, but she understood their feelings. He *was* awfully strict.

Staying just behind Babb's car, Bo-Peep pulled out of the parking lot and headed south out of town on Highway 69, past muddy Mineral Bayou that wound shallow and brown through the green winter-wheat fields. The road then curved into a forest of bare pecan trees, their narrow limbs arching high above the bus in a spiny canopy. As they passed over Moore Creek, a fog set in, the misty kind that rose up off the ground in thin, ghostlike fingers. The sudden chill caused several girls to wrap themselves tighter in their blankets.

Twenty minutes later, the Red River Bridge suddenly emerged out of the fog in front of them. Each girl, including Lucille, crossed her fingers and stared out the window as the bus entered the one-lane, wood bridge that extended across the river that served as the Oklahoma-Texas border. As they passed by the empty tollhouse, a big sign that said CLOSED was posted on the door. Last summer, this bridge had been the scene of an Oklahoma-Texas boundary dispute involving the National Guard. If Oklahoma hadn't won that dispute, they would now be paying a fee to cross into Texas. As soon as they were across, Bo-Peep floored the gas pedal since the bus's top speed was forty-five miles per hour. Over the deep *chug-chug* of the engine, the players chatted about home or closed their eyes to drift off.

After passing through Denison, they entered Hunt County, just a few miles east of the vast East Texas Oil Field, discovered in 1930. Oil wells covered the prairie like long-necked dinosaurs. Enormous trucks would appear out of nowhere and overtake the little bus, creating a wind draft strong enough to send them all flying into a ditch. Bo-Peep gripped the steering wheel more firmly.

Unregulated oil production had spread throughout the region as farmers and ranchers made deals with oilmen to sell mineral rights. Production increased from twenty-seven thousand barrels per year to nine hundred thousand per day with twelve hundred wells. By July 1931, overproduction had driven the price of crude oil from ninety-nine cents per barrel in 1930 to just thirteen cents. Things had gotten so bad that by August 1931, Texas governor Sterling ordered the Texas Rangers and the National Guard to shut down certain wells. Soon angry producers smuggled illegal crude, or "hot oil," via trucks that drove too fast down East Texas highways. The oil bust, occurring less than two years after the stock market crash, had devastated the region. Texas's unemployment rose to 23 percent, somewhat low compared to Oklahoma's thirty percent.

Sooner than expected, Bo-Peep was pulling into a six-room auto court. They hurriedly changed into their basketball uniforms and went to find the Celeste gymnasium.

Once a bustling town of two thousand, Celeste's population had dwindled to eight hundred due to reoccurring economic misfortunes. The basketball team drew girls from small, dusty towns all across the county, and they played to win. That's why Babb had chosen the steady, young team as the Cardinals' opponent for the first game of the season.

The high school gym was easy to find, considering it was the largest building in town. Impatient to get on court, the Cardinals hurried inside to find the locker rooms.

After getting a drink of water from the fountain, Lucille sat on a bench in the locker room and began to wrap her ankles. Doll offered to help, but her incessant chatter just further unnerved Lucille. When Doll got excited, her anticipation filled the room, and she always seemed to talk about Babb. Apparently she was still concerned that some of the players, namely the Dunford twins, didn't understand why he was being so strict with them. He was never mean, like they said. He just expected full dedication to the team. Doll didn't see anything wrong with that. Neither did Lucille. When she was finished, both girls pulled on their warm-ups and headed for the court.

The sight that greeted them made Lucille put her hand over her mouth to hide her smile. Babb was up on a stepladder under one of the goals unwinding a measuring tape that stretched from the hoop rim down to the floor. He took care to measure every inch of the goal space, and when he was satisfied, he walked the court to make sure that every line was within regulation. Some teams had been known to cheat by varying the goal height or free-throw line. The teams that were not trying to cheat had sometimes simply neglected to maintain their playing area. Babb didn't necessarily think that Celeste would cheat to win, but he checked out the court at every away game, just in case.

Finally, Babb put away the ladder, grabbed a basketball, and called his team to attention. They always ran drills to loosen up. Intensity passing, he ordered, and tossed the ball to Doll, who organized the drill. Mrs. Hotchkin, dressed in a pale white blouse and cherry-red skirt to match the Cardinals' uniform colors, hovered near the team bench ready to hand out water to thirsty players.

The Cardinals formed two lines. Lucille and Coral were in front standing about three feet apart. Doll gave Lucille the ball, and she and Coral began snapping off passes back and forth, concentrating on making them crisp and chest high. After reeling off about ten passes in ten seconds, they both stepped back a foot and did ten more. They kept stepping back after each repetition until they were about eight feet apart. Then Coral passed off to La Homa, who was next in line with Vick. Lucille and Coral jogged to the end of the line and waited to go again. The drill was flashy and fast, and no one ever missed.

When it was the other team's turn to warm up, Babb called the Cardinals back to the locker room and motioned for them to gather around him. Babb never criticized nor praised too much. He believed that more could be accomplished through organization and discipline than by frequent, highly charged pep talks.

But he did look every girl in the eyes and said that he was confident that tonight's game would be the first in what would become a record winning streak. How did he know? Because after two months of hard practice and getting up before dawn and braving the bitter morning cold, they were still there. Why did they stick it out? Because right now they loved the game more than anything else in the world. Now go and prove it to Celeste, he said.

"Go . . . Cardinals!" the team shouted as they raced onto the court.

Even though the crowd was small—only a couple hundred people—it was loud. Boos erupted when the Cardinals appeared. Lucille took a deep breath, slipped off her warm-ups, and went to meet the opposing center at midcourt inside the jump circle. As she got in ready position, she noticed that her hands were unsteady. If her nerves caused the Cardinals to lose, Doll would kill her and Babb would move Buena to first string.

"Heads up," Doll yelled. She was standing three feet in front of Lucille, just outside of the circle, waiting to grab the ball.

Lucille crouched low, took another deep breath, and looked up. Seconds later, the referee tossed the ball for the tip-off, and the game was on. She caught the tip and sent it to Doll, who passed quickly to Coral. Within seconds, even before Lucille had made it to her favorite place in the keyhole area underneath the basket, Coral had scored. A Celeste guard, almost as small as Doll, passed the ball down court for her team.

Teny, Vick, and Toka Lee stood ready at guard positions on their side of the court. Even though in girls' rules the guards never crossed the center line, they always knew who had the ball on the other side of the court. Seconds after Celeste whisked the ball down court, Vick cut off the forward's path to the goal, causing her to shoot from outside, and miss. Elbowing the

Celeste forwards out of her way, Teny grabbed the rebound and whipped it to Toka Lee, who shot it across midcourt to Doll.

Lucille snagged the sharp pass from Doll, took the one below-the-knee dribble allowed in girls' rules, and then propelled the ball toward Coral, who passed it over a guard's head and into Doll's arms. The three girls kept the ball in motion for several seconds, whipping it around so fast that the Celeste guards never knew where the ball would go next.

Suddenly Doll whisked it up toward the basket, and scored. The Celeste guards, tired from the workout the Cardinal forwards had given them, quickly sent the ball down court.

After the Cardinals had scored ten points while Celeste had not scored once, Babb called a time-out and replaced Doll and Lucille with La Homa and Buena.

When Buena lost the tip-off, Celeste finally scored. Coral made two more baskets before Babb replaced her with Lera. Soon, Vick, Teny, and Toka Lee were out, too, replaced by Bo-Peep, Monk Mitchell, and Allene West. That night, Babb had every player on the court contributing to the game. At one point, he switched the offensive players to defense, and the defense to offense, anything to make the game more interesting.

Lucille sat on the bench next to Mrs. Hotchkin and felt every move as she tracked the game. She shouted encouragements to Buena and, forgetting herself, nearly fell off the bench and had to be steadied by Mrs. Hotchkin.

When the final gun fired and the Cardinals won, 29–5, Lucille was beside herself with joy. When she came back down to earth, her heart beating so fast that she thought it might pop through her teeth, she knew without any doubt that basketball was magic.

BO-PEEP GOT THE bus started early the next morning, and by 6 a.m., they were eating breakfast at a diner just outside of Greenville on Highway 69. After finishing, they headed southwest on State Highway 34, driving eighty miles on gravel and hard dirt until they reached U.S.

Highway 75 at Ennis, about thirty-five miles south of Dallas. In eight hours, they would be playing the Houston Green Devils sponsored by the Walk-Over Shoe Company. The Green Devils billed themselves as the Gulf Coast champions, but their real fame came from having a six-foot-four forward named Alice Humbarger. In December, newspapers across the country carried a picture of her standing with her arms in a Y position above her head gripping a basketball in each hand. Two smaller players crouched in ready position beneath either arm, and the headline read, "Alice and Her Wonderhands." The caption stated that the giantess "Alice Humbarger of Houston used her six feet four inches of height and a pair of the biggest feminine hands in basketball to help her team, the Green Devils, win second place in the Texas A.A.U. women's tourney."

Vick would be the one to guard Alice, but she wasn't worried about defending against the famous tall girl. During high school, she'd played against boys at least six feet tall. She told her teammates that she knew exactly what to do, and no one doubted her.

But first, they had to get to Houston.

Gripping the bus's oversized steering wheel and keeping her eyes on the road, Bo-Peep was always on the lookout for the bigger rocks that would fatally bust a tire, or the mud holes that sprang up like glittering mirages, turning the dirt and gravel into mucky glue. Other girls would offer to help with the driving, but Bo-Peep didn't want to give up the wheel. She loved to drive trucks, cars, and even old school buses like this one. Although she wouldn't say it out loud, she just didn't trust another girl to have the skill and knowledge she possessed to keep everyone safe. Babb agreed; that's why he had given her this job.

Mostly the landscape out the windows looked just like southeastern Oklahoma: gently sloping prairie with clusters of trees in the creek beds. While on Highway 34, they passed a few hitchhikers, men or boys dressed in shabby clothes heading to or coming from the shack towns built from tar paper, scrap metal, and wood. Upon seeing the families gathered around fires, their faces gaunt and clothes tattered, a few of the girls muttered,

"There but for the grace of God go I," since most of their own parents were one or two crop failures away from financial ruin.

The players took advantage of the drive and caught up on their sleep. Lucille jotted down a few lines in her notebook so that she'd remember certain things when she wrote home. Only Doll seemed on edge, tapping her foot, whispering to Toka Lee, and crawling back and forth through the seats to speak to Bo-Peep. Doll had proved herself to be a fidgeter, someone who couldn't sit still except when she slept. The Dunford twins acted like they were watching a tennis match, turning their heads back and forth as she squeezed by. Once, Doll asked Bo-Peep to stop for a bathroom break among a cluster of trees near the road because there weren't any rest stops.

Finally, they reached the main road to Houston. Turning due south on Highway 75, they drove two hundred miles on the smooth, paved highway, and Doll finally settled down. Along the way, they passed through a dozen small towns, including Corsicana, Richland, Centerville, Madisonville, and Huntsville. Babb and Mrs. Hotchkin were always close behind, but Doll and Bo-Peep both had written down directions to the motel, just in case.

After passing through Huntsville, it started to rain. Big drops that splatted against the window for about fifteen minutes, followed by bright sunlight. That's when everyone noticed the forests on either side of the road so thick that sunlight only trickled through. An hour later, the landscape cleared just in time for downtown Houston to appear on the horizon. Twice the size of Oklahoma City, Houston was Texas's biggest city.

When they pulled into the Valencia Court Motel near downtown at quarter to one in the afternoon, every girl felt her knees creak as she climbed out of the bus. The humid air smelled like car exhaust, and the second thing they noticed was the noise, the constant hum of cars and the occasional siren. Mrs. Hotchkin visited a grocery store nearby and bought enough bread and ham to make sandwiches for lunch. That evening, after their game against the Green Devils, they would eat a substantial dinner. With sixteen players plus Babb and Mrs. Hotchkin, they purchased five rooms for three nights at a cost of about five dollars per room per night. Everyone would have roommates except for Babb, of course. Mrs. Hotchkin used her housekeeping allowance to pay her own way and help the team save money.

Dividing up into rooms and dragging in their luggage, they drew straws to see who would sleep on the rollaway cots. After lunch, they were supposed to be taking naps even though they were too excited to close their eyes. Lera and Vera were staying with Mrs. Hotchkin and kept asking if they could set up a time to talk to their mother over the telephone. Mrs. Hotchkin tried to hide the frustrated look on her face because she understood how teenagers spending their first holidays away from home might suffer from homesickness. She explained that they might as well be asking if they could purchase diamonds because the cost of long distance was very expensive. Instead, she gave every player extra pennies to buy postcards and encouraged them to write home every day.

Sooner than expected, Babb had them all up and out the door two hours ahead of schedule so that they could stretch and warm up before the game.

That night, inside the downtown basketball arena, in front of hundreds of Texas fans, Lucille thought she might hyperventilate. She pressed her lips together and willed her nerves to disappear.

Just like the night before against Celeste, Babb told them that he was sure they could win. There were more fans in attendance on this night, but they seemed more civilized than the rowdy group from last night. That comment made every player grin.

Lucille walked onto the court, still feeling a bit nervous, but ready to play. Alice Humbarger loped into the center circle with Lucille for the opening tipoff. Houston fans cheered her presence. Five inches shorter than Alice, Lucille felt petite for the first time in her life. She widened her stance and sank even lower than usual so that she could spring up quicker than Alice when the referee's whistle blared. Lucille won the toss. Coral caught Lucille's tip, turned on a dime, and made the first score of the night.

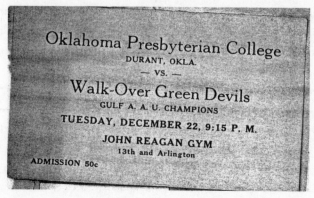

Ticket to the Green Devils' game from Doll's scrapbook

During the first half, Coral and Lucille worked together so well that Lucille thought her roommate had gained psychic ability and was reading her mind. Doll was another matter entirely. She made daring shots from the sideline or half-court that bounced off the rim. Even though she was missing shots, she wouldn't feed the ball to Lucille or Coral even when they shouted that they were open. She would never admit it, but Doll liked the attention.

To make matters worse, the Green Devils were using their elbows like weapons and the referee didn't call one foul. Back at the bench, Babb held his tongue because the rules prevented him from sideline coaching.

With the six-on-six game under girls' rules, twelve players were on the court at one time. The guards had to finesse the ball, pass with flow and continuity, and dominate the opposing team in order to feed it to their offense on the other side of the court. When the guards were trying to get the ball to the forwards across the half-court line, and all twelve players converged, the play became brutally close, elbows in ears, toes being crushed, more like football than basketball. Tonight the center line became a battle zone.

The OPC guards, Bo-Peep, Vick, and Toka Lee, worked hard to shut down Alice and her teammates, but the rough play disrupted their footwork. They seemed to be out of step and behind the ball.

By halftime, the game was tied, 10–10.

Babb took Doll aside during the break and spoke to her quietly. When they were finished, Doll looked subdued but determined.

Gathering the rest of his team around him, Babb told the Cardinals that he and Doll had discussed teamwork. Doll, standing next to Lucille, looked defiantly at the other players, daring them to criticize.

But Babb said that the entire team needed to exhibit better cooperation, not just Doll. Calmly, he told them, "You can beat Houston with one hand tied behind your backs. The score is tied because you're being too selfish." To overcome selfishness, they had to trust each other. As a team, they could win. But as individuals on court showing off for the crowd, they would lose. "Focus on the play, not the results," he said.

Babb's words made Lucille feel proud to be a Cardinal. Out of impulse, she caught Doll's hand and squeezed. Doll looked surprised. Then she nodded at Lucille, let go of her hand, and the two trotted onto the court. Soon the rest of the players were ready, and the referee blew the whistle.

In the second half, the Cardinals were a different team. Doll, Lucille, and Coral quickened the pace by zigzagging footwork, faking passes, and making basket after basket.

Teny, Vick, and Toka Lee stayed alert and seemed to know where the offensive player was going before she even took a step. Their actions were quick and aggressive, forcing the offense to react. Alice Humbarger and her extraordinary height couldn't overcome the Cardinals' momentum.

The Green Devils looked confused, and their confidence waned. When the night was over and the final whistle sounded, the Cardinals beat Houston, 33–18.

The next night, in front of another big crowd, the Cardinals proved that they were a team to be reckoned with, soundly defeating the Green Devils, 39–16. Doll played a perfect game, scoring twenty points. Afterward, they showered and changed into their clothes, then headed out for dinner. Babb decided to ride on the bus and let Mrs. Hotchkin drive his car to the restaurant.

Before letting Bo-Peep start the engine, Babb spoke to his team.

Beating the Green Devils two nights in a row was very significant, he said. "I'm very proud of you."

"Winning against the Green Devils is like firing off a gun in the middle of a crowd," Doll said, too excited to remain quiet. The better teams like the Golden Cyclones and the Sun Oilers would be paying attention from now on. "Just you wait," she said.

"Is that true?" asked Coral.

Babb shrugged and said that he admired Doll's enthusiasm. "Let's not worry about any other teams right now. Better to start thinking about the game tomorrow against the Galveston Anicos."

Right then, someone's stomach growled loud enough for Babb to hear. He laughed and told Bo-Peep to get going. They would stop at a diner for a light supper. But when she turned over the engine, it wheezed and then stalled. Used to the routine, everyone hopped out to push after Bo-Peep used both hands on the crank so that she wouldn't be forced backward. It took two tries to get it started.

The Cardinals might be a team to be reckoned with, but their bus could fall apart at any moment.

When they had eaten dinner and were back in their motel rooms, the first thing every girl did was take care of her Converse high-tops. Since they all owned only one pair, and they were soaked through after a hard game, they had to get them dry especially if they had a game the next day. Damp shoes increased the chance of getting blisters that could become infected. So every night, each girl removed the laces and sometimes covered the worn canvas with shoe polish. Then she pulled the tongue forward and set the shoes next to the steam heater so that the sweat-soaked insides would dry overnight. It worked like a dream.

After falling asleep sometime after midnight, Lucille awoke to a banging sound outside her room at the Valencia Court Apartments. The sun was just coming up. She hopped out of bed, opened the curtains, and saw Bo-Peep leaning over the bus's engine and whacking it with a socket wrench. She was hitting it so hard, the hood, propped open with a flimsy-looking pole, shook back and forth. Lucille slipped on her robe and went outside.

"What're you doing?" she said, grabbing the hood to steady it.

"Changing spark plugs and wires," said Bo-Peep.

She handed her wrench to Lucille and stepped behind the wheel. With Lucille gripping the crank with two hands and Bo-Peep pumping the gas pedal, the old bus finally started. Lucille gave a victory whoop.

"Well, at least you'll get a ride to breakfast."

Lucille turned around and found Babb standing behind her. Mrs. Hotchkin, wearing a bright green housecoat and curlers in her short hair, looked stricken standing beside him. She insisted that he find some other mode of transportation for the young ladies. Then she told Bo-Peep that she had to wash off the engine oil covering her face and hands before setting foot in a restaurant.

Babb had a few ideas about replacing the bus when they got back home. "Next time we'll get a mechanic to fix the engine," he told Bo-Peep.

She pressed her lips and nodded at Babb. As she and Lucille walked back to their room, Bo-Peep mumbled, "I can fix this bus better than any mechanic."

Lucille agreed.

At the restaurants, they usually filled up two or three big tables and always gave the waitress a nice tip. This morning, Babb was late. But that didn't keep anyone from ordering food. In the meantime, Toka Lee was keeping everyone entertained.

"Covering the court like a red plague, the Oklahoma Presbyterian Cardinals completely annihilated Houston's home team," Toka Lee read from an enthusiastic article written by popular Houston sports columnist Johnny Lyons and appearing on the front page of the *Houston Post-Dispatch* sports section. She had the newspaper spread out on the breakfast table in front of her. The rest of the team sat listening. "Doll Harris, a sensation on court, was the individual scoring star with 20 points. Coral Worley followed with 10 points, and Lucille Thurman scored the remaining 9.

Toka Lee Fields, Hazel Vickers, and Ernestine Lampson set up a defense that had the Texas girls completely baffled."

Toka Lee beamed at Teny and Vick, who seemed happy to get the accolades. The rest of the team buzzed over the good press until someone appeared to take their orders. Lucille dug in her purse for a nickel so that she could buy a copy of the newspaper. Other girls were doing the same thing, and this morning the restaurant would sell out of the *Houston Post-Dispatch*.

Doll asked where Babb was. He was usually twenty minutes early to every meeting, and never late for a meal. Mrs. Hotchkin reminded her charges that today was Christmas Eve, and maybe Babb was making special arrangements for their holiday. Then she blushed a deep red because she had just given away a big secret. The buzz at the table grew louder as they discussed what their surprise could be. They were scheduled to play against Galveston this afternoon but had the next three days off.

Lera thought they could get back home in time to eat Christmas dinner at her house if they started right this minute. Doll dismissed her comment as preposterous and reminded her that they had already ordered the Christmas telegrams. Vera hadn't spoken since she'd heard that it was Christmas Eve. She was in shock that she had completely forgotten.

Several girls asked which church service they could attend after the game. Everyone was talking at once when Babb's voice broke through the hubbub. He wanted them all to meet someone.

When they saw the young man standing next to Babb, their eyes widened with surprise. Teny gulped in enough air to make her hiccup. The Dunford twins giggled, and Ginny Hamilton kicked them on the shins to make them stop.

It turned out that Babb had invited John Murphy, a young sportswriter from Galveston, to join them for breakfast. He had driven into town early but would be covering the game against the Anicos later that day. But introducing them to a handsome and successful young man wasn't the surprise that Mrs. Hotchkin had mistakenly revealed.

Babb kept standing so that all three tables of girls could hear. He told them to return to their rooms and pack their bags. Right after the game, taking place in the Houston arena this afternoon, they would be making the hour drive to Galveston Island and spending Christmas on the beach. It turned out that Galveston was Babb's most favorite place. He loved to travel more than he loved basketball, and he'd been across the western half of the United States, from Chicago to California. Except for Oklahoma, though, where most of his siblings had ended up, no place felt more like home than Galveston.

The Cardinals were speechless. Lucille sat blinking, letting Babb's words sink in. Like most of the other freshmen players, she had never seen the ocean and couldn't wait to taste the salty water. Suddenly everyone was talking at once, asking Babb about bathing suits and towels.

That afternoon, after an easy win against the Galveston Anicos, they drove the sixty miles south to Galveston Island. When they reached the causeway road that crossed from the mainland to the island, they all fell silent and stared. They had never seen this much blue sky and water. After arriving at their destination, several of the players forgot about luggage and stood puzzling at what turned out to be a stout palm tree. The basket-weave trunk was almost three feet in diameter. Large fan-shaped leaves sparkled blue-green in the sunlight. The Miramar Courts' single-story duplex apartments, built Spanish style with yellow bricks and beet-red window awnings, spanned an entire block. The Miramar was part of a number of hotels owned by Galveston entrepreneur W. L. Moody, who also owned the newspaper where Murphy worked. His businesses sponsored the Anicos basketball team. Babb had met Moody last year at the AAU national tournament held in Dallas, and now, due to their fast acquaintance, the Cardinals were getting a special rate for their motel rooms.

ON CHRISTMAS MORNING, even during the slow winter season in Galveston, a few restaurants stayed open to accommodate guests. During breakfast, Babb encouraged everyone to send their parents a postcard and let them know how well they were doing. But before anyone wrote a word, they hurried back to the motel and rented swimsuits. The morning had grown warm, and the temperature could reach almost seventy degrees.

Wrapping themselves in the thick motel towels, the Cardinals, followed by Mrs. Hotchkin and Babb, crossed the street from the Miramar to visit their little beach, several blocks away from the main swimming area. It didn't matter. Only a few people walked along the water's edge. When the Cardinals discovered that the water felt temperate and not cold, they all waded in. Lucille splashed Coral in the face and participated in a dunking war with Vick against the Dunford twins, who suddenly weren't homesick at all. Vera took a breath too early and swallowed some seawater. She said it tasted just like pickled cucumbers.

By the end of the afternoon, they could dive beneath the waves, which weren't very big, and then pop up behind them as they lapped toward shore.

Babb sat on a wooden beach chair the whole time and talked with Mrs. Hotchkin, who was wearing a swimsuit but had a thick cotton blanket wrapped around her shoulders. She would get up from her chair every once in a while and stick her big toe in the water to see if it was any warmer. Doll didn't swim very much, either. She was always within conversation distance from Babb, lying on her towel and drying off in the sun. But then, she *was* the team captain.

Once, Lucille swam a little too far from shore, and on her way back in, she began to imagine huge sea creatures hovering in the deep, murky water—poisonous eels, maybe, or sharks. Suddenly she felt microscopic, like a flea on an elephant. She raced back to shore, pulled herself onto the sand, and sat dripping wet and shivering. But then, as she gazed out at the never-ending water, her fear suddenly disappeared. She took a deep breath and thanked God that the Cardinals were winning and that nothing too bad had happened to them, at least not yet.

CHAPTER 9

End Game

Doll stirred a teaspoon of sugar into her coffee, added a dollop of cream, and took a sip. Then she opened her menu hoping that she would find poached eggs. After eating at so many different restaurants in the past two and a half weeks, she had discovered that this style of eggs was her favorite. Sitting in the coffee shop of the Harris Hotel in Harris, Louisiana, she waited for Babb to arrive so they could start. She looked forward to these breakfast meetings every few days, getting away from her teammates, hearing Babb's opinion about things. She always arrived early so he wouldn't catch her adding sugar to her coffee.

It was Doll's job to research their next opponent. If she couldn't find any recent newspaper articles, she would ask the townspeople. They were generally happy to describe recent games, brag about the top players, and discuss who was on a hot streak and who was injured. Babb was often friends with the coach if they were both members of the AAU. Doll had come to realize that Babb did far more than coach his team and teach psychology. He arranged for the games themselves and took care of all the politics that went along with playing competitive amateur sports. He handled problems by anticipating them and did everything possible to ensure that a fair game took place. Along with Dr. Hotchkin, he wrangled funds, sought publicity, and coached in a manner so understated that none of his players, except for Doll, ever knew the amount of time and effort he put into it every day.

After the team's excellent performance on the road, winning every game so far, better teams like the Dallas Shoe Shop "Slipper" Girls and the famed Golden Cyclones would want to add the Cardinals to their schedule. Doll couldn't wait to face them.

She left her vision of pummeling the Golden Cyclones to focus on Babb, who had slid into the booth across from her. He opened his menu, and when the waitress arrived, ordered hot tea, scrambled eggs with onions, and buttered toast. Then he asked Doll to tell him about the Harris team.

"It'll be another smasher," Doll said. Not as easy as Bastrop, though. The Cardinals had beaten Bastrop, Louisiana, 69–22. The Harris team had no defense. Their best guard was injured. Most of their forwards were no taller than Doll, and they lost to Athens, whom the Cardinals had beaten, 41–10.

Babb expressed his approval and watched as the waitress set down their plates of food. Between eager bites, he asked Doll how everyone was getting along. She wrinkled her eyebrows and frowned. She had expected Babb to scold her for underestimating her opponents. Now she felt like he was asking her to squeal on her teammates. Back at school, he assigned certain students to keep watch and make sure that his athletes made curfew and were in their rooms by 10 p.m. These dormitory spies never revealed themselves because who in their right minds would want to be known as a squealer?

But the truth was, except for Toka Lee, Doll didn't know her teammates well enough to have access to their secrets. She just wasn't that interested except when they were on the court. She would never tell Babb, but most of her good friends had been boys in her high school class, plus her high school basketball coach, and now Babb. But she took a stab, anyway, at reporting about the emotional stability of her teammates. Everyone had forgotten about being homesick. Lucille and Coral were hard workers. La Homa seemed boy crazy. The Dunford twins were never serious about anything. Stuff Babb already knew, but Doll wanted to seem like she at least was trying when it came to her teammates. But what did it matter? They were winning. That's how she really felt.

"There's more to life than winning," he said.

Maybe. But it sure seemed like Babb's concern over discipline and practice was fueled by a desire to win. Even on the road, he made them keep up with running one mile every day and making one hundred free throws. That didn't earn him any "nice" points from some of her teammates.

Doll took a bite of toast and watched Babb as he finished his last bit of eggs, scooping them up between his fork and a piece of toast. His hands were big, like bear paws, and calloused, something she'd never noticed. And his eyes were dark, the color of black coffee.

There's nothing better than winning, she thought with satisfaction. Except maybe eating poached eggs and talking basketball with Mr. Babb.

THAT NIGHT, AFTER a 54–20 victory over Harris, Doll and Toka Lee arrived back at their motel room with Susie Lorance. Tomorrow they would travel to Eureka Springs in Arkansas, where they had reservations at the famous Crescent Hotel, a real step up after staying in the dusty and cramped motor courts along the roadside. After two quick games with the local team, they would be going back to Durant.

Chatting about the game, Doll and Toka Lee stripped down for a shower. After taking turns bathing before the hot water ran out, they put on their pajamas, brushed their teeth, rubbed night cream on their faces, and brushed each other's hair one hundred strokes with Toka Lee's fine, wooden brush. Then they turned out the light and crawled into the bed they were sharing. Neither one closed her eyes.

"Say, where'd your name come from, Toka Lee?" Doll said.

"My mother named me after Atoka, Oklahoma," Toka Lee answered, surprised by Doll's sudden interest. Most of the time, their conversation started and ended with Doll as the main topic.

"I like it."

"Thanks." Then she added, "You know, Doll, you're the closest friend I've ever had."

Toka Lee's words caught Doll by surprise. They had been through one and a quarter seasons of basketball together. She turned onto her side so that she was facing Toka Lee and asked her if she had ever wanted to be a boy. Toka Lee yawned and said, What do you mean?

Doll said that when she was younger, she wanted to wear pants all the time and go without a shirt in the summer when it was so hot and humid. She didn't want to have to worry about how she looked but only wanted to be accepted because of her skill on the basketball court or her good grades in school. She wanted to be a boy, for a little while. But not anymore.

From the other side of the room, Susie said, "Lights out." Toka Lee yawned and then turned off the bedside lamp. Doll pulled the sheets up to her chin, and soon they all were fast asleep.

AT THE SAME time the Cardinals were growing into a team to be reckoned with, the Women's Division of the NAAF—with Mrs. Hoover still at the helm—had begun referring to itself as, among other things, a publicity organization. Its goal was to spread its core beliefs, called the Platform, through all available channels. At the organization's main office in New York City, the only paid worker, office executive Mary Van Horn, had started a scrapbook collection of all printed publicity and promotion in magazines, state journals, high school bulletins, and newspapers. She also kept an "enemies" file that contained points of view opposite to that of the Women's Division.

The newest field secretary, Anne Frances Hodgins, was in the midst of traveling to forty-five states, giving hundreds of speeches to thousands of people about special play for girls and the evils of competition. The relentless publicity, along with the work of Hodgins and the Women's Division members who helped promote the Platform in each state, had been immensely successful. Hundreds of high schools, colleges, and universities had either discontinued or were in the midst of eliminating all basketball tournaments and intercollegiate athletic contests of any kind. Play days were growing numerous, and any young woman who wanted to become a top athlete was advised that she would never achieve any notice as a champion in the athletic field. If she wanted to have fun and learn a few skills, she should participate in more acceptable venues like dance, swimming, and tennis.

The Women's Division would have probably mailed out hundreds of Most Wanted posters with Babb's picture had it known about the Cardinals' barnstorm. The only travel the organization sanctioned for female athletes was a trip a few miles away, perhaps to a neighboring school, and only for a scheduled play day. What the group did not sanction was a basketball team with very limited funds all crowded into an unreliable old bus, gallivanting halfway across the continent and chaperoned by their male coach. To leverage support for their cause, members of the Women's Division would paint a portrait akin to the shocking romantic comedy *It Happened One Night*, except with a younger version of Clark Gable as the chaperone leading underaged, innocent young women astray.

In reality, the Cardinals were in no danger of being ruined. They had no time for boyfriends and were well supervised during their Christmas barnstorm. And even though they were merely students on financial aid with popular extracurricular skills that stirred up a hopefulness for the future among other students and townspeople that only underdogs could achieve, according to Mrs. Hoover and the Women's Division, the Cardinals and their male coach were desperadoes similar to their contemporaries Bonnie Parker and Clyde Barrow. Instead of robbing banks, the team skirted the back roads in a rundown bus and barnstormed for cash. Outlaws of the worst kind.

So powerful was the influence of the Women's Division that even the

AAU would sometimes bend to its wishes. In January 1932, at about the same time the Cardinals were playing their last game on the road, the AAU ordered the elimination of all references to women athletes by nicknames, citing such use as unladylike. Some Texans, including Babe Didrikson, believed that the rule was aimed at the star athlete, a candidate for the 1932 U.S. Olympic team. The Women's Division had spent the last three years protesting the inclusion of women's athletic events in the Olympics. Babe responded to the AAU by writing a letter that said, "I am sorry to foil your plans, but my birthright name is officially Mildred Babe Didrikson. Babe is not a nickname." When discussing the new AAU rule with sportswriters, she issued an ultimatum: "The first one of you guys referring to me in his stories as *Mildred* instead of *Babe* is going to get a punch in the nose."

This new AAU rule could have been part of the reason that Doll, who felt the same way about her name—Velma Bell—would soon legally change it to Doll Harris. And, as it turned out, no sportswriter ever called her Velma Bell.

THE CARDINALS' FINAL game was against the Crescent Comets. Located in Eureka Springs, Arkansas, the Comets played for Crescent Junior College and Conservatory for Young Women that operated out of the Crescent Hotel from September through May. This exclusive boarding school advertised for students in *Cosmopolitan* and other prestigious magazines.

Eureka Springs sat in the middle of the lush Ozark Mountains. Built into the side of a steep hill, this quaint town had twenty-three hundred permanent residents, but the population swelled with tourists during the summer. The roads wound around on precipitous ledges, some with three-hundred-foot drops. Wealthy owners had built prominent Victorian homes along these ledges. Other, more modest homes, European-style restaurants, and numerous shops were nestled along the roads and in the shady hollows. The famous Crescent Hotel stood guard at the highest point on the mountain.

Bo-Peep had to put the bus in low gear as it climbed up the winding road that led to the hotel/college. Doll sat directly behind Bo-Peep. It was midmorning, and the sun was just breaking through the cold January fog. Doll glanced out the front window and saw the hotel appear suddenly at the top of the hill. Frost glistened on its steep and massive roof. It was a large, gothic Victorian structure, built in the 1880s, a castle in the sky that also resembled Dracula's fortress to those who had seen the latest Bela Lugosi picture.

Built in the middle of the Ozarks when most people didn't have indoor plumbing, this hotel attracted the "carriage set" with its steam heat, luxurious spa, and gourmet meals. The college was opened in 1908 to provide extra income needed to keep such an extravagant hotel in business. The owners had to close the college in 1924 due to lack of funding, but it reopened in 1930, and this time it included a basketball team led by famous Arkansas player Quinnie Hamm, who had graduated from Sparkman High School. The Sparkman Sparklers had played into the finals of the AAU national tournament for two years in a row, with Quinnie being named an All-American. The Sparklers had placed the town of Sparkman on the map, and when they were winning, funds had poured in, growing the school from two rooms into a fully functioning high school by the time Quinnie graduated. In fact, Crescent College had taken in the whole team of players including Quinnie's sister, Irene, Cosie Fite, and Marjorie Leonard. The owners hoped that the team would help keep the struggling school and hotel in business.

Finally, Bo-Peep pulled into the parking lot, and the Cardinals piled out of the bus and into the hotel lobby. It was immense, with polished wood floors, a stone fireplace ten feet high, and crystal chandeliers. There was a formal dining area, and all the tables had white tablecloths and sparkling china and silverware. A few other guests were milling around, but January was a low season for Eureka Springs. Since the Cardinals were scheduled to play against the Crescent Comets, the school had given them room and board at very low cost. But when Babb was checking in, he found a telegram waiting for him from the coach stating that both games were canceled because of a flu epidemic. The players were ill, and the coach himself was confined to his room with the bug.

Thus, they would be heading back to Durant first thing in the morning.

After they had settled into their rooms, Mrs. Hotchkin offered to drive a few girls into town and let them shop for souvenirs. Lucille, the Dunford twins, and La Homa were all that could fit into Babb's car. Toka Lee managed to squeeze into the car and go along, too, so Doll was left to fend for herself. She waved good-bye, then set off on an adventure of her own, determined to explore this majestic hotel, flu or no flu. First, she climbed up the stairs to the next level, where she could gaze out over a balcony at the first floor. She continued to wander down hallways, and up more stairs. Old-time photographs lined the walls showing women dressed in Victorian clothes, men in dark suits and bow ties, and the many Victorian homes that dotted the cliffs that surrounded Eureka Springs.

The girls who attended Crescent College all resided on the fourth floor. Doll wondered what it would be like to live in such a place and go to school. She had noticed horses stabled in a barn near the hotel and felt jealous as she walked down the carpeted hallway. In addition to horseback riding, students could attend dance classes in the ballroom. Doll loved to dance and took every free lesson that Durant had to offer. Why couldn't this plush hotel have been her school? She imagined winning a spot on the team and moving to Eureka Springs, riding horses, climbing mountains, and learning to dance from the best teachers.

Thinking about leaving OPC and everyone she knew made her feel suddenly lonely. She remembered the stories she'd heard about the hotel's ghosts, like the spirit of the beautiful young student who fell from the fourth floor balcony. The gossip said that she jumped because she had gotten pregnant, but other darker rumors suggested that she had been pushed. Just then Doll thought she saw movement out of the corner of her eye, but when she turned her head nothing was there. A door slamming down the hallway made her jump. She felt cold air whoosh by and imagined it was the sad spirit of the poor woman who had jumped to her death. She wanted to call for Mr. Babb. The son of a preacher, he should know what to do if a malignant ghost ever materialized.

She walked along yet another hallway, only this one seemed narrower and darker than the others, with more shadows and doors. She began to feel like Mina Harker right before Dracula attacked. She wished Toka Lee would appear, or even her other teammates, Lucille, Coral, and Teny. It surprised her to realize that she thought of them when she was feeling vulnerable. Not wanting to be alone in the hotel anymore, she leaped past a door that said LADIES' SPA and scooted down some stairs that led out a side door and into the fresh air.

THE NEXT MORNING, the Cardinal team plus Babb and Mrs. Hotchkin were the only people eating breakfast in the dining room. With the wait staff all to themselves, they felt like royalty. All the girls, but especially the Dunford twins, seemed excited about going home. They talked about their plans to see their families during the few days remaining of their holiday break. La Homa said that she hadn't spoken to her parents since before Christmas. She needed to get home, too. Other girls admitted that they had missed opening presents and celebrating the new year with their relatives.

After finishing breakfast, they stowed their luggage and boarded the bus. Now that it was actually happening, everyone seemed ready to go home.

Bo-Peep started up the bus and pulled out of the parking lot. The road into town was steep, and she touched the brakes often to slow down the heavy vehicle. Doll sat in the front seat, her usual spot, looking out the window, watching the trees go by. Soon they were going by so fast, they were almost a blur.

"Bo-Peep, slow down," Doll yelled.

"I can't. Brakes are gone."

Doll leaned forward and saw that Bo-Peep's foot kept pressing the brake, but nothing was happening. Bo-Peep pulled the emergency brake, but it didn't work. Doll yelled for everyone to hold on. She could hear the continuous honking from the car behind them, and thought that Babb and Mrs. Hotchkin must be frantic. Bo-Peep whipped the bus around a turn, and the back of the bus careened over the road's edge. Susie Lorance screamed, but Bo-Peep held on to the huge steering wheel with a grip of iron.

"Hang on," Bo-Peep yelled. She steered the bus to the left, like she was going to drive it right off the mountain, and then skidded into a sharp right turn. Gripping the steering wheel even tighter to prevent the heavy vehicle from flipping onto its side, she guided it onto a side road that was really just a long driveway. The road ran up a slight elevation, and soon the bus slowed to a stop. Bo-Peep then put the bus in reverse, gingerly backed it all the way up the hill to the hotel, and slowed to a halt on a level spot in the parking lot.

Babb pulled up behind the bus, and he and Mrs. Hotchkin flew out of their automobile.

"Is anybody hurt," he shouted, looking over the girls.

Everyone said no, but Toka Lee and Susie, who had both been sitting in the backseats, had turned the color of skim milk, and looked like they might throw up.

"Bo-Peep saved our lives," Vera shouted, and she threw her arms around the red-faced girl. Lera followed suit, and soon everyone was hugging and thanking Bo-Peep, who brushed off the praise by saying that she only did what anyone would have done.

Babb entreated the hotel concierge to find the best mechanic in town to fix the brakes. When the players started to reach for their suitcases, assuming they were stranded, Mrs. Hotchkin asked everyone to wait. The mechanic arrived shortly. With Bo-Peep and Babb looking on, he spent two hours replacing brake lines. Even though he guaranteed his work, Babb still didn't trust the old bus. He and the mechanic took all the players and Mrs. Hotchkin into their cars and drove them down the hill and into town. Then the mechanic carefully drove the bus down the hill. After

Babb paid the mechanic, the girls boarded the bus and settled in for the six-hour drive home, trying to relax. Soon enough, the familiar *thump, thump* of the blacktop soothed even the most frayed nerves.

EXHAUSTED AND EXHILARATED, the Cardinals had never thought they'd end up cheering when they saw the DURANT CITY LIMITS sign after spending three weeks on the road. The old crank-start bus, after nearly killing them, had stalled once and gotten a flat tire (which they all helped change), but they made it, and the girls felt that they had just been on the biggest adventure of their lives. The Cardinals averaged sixty-five points per game to less than ten for their opponents. They had hoped to win some, but none of them had expected to be this good.

Upon their arrival, Dr. Hotchkin met them at the parking lot and made sure that his wife was still in one piece after her weeks on the road. The school dorm was empty since it was still the holidays, so Dr. Hotchkin invited everyone over to his house, and he and Aunt Lucy cooked the first homemade meal that the weary travelers had eaten in weeks.

The next morning, the *Durant Daily Democrat* interviewed Mr. Babb and a few team members about their success. The subsequent articles described how Coral was becoming a great assist player and how Vick was a pistol. She was strong and fast, one of the best ball handlers on the team. Vick, Teny, La Homa, and the Dunford twins stuck together like glue. Toka Lee had turned out to be the team's mighty mouse, a nickname Teny had bestowed upon her even after the AAU outlawed such endearments. Toka Lee was probably the Cardinals' most feminine player off the court, but on the court she did everything short of knocking the ball down her opponent's throat. She had committed the most fouls so far this year.

As for Doll, well, she scored fifty-seven points against Jasper, Texas. The Cardinals had crushed them, 111–4.

That afternoon Babb called a short team meeting where he revealed that Melvin J. McCombs, the coach of the Golden Cyclones, had telephoned that very morning. His words perked up everyone's ears. The game was set for later in January. School started a week from Monday. To keep up the team's momentum, Babb asked that every girl stay for practice throughout the rest of the break. Doll looked smug. Lucille winced at the butterflies knocking against her insides. Coral asked if it was okay for her parents to come and visit her at school. Babb said that they could stay in an empty dorm room. Lucille thought that maybe her sister and mother could ride out with Coral's parents. Other team members seemed excited, but Lera and Vera didn't say a word, and La Homa, who usually was the most cheerful Cardinal, stared at her hands resting in her lap.

Some of the girls had plans to catch a movie that night—*Cimarron*, which was based on a novel by Edna Ferber and told the pioneer story of the Oklahoma land run in the 1880s. Lucille had asked La Homa if she wanted to come, but she declined. Coming home from the picture show, Lucille stopped in the dorm lobby to check her mailbox and found a message that was scribbled in Aunt Lucy's handwriting: "Lucille, Dink called for you tonight at 7 p.m. She said that she would call back tomorrow morning at 10 a.m."

Lucille clasped the note in her hand. She hoped it wasn't bad news that would put her family's visit to Durant in jeopardy. She and the other girls headed upstairs. Usually, the dorm was bustling with college girls, but now everyone was at home on break. Only the basketball players and Aunt Lucy remained. When they had reached the fourth floor and were halfway down the hallway toward their rooms, Coral put her hand on Lucille's arm and asked her to be quiet for a minute. Lucille held her breath and listened. Vick said she heard it, too. Someone was crying.

The three crept down the hallway until they came to La Homa's room where the loud snuffling seemed to be coming from. Coral knocked and the sounds became louder. She pushed open the door to reveal La Homa sitting on her bed in her long woolen underwear. Her pretty face was covered with tears. When she saw her friends standing there with concerned looks, La Homa held out a letter that she had been reading. It was a Christmas greeting from her mother, and the letter described the celebration that La Homa had missed at home.

La Homa said she needed to wash her face and rushed past them and out her door. Lucille, Vick, and Coral followed her into the bathroom where they found her in the arms of Lera and Vera, who were now in tears themselves. They were crying about how much they missed their mother's cooking. La Homa wished she was eating pecan pie right this minute.

Coral decided to go find Aunt Lucy. Lucille helped La Homa back to her room, followed by Vick and the Dunford twins. After making sure that Vick could handle the situation, she went to find Doll, who was after all their team captain and should know about this mess.

Halfway down the stairs, she ran into Doll who was already on her way up. Apparently Coral had stopped off at Doll's room on her way to get Aunt Lucy. Doll asked if things were as bad as Coral had described. Lucille admitted that La Homa seemed very upset. As they approached La Homa's dorm room, Lucille could hear loud moans from within. She and Doll exchanged looks and then entered the room. Lucille gasped at the sight, and Doll bit her lower lip. La Homa was now outstretched on the floor, her eyes closed. Lera and Vera were pacing back and forth complaining that Mr. Babb had murdered La Homa. Teny was there, too, the back of her hand placed dramatically against her forehead and her eyes bright with tears. Vick, her eyes wide in disbelief at the chaos, had her arms outstretched in front of the open window to prevent anyone from leaping out.

Somehow the grief at missing Christmas celebration with their families had grown into a dramatic outburst. Stored up emotions poured out, and they were incensed at Babb for keeping them at school.

Doll couldn't believe that these crybabies were great basketball players. If a representative of the Women's Division had been present, this emotional display would have confirmed their worst fear—that women were too fragile to handle the demands of competitive sports. But the Women's Division would have never acknowledged that under the exact same circumstances young men might have been just as emotional. Feeling sad and vulnerable sometimes didn't mean that anyone should just give up on their dreams.

Disturbed by the noise, Buena, Susie, Allene, and other girls dressed in their pajamas came to investigate. Seeing their teammates so miserable, they started blinking back tears of their own.

At that moment, Aunt Lucy rushed into the room and headed straight for La Homa. She kneeled down and waved smelling salts under the girl's nose. When La Homa's eyes popped open, she became embarrassed and hid her face in her hands. Through split fingers, she glanced over at Lera and Vera, who were staring down at her with glowing smiles.

"We're here, honey," Lera cried, and she and Vera kneeled on each side of La Homa and helped her to her feet.

Aunt Lucy tucked La Homa into her bed after giving her some water and an aspirin. Then she took Doll's arm and said, "We're taking a little walk." When she saw Lucille and Coral, she indicated that they should accompany her, too.

Mystified, the three girls followed Aunt Lucy down the stairs and out of the building. They could barely keep up with the dorm mother as she scurried down a path toward the Hotchkins' home. Without cap and coat, she looked like a tiny, magnificent nun in her white and black cotton dress, dark stockings, and shoes.

Several yards ahead beneath a streetlamp, Babb, Dr. Hotchkin, Mrs. Hotchkin, and a young woman no one recognized were bundled in coats and hiking down the stone path. Aunt Lucy shouted breathlessly and then waved to get their attention. Seeing his younger sister running toward them in the dark, Dr. Hotchkin called for her to stop right this minute because she might turn an ankle. She halted in front of Babb and caught her breath. Dr. Hotchkin beamed at the girls, taking the hand of each in a firm grip and shaking it up and down like he was pumping well water. Keep up the good work, he kept saying. It took a minute for them to realize that he was congratulating them about their wins playing basketball. The local newspaper had kept the whole town informed.

Lucille grinned back at him and then began stamping her feet to keep warm. Coral had managed to grab her coat, and she handed Lucille the gloves from her coat pocket. Doll thanked Dr. Hotchkin politely but seemed distracted by the young woman standing next to Babb.

After catching her breath, Aunt Lucy told Babb and Dr. Hotchkin that they better listen closely to what she had to say or else they would be in real trouble. La Homa was wrought up and in bed. The Dunford twins were broken apart, too. She had seen it before, of course. Young ladies away at school always missed their families. Then Aunt Lucy said point blank that Babb needed to turn loose of these young ladies and let them go home.

Dr. Hotchkin looked surprised and asked if Aunt Lucy had called the doctor. She reassured him that every girl was perfectly well. Just a bit distressed.

Babb frowned and looked at his feet. He didn't believe Aunt Lucy had gotten at the whole truth of the matter. He figured that whoever was causing the disruption just wanted attention. Once they had rested, the girls would be fine, he told Aunt Lucy.

She folded her arms across her chest. "Young man," she called him, and then started *her* lecture at Babb. The Cardinals had performed so well over the past couple of weeks, had it escaped his mind that most of them were just teenagers? Maybe if he wanted them to keep winning, he needed to allow them some time on their own away from basketball. Maybe he should listen to her for just one minute because he may know about basketball, but she knew about young women.

During Aunt Lucy's speech, Lucille and Coral stood wide-eyed, and Doll had her mouth open. Dr. Hotchkin kept saying, "Now, Lucy," but she didn't stop until she wanted to. When she finished, no one said anything for several minutes.

"My goodness, Sam, cat got your tongue?" said the young woman standing next to him, breaking the awkward silence. To lighten the mood, she began to tease him in her deep southern drawl and pronounced his first name as if it contained two syllables—*SAH-um.*

If it hadn't been nighttime, everyone would have noticed that Babb was blushing. He introduced the woman as Atha Segroves. She nodded toward Coral, Lucille, and Doll, and the delicate finger waves in her bobbed hair bounced up and down. Looking not much older than Doll or Coral, Atha had a trim figure, small hands and feet, and huge eyes behind fragile,

silver wire-rimmed glasses. The scent of violets and honeysuckle floated around her, and she resembled motion picture star Jean Arthur.

Maybe Aunt Lucy had convinced him, or maybe his attitude was softened by Atha's presence, but Babb gave in and canceled Monday-morning practice. The girls could now make arrangements to spend the rest of the break at home if they wanted.

Atha grabbed his shirt sleeve, stood on her toes, and whispered something in his ear that made him start grinning. When she had finished telling him her secret, Babb turned toward Aunt

Sam and Atha, most likely on their wedding day, 1932

Lucy and announced that tomorrow afternoon, if time allowed, they would throw the girls an ice-cream social in the middle of January. After a moment of stark silence, someone pointed out that there's a depression on and cream is almost as costly as gold. Babb shrugged and said he had a few ideas.

Aunt Lucy's face instantly brightened. She liked the notion of a celebration, and she was positive that Mrs. Hamilton, Alice and Ginny's mother, would be happy to host it at her house across the street from OPC. The players treated Mrs. Hamilton like their second mother, anyway.

When everything had been decided, Babb and his group continued on to the church, where members were holding a potluck supper to collect money for Durant's poor families.

Doll stared after them, a stony look on her face. Lucille wondered if Doll had met Atha before tonight. As Aunt Lucy motioned that it was time to get going, Doll followed Lucille, Coral, and Aunt Lucy back to the dorm. When Coral mentioned that she loved ice cream, Lucille said that she hadn't tasted anything sweet in months. The girls were shocked that their strict coach was going to let them indulge, even throw the party. Doll was quiet. She looked like she was far away, thinking about something else.

THE NEXT EVENING, every Cardinal trotted across to the Hamiltons' home during a cold, clear January sunset that shot fading bits of golden sunlight through bare tree branches. The girls were dressed for a party. Winter wool coats hid cotton and rayon Sunday dresses. Rubber boots covered leather pumps and Mary Janes. Lucille had put on her favorite red dress. Doll had pulled on a pair of white dress gloves bought with money she had earned giving weekend basketball lesson to young girls. Toka Lee wore earrings that sparkled. Even Vick left her warm woolen trousers folded in her dorm-room closet and wore her navy-blue flannel jumper over a white sweater, belted at the waist. Most had not ingested anything sweeter than orange juice since August. By the time everyone had tromped through Mrs. Hamilton's front yard, they were nearly drooling.

La Homa threw off her coat as she hurried inside the Hamiltons' small front room. Her nose told her that Mrs. Hamilton was serving other desserts besides ice cream. Brownies! And gingerbread! Bo-Peep followed La Homa into the living room—still decorated with red, green, and gold

Christmas ornaments. The rest of the Cardinals—Lucille, Doll, Toka Lee, Teny, Vick, Coral, Lera, Vera, Allene, Buena, and Susie—rushed in through the front door.

Mrs. Hamilton greeted them all with a warm, welcoming smile, thrilled to be celebrating Christmas Day and New Year's Eve all over again. Tall and slender like her daughters, with long arms and strong hands, a stout Roman nose, and graying hair, Mrs. Hamilton was wearing a red wool dress covered by a green-and-white striped apron that resembled peppermint candy. Aunt Lucy, who had lugged over her Victrola and her favorite records with the help of the Hamilton girls, collected coats and put them all in Ginny's bedroom.

Someone asked where that gingerbread smell was coming from.

"I smell boys," said Lera.

Vera, who had just handed her coat to Aunt Lucy, threw up her head like a stallion sniffing the wind. The rest of the Cardinals burst out laughing. What did boys smell like, they all asked.

"Barn dust or chewing tobacco," said Lera. "Some smell like Bay Rum cologne, when they dress for church."

Mrs. Hamilton waltzed into the room carrying a platter filled with pecan brownies and gingerbread men. Her two sons, who played basketball for Southeastern Teachers College, were close behind carrying a large bowl of apple cider punch and cups. Five of their male college friends dressed in coats and ties and reeking of Bay Rum cologne soon followed. One of them brought the fresh-cranked vanilla ice cream and began arranging the food and drink on the Hamiltons' large dining room table set up near the back of the living room.

The Cardinals inched together like a herd of deer and watched. Vera commented that there might not be enough to go around. La Homa said that it looked like there was plenty of cookies and ice cream for everyone. But Vera had been talking about the *boys*.

Lera and Vera pounced on the two tallest fellows and found out that they played freshman basketball for Southeastern. All the other girls giggled in whispers, smoothing their hair in place and pulling up their hose. Aunt Lucy put on Bing Crosby's "Dancing in the Dark." After giving the Victrola's turntable a good crank, Crosby's smooth voice filled the living room.

"It's awfully kind of you and Mrs. Hamilton to do this for us," Lucille said. She was standing near Aunt Lucy's elbow, Vick and Coral at her side.

"Oh, we're just carrying out orders," said Aunt Lucy. Then she explained to everyone how Babb was responsible for this party.

Vick shook her head in disbelief and said that he must have a heart after all.

You're like daughters to that man, Aunt Lucy said, raising her voice because Vick's comment had gotten her upset. That morning, Babb had searched all over town to hunt down the ice-cream makers and ice, and he'd driven six miles to the nearest dairy farm for fresh cream. Then he and Hotchkin cranked the cream for hours so that there would be enough for everyone. At the last minute, Babb had decided that his team might like a night of fun *away* from their coach, so he had made other plans.

Aunt Lucy looked at Vick with an expression meant to silence further comments about Babb's lack of heart.

Vick was relieved to hear that Babb had decided to skip his own party. She would be spending the day with him tomorrow because he was driving Lucille, Coral, Doll, and Vick home to visit their families. It turned out that those four lived on the way to Mangum where his brother resided. First, he would drop off Lucille and Coral in Cookietown, and Coral's parents would drive down from Cache to fetch their daughter home. Next, he would drive north sixty miles to Cement and deliver Doll to her family. Cooperton, Vick's hometown, was halfway between Cement and Mangum, about forty-five miles due west. She would be sitting alone with Babb that last leg of the journey, from Cement to Cooperton. Nervous about riding with her coach whom she didn't like too much, she hoped she could think of things to talk about, or maybe he would appreciate the silence.

Doll had poured some punch for herself and Toka Lee. The two were sitting on the divan and sipping the fruity drink with their pinkies held straight out from the cup. They looked like mirror images. But Doll hadn't told even her best friend about Babb's lady friend named Atha. She was still feeling confused about meeting the young woman last night under such strange circumstances. Until last night, Babb had never mentioned Atha, not even to Doll. She hoped that he hadn't noticed her unfriendly reaction. For the past few months, Doll had been nursing certain romantic feelings toward her coach that she had kept hidden even from herself. Meeting Atha had shaken her deeply. She had gone straight to bed, and tossed and turned all night trying to decipher her feelings. Having more access to Babb than the other players, acting as his sounding board, and giving him her own ideas, she had begun to feel like Babb's basketball wife, and the players were their children. This realization made her cringe with embarrassment. She hoped she hadn't given herself away. Now she would deliberately end her schoolgirl crush and become great friends with the charming Atha Segroves.

Just then, Bing Crosby's croon started to sound like a slow groan, so Vick began cranking the phonograph back up to speed. Someone from behind her with a deep voice wondered if she'd like to dance, and she looked up from the phonograph, surprised. Others, including Doll and Toka Lee, wanted to join in, too, and asked Aunt Lucy if it was okay. Oklahoma Presbyterian College for Girls, being a church school, did not hold dances or other co-ed events on campus and did not encourage its students to attend dances elsewhere.

Aunt Lucy looked at the girls in front of her for a moment and then said that since they were not at OPC, they could go ahead and dance if the spirit moved them. She would never tell.

CHAPTER 10

Babe Didrikson and the Golden Cyclones

The old Texas Road that had drawn thousands of immigrants through Indian Territory before statehood, passed through Durant and, fifteen miles southwest, crossed into Texas just north of Denison. Before the Civil War, a Chickasaw citizen named Benjamin Colbert built a ferry at this point and transported travelers, including cattle drives heading to Kansas, across the Red River. He charged ten cents a head for horses and cattle, twenty-five cents for a man and a horse, and between $1.00 and $1.50 for wagons depending on how many horses were involved. His profits allowed him to build a mansion called Riverside.

In 1872, the Katy railway constructed a bridge across the Red River, and Colbert's business faltered. So two years later, he bought a charter and built his own toll bridge that soon gained paying customers when a flood washed away the Katy passage. The Texas Road turned into Highway 69, and Colbert later sold his charter to the Red River Bridge Company, serving as its first president. The company collected tolls until 1931, when Texas and Oklahoma jointly built a free bridge about a mile north of the existing toll bridge.

On July 10, 1931, the Red River Bridge Company filed an injunction against the Texas Highway Commission that prevented it from opening the new free Denison-Durant bridge. Apparently the highway commission had promised to buy the old toll bridge for eighty thousand dollars.

Honoring the injunction, Texas governor Ross Sterling ordered the free bridge barricaded on the Texas side. On July 17, Oklahoma governor William Murray, who was known as "Alfalfa Bill," because every speech he gave contained information about planting alfalfa to restore nitrogen to Oklahoma's depleted soil, took action against the Texas governor. He sent Oklahoma highway crews across the bridge to demolish the barricades and reopen Oklahoma's lengthwise half of the bridge to traffic. Murray justified his action by claiming that Oklahoma owned both sides of the bridge as designated in the Louisiana Purchase.

Governor Sterling told Murray in a telegram, "I feel you have extended your jurisdiction beyond all reason," and ordered Adjutant General William Warren Sterling and three Texas Rangers to the bridge to guard the Texans who were rebuilding the barricade.

In response, Murray had Oklahoma crews plow up the road leading to the old toll bridge, making it impassable. Now no one could get across either bridge.

Newspapers across the country ran daily articles keeping track of the heated Oklahoma-Texas battle. Headlines read, "Sterling Wires Governor Murray He Goes Too Far," "Murray Defies Federal Order Opening Bridge," "Battle Rages over Bridges at Red River: Texas Rangers, Crews of Highway Police Battle On," and "Murray Extends Martial Law Zone of River Bridge Dispute."

On July 24, Murray declared martial law on a strip of land between the two bridges over a mile long and two hundred feet wide. He then called out the National Guard to defend Oklahoma's sovereign state's rights. The state adjutant general, Charles Barrett, called down five companies that totaled 250 men who were all housed in Durant.

Sporting a walrus mustache and carrying a loaded pistol, Murray stood in front of the toll bridge, declared martial law, and led the National Guard from Durant to confront the Texas Rangers. He requested a news conference, and surrounded by the men in uniform, he stood in front of the barricade as a symbol of freedom and got his picture taken. Eventually, a federal judge in Houston ordered the free bridge opened, and Murray rescinded the martial law order. The *Durant Daily Democrat* proclaimed Murray the victor.

Time magazine ran a story that began, "Texas and Oklahoma are not independent Balkan powers. If they were, they would have been at war last week. . . . The real fighting, however, was done in the columns of the Press."

"Alfalfa Bill" won because he was a skilled propagandist. By the end of his administration in 1935, he had called out the National Guard forty-seven times and declared martial law almost as much.

The ruckus triggered by the Red River Bridge War was said to have caused the ever-vigilant Hitler, formulating his future war plans in Germany, to believe that America was a weakened nation plagued by domestic conflict.

THE BRIDGE INCIDENT brought a carnival atmosphere to Durant and was a welcome distraction from the mounting bad news that plagued daily lives. Crop prices had begun to sink lower. Landowners' profits turned downward, and tenant farmers and sharecroppers began to fear for their jobs. Some started thinking about loading up their belongings and migrating west but would stick it out for a few more years. Local newspapers published the column Will Rogers Says, the daily telegrams of Will Rogers, the world-famous cowboy, actor, and philosophical humorist born in Indian Territory near present-day Oologah, Oklahoma. One telegram with a dateline of Durant, Okla., Feb. 4, 1931 read:

> I see by tonight's paper where Mr. Hoover dispatched a flyer to Arkansaw [*sic*] and the stricken area to see how bad things were. He could have sent a blind man and found out.
>
> The Red Cross is feeding seventy counties in this state. Every town is feeding people, yet the ones that have it sure do help. We played morning,

afternoon and night in three small towns, all under six thousand population, and the three paid over ten thousand dollars in admissions.

They did that because they know it's needed. If the rest of the country could just get woke up like that and quit waiting on the government! Look at the farmers; they been promised relief since Lincoln's first administration.

Yours,
Will Rogers.

With peace returning to the Red River Bridge, Durant needed another reason to join together and keep spirits strong.

DOLL HAD BEEN back at school for two weeks after the winter break, and now she was staring at an empty dorm room and wishing that Toka Lee would hurry up and finish studying so they could go to supper. She decided to straighten up, so she swept the floor, put clean sheets on her bed, and hung the homemade curtains that she had taken home to wash. Girls were running and giggling outside her door, and she could hear them gossiping about the holidays.

On the first day back at school, the pep squad had led the student body in a demonstration of welcome to the returned Cardinal basketball players. It was a raucous event. Students put up colorful posters that read, WELCOME HOME CARDINALS and OPC BASKETBALL QUEENS. Teachers offered lengthy victory toasts, and Babb and Dr. Hotchkin, who had heard all about the excursion from Mrs. Hotchkin, gave highlights of the Christmas barnstorm. The Cardinals all were thrilled to be back at school and by the end of the night had sworn to keep up the winning streak to the best of their abilities.

Doll had spent her weeklong break getting over the crush she had on her coach. She couldn't stop thinking about how pretty Atha had looked. But when she stared at herself in her bedroom mirror, she liked what she saw—a girl part Irish, part Cherokee (on her mother's side) with wavy shoulder-length black hair; high cheekbones; a face covered in freckles; chocolate eyes set wide apart; slender neck; long muscular arms; a small waist; soft, round hips; muscular legs; and small feet. Being so petite, she looked younger than her nineteen years. She vowed to always look her best no matter what.

"Think pretty, look pretty, be pretty," she said out loud.

She ought to be thinking about the Cardinals' upcoming clash with the Golden Cyclones. She *ought* to be figuring out how to beat that Babe Didrikson. Suddenly an idea hit her that hurled thoughts of Babb into oblivion.

Doll knew that Babe was a crowd-pleaser, especially since she had gained fame from her wins last summer at the AAU track-and-field tournament. Her notoriety lit up newspaper pages across the country. Sportswriters loved her because she often made outrageous comments, but they weren't always kind. She had been described as thin and muscular, boyish-looking, with the manners of a rancher's hired hand. The worst thing that could happen to any female athlete was to be described as masculine because that would fulfill society's worst fears—that competitive sports would turn young women into men. Doll made a pact to never let any article disparage her like that. To gain an edge, besides her talent on court obviously, she decided to dress up her looks while playing basketball by wearing ribbons in her hair, pink, yellow, and green ones especially. Everyone would see a newer, prettier Doll.

What Doll didn't know about her upcoming and fiercest opponent was that Babe's only, modest goal was to be the greatest athlete that ever lived. Unlike Doll, she didn't have school studies to take up her time, and some said that she didn't perform her job at Employers Casualty. All she did was train for competition. Not only was she gifted with enormous athletic ability, she also knew how to leverage publicity. Babe grew up poor, just like Doll, and when Melvin J. McCombs recruited her to work for his company, Employers Casualty Insurance, and play basketball for the Golden Cyclones, she accepted. He didn't think she would at first because while he was describing her job duties, she was leaning out of his office window and spitting on the heads of people passing on the sidewalk below. Of course she kept a running total in her head of how many she hit.

Employers Casualty paid her seventy-five dollars per month to be a typist, more than a teacher's salary. Babe wanted more money because her family really needed it. So she cultivated a hustler attitude and set out to get herself a manager. When the AAU informed her that having a manager violated its rules for amateur standing, it didn't matter because she was already being quoted in newspapers across the country. Everyone knew who she was: a hard-training athlete who was unbeatable.

Babe was twenty, a year older than Doll. They both liked to be the cen-

Babe Didrikson

ter of attention. And they shared a hubris that alienated their teammates who mostly thought they were bigheaded and lacked a necessary team spirit. The only difference was that Doll had Babb, and he valued teamwork over anything else; Babb kept Doll's ego in check . . . most of the time.

Restless after cleaning her room, Doll decided to fill up some empty pages in her scrapbook with recent newspaper clippings. Besides articles, the large bound book contained letters, school records, movie tickets, and other memorabilia. She just couldn't let go of certain things.

When the Cardinals left three weeks ago for their holiday break, they had thought they would be up against the Cyclones by the end of January. But it was another champion Dallas team that came instead—the Slipper Girls. Doll had clipped her favorite article from the *Durant Daily Democrat* about the game. Adding some paste to the other side, she pressed it into the book's pages.

CARDINALS WILL MEET STRONG
DALLAS SHOE COMPANY TEAM TONITE

DURANT AND SOUTHEASTERN OKLAHOMA basketball fans will have their first opportunity of seeing the Oklahoma Presbyterian College Cardinals in action tonight when the local girls clash with the Dallas Shoe company sextet, which last year represented the Sun Oil Company. The game will be played at the Southeastern gym, beginning at 8 o'clock.

The Cardinals have attracted a great deal of attention on account of the wonderful record they made on the recent road trip on which they played and won 15 games. What manner of team does Babb have this year that has taken on all comers alike and won from all hands down? Is the question that has been asked around here.

Tonight these interested fans will find out how good the Cards really are for they will meet one of the toughest teams in the nation and they will have to be good to win.

Outstanding Cardinal players who will get into tonight's game are Doll Harris, high scorer in most of the recent games, Lucille Lampson [sic], Buena Harris, Coral Worley, La Homa Lassiter, and Toka Lee Fields.

The [C]ardinals' opponents tonight will comprise a number of all-American girl players including Carrie McLeroy. This little girl is fast and smart and is credited with being the best shot in the country from the foul line. Local fans will remember her hitting eleven goals out of eleven chances from the foul line in a game with the Cardinals here a few years ago. Lura McElreath Calhoun is another all-American miss who must be watched close tonight.

It seemed like the whole town had turned out to see the Cardinals take on the Shoe Shop "Slipper" Girls. OPC's *Collegian*, the school newspaper, wrote up the game afterward, but in the author's hurry to praise her team, she had forgotten to publish the final score, 43–25 in favor of the Cardinals. The *Collegian* predicted nothing but future glory for the school team, "With this victory in hand—and it does not seem an impossible thing to reach out now for the larger honor enjoyed by the Cyclones."

Last March, when the Slipper Girls were known as the Sunoco Oilers, they had beaten the Cardinals by twenty points and gone on to place second in the national tournament finals, losing to the Cyclones. The Oilers had won the AAU championship three years in a row, 1928 through 1930.

While Doll was busy adding to her scrapbook, a handful of her teammates were gathered in La Homa's room up on the fourth floor. Still excited by their recent win over the Slipper Girls, Lucille, Vick, Coral, Lera, Vera, and La Homa were talking all at once.

"You've got to see yourself winning games," said Vick. "It's like a moving picture in your head, and you're the star. That's what I do."

"Look at Doll," said Coral. "She believes in herself more than anyone I know."

"That's how she can play the way she does," said Lera. "She's so short that she'd never be able to compete otherwise."

"Doll's a great player," said Coral.

"The best," said Lucille. "She knows how to read an opponent. No matter how we feel about her, she's our captain."

"You'd make a better captain." Vick folded her arms against her chest. "At least you care about your teammates."

"Doll may think she's hot spit," said Vera, "but she's good at her game."

"Doll is happy to be my friend as long as I throw the ball to her," Lera said. "She never speaks to me unless I'm on the basketball court."

"Do you see the way Coach Babb treats her?" said Vera. "I think he's in love with her."

"He's not," said Coral and Lucille at the same time.

"She's his team captain," said Lucille. "They're bound to be close. Besides, we have to work together and support Doll, for the sake of the team.

You may not be too keen about having her as a friend, but would you want her as an enemy?"

"Nope," said Lera.

"Not in a million years," said Vera.

On a bitter cold Tuesday morning in February, the day before the Cardinals were finally set to play against the Cyclones, a bright sun spat through gray clouds, illuminating the glittering frost that blanketed the town's fields, roofs, and trees. By noon, the temperature had shot up to 60 degrees. For the first time in over a week, bushy-tailed squirrels crawled from their tree-hole bungalows to scatter among the birds' chirping arguments. Doll was sitting in her Advanced Algebra classroom when a cardinal landed abruptly on the windowsill beside her and trilled out its greeting with full plumage and outstretched neck. Doll grinned and took the bird's appearance as a sign of good luck.

Professor Scroggs had just written on the chalkboard. He brushed the palms of his hands together to rid them of chalk, and the white substance clung to his black fur coat like dandruff. When he asked if Lucille would come up and solve the problem, he called her Lucy. Doll watched her teammate set her teeth and walk to the front of the room. In addition to despising math, Lucille hated being called Lucy.

As Lucille worked out the problem on the board, Doll found her thoughts drifting, as usual, to basketball. She couldn't shake the image of Babe's angular face and what awaited them at tomorrow night's game against the Cyclones. Doll snapped out of her reverie and had a sudden desire to skip her next class. She loved art and had a talent for sketching, but she knew that her teacher would believe her if she said that she was feeling feverish and wanted to rest. After all, the Cardinals' captain and best player couldn't miss the most important game because of illness.

When the bell rang, she ran to her dorm, just a few yards away from the classroom, grabbed her sketch pad and pencil, and fled through the side exit. Racing through the cool air, she ran several blocks past campus until she stood looking up at a massive red oak standing tall and alone in a field. Making her decision, she put the edge of her drawing pad between her teeth, dropped the pencil in her dress pocket, put bare hands to bark, and climbed.

Wrapping her arms around the highest branch, she felt like a bird, an eagle with its hooked beak and huge wings spread. She settled into the branches and cast her gaze across the field—the day had turned so clear and bright that Doll could see the Buzzard's Roost. Farther east, the clock tower of Southeastern State Teachers College rose into the sky. Everything felt full of possibility; she felt strong.

Climbing trees was good for playing basketball because it built strong shoulders and arms, vital for good passing and shooting. Coach Babb, who seemed to be an expert in human physiology, had explained that passing the ball with strength and precision is a combined function of the upper body torso. The shoulders, elbows, wrists, fingers, and thumbs all worked in a smooth, rhythmic motion and follow-through.

Doll had said in reply that she wanted to study ballroom dancing to help improve her physique. She failed to mention that she wanted to take dance lessons for another reason. Doll might have a natural athletic talent, but when she was a kid one of her older sisters had teased that she walked like a raccoon, squatty and awkward. The image had stuck. To acquire a more graceful gait, Doll had practiced dancing. Her family had no money for lessons, so she copied steps from instruction books and invented her own moves and stretches. When she could find a ride, she attended the weekly square dances in Anadarko, fourteen miles north of Cement.

Doll worked to improve herself because she knew in her heart that she was destined for a larger life. Ever since she first started playing basketball back when she was in grade school and sunk fifty free throws in a row, she knew that one day everyone would know her name. On special days, like today, she'd call up that memory and relish it, turning it over and over, like a bit of sweet, hard candy.

After the Cardinals' successful Texas tour, Babb was busy arranging games with the top teams in the country. Just a week ago, Quinnie

Hamm and the Crescent College Comets had come to town to play their rescheduled matchup. Every team member had gotten over the flu and looked healthy and strong. Just not strong enough to beat the Cardinals. Doll had achieved her average of twenty-six points per game, and the Comets lost.

Doll couldn't wait to meet Babe on the basketball court. She began to imagine a great victory, with Babe so humiliated that she quit sports for good. Then she remembered something Babb had said. Keep your feet planted on the ground at all times. She laughed. If only he could see her now. Doll usually did what Babb told her. She understood that without his help, she would never achieve fame. Anyone who could find the financing for a girls' basketball team at a tiny Oklahoma church college during a depression must be the smartest person alive—and the wiliest, short of dishonesty, of course.

"Dishonest people are lazy people," Babb had said once during his psychology class.

Doll was still struggling to put Babb out of her heart. She had even started holding her breath when he was near, like people did to get rid of the hiccups. But every time she was with him, every time he spoke to her or acknowledged her expertise about something, she felt warm with excitement. She started to picture him sitting on the branch next to her, telling her that she was the best ballplayer he'd ever seen, but she caught herself. He wasn't a man who could climb trees. Every time she saw Babb, she noticed his pronounced limp and could sometimes see beneath his shirt the outlines of the leather shoulder straps that held his prosthetic in place. More than anything, she yearned to know how he had lost his leg.

She opened her sketchbook and began to outline a portrait of her coach with the edge of the charcoal pencil she'd stowed in her pocket. His face began to take shape—dark, deep-set eyes, a broad forehead. Doll knew every line in his face, every contour. Full of boyish energy and optimism about each day, he was giving her the best times of her life.

THE ATHLETIC DIRECTOR for the Golden Cyclones was Melvin J. McCombs, a safety engineer turned advertising whiz. One way to attract national recognition for his employer, Employers Casualty Insurance Company, was to sponsor competitive basketball teams for men and women with games and tournaments organized through the AAU. Employers Casualty also sponsored other sports, including softball and track and field. This year, McCombs was determined to eclipse the Sun Oilers' dominance of the industrial league. By 1929, McCombs had enticed seven All-American athletes with both basketball and track-and-field records to join the Cyclones, making them the only sports team in the nation to have national records in both basketball and track and field. He then hired Danny Lynch, a professional baseball pitcher, to coach the team. Coach Lynch had drawn up a team strategy notebook for the Cyclones that was two hundred pages thick, full of tactical schemes for passing and defense. In addition, McCombs employed a business manager, trainer, mascot, and chaperone. But it was only after Babe joined the Cyclones in 1931 that they finally claimed the basketball championship, beating the Sun Oilers at the AAU national tournament. They played more than forty games per season, averaged thirty-eight points per game, and held their opponents to an average score of eleven. The Cyclones boasted the highest score ever recorded at the national tournament, ninety-seven points.

The Associated Press had named Babe Woman Athlete of the Year in 1931, the year she led her basketball team to the AAU national championship and set national records in AAU track and field, including the 80-meter hurdles, the javelin throw, and the long jump. At twenty, she was the Cyclones' youngest player.

Compared to the schoolgirl Cardinals, the Cyclones were royalty.

On February 10, the day they would battle the national champions, every Cardinal, including Doll, attended all of her classes. Even though sportswriters as far away as Dallas and Oklahoma City had printed brief notices about the upcoming matchup between the Cyclones and Cardinals,

This photograph of the Golden Cyclones was taken the year that Babe Didrikson joined the team. She is the third woman from the left standing in the back row.

none thought that OPC would win. They didn't give the game much thought.

But word of mouth and loyal fans won the day. Durant citizens were making their own predictions about the night's outcome—in barbershops and beauty salons, church meetings, the ladies' sewing circles, and canning clubs. They compared the records of both teams, gossiped about the strength and prettiness of the players, and finally decided that in the end the Cardinals might prevail given the right circumstances. But one thing was certain—everyone in attendance was anxious to see the great Babe Didrikson meet Durant's pint-size heroine, Doll Harris.

An hour before the game was scheduled to start, fans began showing up at Southeastern's gymnasium. Dr. Hotchkin arrived escorting members of the Presbyterian board who oversaw the financing of OPC. Mrs. Hotchkin, dressed in her Cardinal red-and-white colors, also accompanied the group. Almost the entire OPC student body was in attendance, with Aunt Lucy sitting right up front.

This matchup had attracted a whole new class of audience. Schoolteachers, farmers, ranchers, shopkeepers, and several city and county newspaper editors sat cheek by jowl with doctors, lawyers, and professional businessmen all dressed in three-piece suits. They were accompanied by their wives, who wore delicate wool hats and pearl chokers. The Durant Chamber of Commerce and business and community clubs sent its members to take advantage and query the wealthy fans about future funding for the team, especially if the local girls happened to come out on top.

Soon it was standing room only. Durant had turned out en masse to see their home team take on the national champions, and it would turn out to be one of the largest crowds ever to stuff themselves into Southeastern's field house.

A boisterous cheer went up when the Cardinals took the court to warm up. Babb lined his players up, and on his whistle they started performing their regular showy drills that pleased the crowd. Right before finishing, Babb let his team make a few extemporaneous shots at the goal. Taking her guard position, Toka Lee crouched with her arms held up in front of her, elbows crooked, palms flat, fingers spread. Doll let the ball fly. It arced upward and down toward the goal. The breath of the ball's passing barely touched the net. The crowd gasped.

While Doll and Toka Lee continued to show off, there were sudden bellows and shouts, and those in the crowd started chanting, "Babe, Babe."

The Dallas players were jogging onto the court for their warm-up. Doll whirled around to find herself face-to-face with Babe Didrikson. She measured herself against the Cyclones' basketball star and was surprised to discover that the famous athlete was only a couple of inches taller than she was. Babe was wiry. Doll had a touch of baby fat. Babe's light brown hair was parted on the side and cut boyishly short. Doll wore her shoulder-length black hair pulled back and tied with a pink satin ribbon that touched her shoulders. She saw that Babe's hands were rough and strong, dirt under the fingernails. Her angular nose and chin looked awkward next to Doll's petite features.

Doll stuck out her hand. Babe took it in a ferocious ice-cold grip and gave a short nod before walking to the bench.

After Dallas had finished warming up and galloped off the court, the game's announcer introduced both teams. The Cardinals and the Cyclones took their positions. Lucille jumped center and missed. The Cyclones bolted down the court, and Babe scored two points, her eyes fierce and unblinking.

The Cardinals had possession and in a flash Doll fired off a shot. She knew when it left her fingers that she would miss. The ball bounced off the rim into the hands of a Dallas guard who sent it quickly back down the court. Babe scored two more. Vick, who was guarding Babe, cursed under her breath. Dallas had secured an early lead.

Cheers echoed from the gymnasium rafters like ecstatic sighs. Wooden support beams shuddered. Lightbulbs dangling on cords with green aluminum reflector hats shivered and danced in the air. Doll took a deep breath and let it out slowly, eliminating from her mind any emotion that might rattle her. The little black-haired, freckle-faced forward from Cement, Oklahoma, kept a simple game plan in her head, one that she had developed years ago when she first learned to play basketball: she closed her eyes for a second and in the very depths of her heart, the crowd's roar would vanish and she'd claim quiet ownership of the ball. It always worked.

She kept her eyes on the ball now, in enemy territory yet heading back her way. She had the ball in her hands, but it didn't feel right. Passed it to Lucille. Lucille passed it to Coral. Coral fed the ball to Doll, who was now in a better position under the basket. She took the shot. The ball went in. *Swish!*

Doll's fingertips were red-hot. She had established her rhythm. She felt rather than saw the other players, forgetting that Babe Didrikson even existed. The rest of the Cardinals moved with her through space, weaving shots together like tapestry. At the quarter, Babb sent in La Homa as a substitute for Coral, who seemed a bit off her game.

At halftime, the score was tied, 13–13. Those in attendance basked in the electric thrill of watching the game unfold. Sitting on the hard benches waiting for the second half to start, they would be forever connected to each other and this place and time. These young women who came from no better circumstances than their own gave them a link to greatness and a hopefulness for the future. There was no room for cynicism or selfishness during these hard times.

When she huddled with her team during the ten-minute break, Doll was quiet and focused. There was an air of intensity about her, like a hawk zeroed in on its prey. Babb gave them instructions from his notes. They came back for the second half with one game plan: give the ball to Doll. She was hot.

The Cardinal offense, with several short passes and quick footwork, set up Doll to score. She crouched in a shooting position, holding the ball low on her right hip, her right hand behind the ball, her left hand underneath it. Then she took her shot, a soft, fluid release. The ball dropped in without touching the rim. The Cyclone guards stood hypnotized. How could someone shoot like that, in such a wildly graceful, unorthodox manner, and score?

The Cyclones took possession, and Babe made two points with a masterful jump shot twenty feet from the goal. The crowd erupted in cheers. Babe grinned, basking in the noise. But she was Vick's girl to guard, and that would be the last time she would allow Babe to make a goal on this night. Babe's points for the game would total a measly six.

Babe's teammate, Clara Mansfield, took up the slack and sank two more. Toka Lee sent the ball back down the court toward Doll, Lucille, and Coral, back in after Babb removed La Homa. Lucille caught the pass and lost her footing. The ball flew in the air and took a sudden spin that sent it soaring into Clara Mansfield's hands. Durant fans moaned.

"Come on, Cardinals!" screamed OPC's pep squad, its members seated across the first two rows. "Get that ball back. Get that ball back." Several cheerleaders jumped and yelled, vigorously conducting their charges. Some Indian kids from OPC's secondary school, all wearing clodhoppers—high-topped leather work shoes—stomped on the wooden bleachers—*wham, wham, wham.* Others joined in without thinking. A few concerned onlookers glanced up at the auditorium's wood-framed glass windows to make sure none had shattered.

The Cardinal guards fought for the ball, sweat pouring off their bodies. One Cyclone fouled Vick by shoving her out of the way, and Vick's hands clenched into fists. But then she got revenge by expertly sinking both of her free throws.

The game went into its final minutes. The score was tied, 28–28. The Cardinals' forwards completed pass after pass. La Homa, back in for Coral, passed to Lucille, who scored two and was fouled. She made her free throw. The Cyclone guards fought against the passing of Doll's teammates. The minutes ticked away. Then, in the last few seconds, Vick stole the ball and sent it sailing in a crosscourt pass.

Doll raised her arms up high, jumped with all the power she could muster, and caught the wild pass. She planted her feet when she landed so that she would not commit a traveling foul. Then she focused for two of the three seconds remaining, crouched in shooting position. The ball flew from her hands and arced perfectly upward. It sank clean.

The Durant crowd roared its approval. Dignity was ignored. Lawyers and doctors, college professors, farmers, ranchers, and schoolkids forgot everything and stood and yelled their hearts out in the thrill of seeing Doll make that final score. Even the ladies dressed for tea could not keep their seats and shouted with gusto. Everyone swore it was the best brand of basketball they'd ever witnessed.

To Doll, when the gun sounded, the game had passed by in an instant. She looked up at the scoreboard. The Cardinals had won, 33–28. Durant fans surged onto the court, unseating Leland Evans, the diligent editor of the *Durant Daily Democrat*, who was still scribbling notes onto his notepad. OPC students hugged each other; many waved pointed fingers at the shocked Dallas fans, indicating that the Cardinals were now number one.

Doll felt strong arms grab her shoulders, and she turned to find Toka Lee with great tears of joy running down her face. Doll gave her friend a hug and wiped at her tears and told her that bawling would turn her nose red. Then Doll dragged her friend across the court to join the other Cardinals, all jubilant in their hard-fought victory. Fans had gathered around the team, offering congratulations and asking for autographs.

"No, I'm not surprised," Babb said again and again to reporters. "I knew we'd win." The next day, those words would be repeated on sports pages across the country.

When he and the Cardinals walked over to shake hands with the Cyclones, Coach Danny Lynch looked pale. The Cyclone players were unsmiling. One thing was certain, the Cyclones would be more than ready to face the Cardinals when they played a rematch scheduled at the Fair Park Auditorium in Dallas the following Saturday.

"Great game," Doll said solemnly to each player.

Doll looked around at the group of golden-clad Dallas players, searching for the wiry athlete with the boyish haircut and smirking grin. Babe was nowhere to be found.

A glint in his eyes, Babb asked Doll if she wanted her game stats. When she nodded, he said, "Twenty-seven points."

Doll couldn't believe it. She had beaten her average. And then she heard Babb say something even she couldn't believe. She had scored all but six of their points. Against the toughest women's team in basketball history. After congratulating Doll, Babb went on and praised every player for her contribution, even those who had sat on the bench.

Caught up in the emotion of having played a game for the history books, Doll wondered why Babb even bothered with the other girls, who just weren't in her league. But as she slipped on her warmups and accepted

From left to right: *La Homa Lassiter, Ernestine Lampson, Lucille Thurman, Hazel Vickers, and Coral Worley*

praise from Aunt Lucy and other schoolmates, she found herself looking around for Coral, Lucille, and La Homa. Without their skill in passing, feeding her the ball, and setting her up to score, she would never have achieved what she did today. Anybody else, and the game might have turned out differently.

Finally, she was beginning to understand the gift of teamwork.

CHAPTER 11

Guts and Glory

The good people of Durant didn't sleep much that night after the game. They stayed up talking in restaurants, living rooms, and front porches about the miracle that had just taken place at the Southeastern field house. Some even dreamed about it after finally dozing off with visions of Doll Harris sinking basket after basket against the All-American Cyclone guards.

Doll made the headlines, but Vick made history. Holding Babe Didrikson to a fraction of her usual scoring rampage caused the sociable and opinionated Cardinal guard to become a sensation overnight. Not used to the accolades, she was surprised that sportswriters even knew her name.

The next day, Babb received the Cardinals' invitation to the AAU national tournament to be held March 21–25 at the Dallas Fair Park Auditorium.

Well-wishers visited Graham-Jackson Hall in hopes of catching sight of Cardinal team members. Aunt Lucy, standing guard, thanked those who visited but informed them that the girls had to study for exams because they were students first and star athletes second.

Overnight, the OPC Cardinals had transformed from a pretty-good schoolgirl basketball team into heroines in quest of national honors. And the whole of Bryan County was on edge about the rematch against the Cyclones on Saturday.

Sportswriters claimed that the Cyclones were all set to avenge their surprising defeat by the young upstarts on Saturday at the Fair Park Auditorium in Dallas. The minute they got home, Coach Danny Lynch began drilling the Cyclone guards, Kathleen Peace, Lucy Stratton, and Agnes Robertson on how to keep Doll from scoring. He didn't have to put Babe through any drills. Not wanting to be humiliated a second time, she practiced on her own for hours.

Dedicated Cardinal supporters volunteered to transport team members down to Dallas, and more than one hundred Durant fans crossed over the Red River Bridge and followed caravan-style in their own cars. Even though it meant spending precious funds on gasoline and tickets, they didn't want Babb's girls to meet the Cyclones again without their own cheering section.

Nearly a thousand Dallas fans showed up at the Fair Park Auditorium, a thirty-five-hundred-seat arena best known to Texans as one of the grandest concert halls in America. The architecture was striking. Built in Spanish Baroque style with both Moorish and art deco influences, the auditorium was framed with six soaring stair towers each crowned with cast drum and dome. Five great arcade porches allowed views of Fair Park at every angle. In the fancy postcards sold around town to advertise the state fair, the tinted photograph made the auditorium look like a fortress, a combination of the Taj Mahal and the Alamo.

Across the way from the auditorium, construction workers were busy laying the groundwork for a forty-six-thousand-seat stadium that in 1937 would hold its first Cotton Bowl football game.

Both the Cyclones and the Shoe Shops called Fair Park Auditorium their home court. The previous year, in 1931, Dallas held the women's AAU national championship at Fair Park and, due to its success, planned to sponsor the event again for 1932.

On this Saturday, February 13, Fair Park proved to be a struggle for the Cardinals. The contest started out slow, with each team scrambling to get ahead. Forwards on both sides made bad passes that were easy to intercept. By the end of the first quarter, the game was tied, 5–5.

In the second quarter, Babe found her rhythm and sank three baskets in a row. Vick stuck close, but in this game the Cardinal guard moved without her usual precision. She looked pale. Something was wrong, but she never complained. The expression on her face appeared to be more determined than ever. Still, the Cyclones led 12–9 at halftime.

The third quarter brought a rally from the Cardinals that gave hope to their one hundred fans. First, Lucille sank a basket for two points. Toka Lee stole the ball from forward Ruby Mansfield and sent it back down court. Moments later, Doll scored, giving the Cardinals a one-point lead. But in the final seconds of the third quarter, Babe sank a layup, and the Cyclones led by one.

During the fourth quarter, the Cyclones leaped ahead by six points. The crowd was on its feet, and no one would sit back down until the game was over. The cheers, whistles, claps, and shouts sounded even rowdier in Fair Park, built with acoustics for music. Everyone was certain that by this point, the Cyclones were safe and had won the game.

Then something happened that no one predicted.

It turned out that the Cyclones' plan to beat Doll boiled down to fouling her almost every time she got the ball. It worked. Even in the fourth quarter, they wouldn't let her try for a goal. Cyclone guard Stratton committed a foul, and Doll scored a free throw. When Robertson fouled her, she sank two more, and now the Cardinals were within two points.

Vick returned the favor and fouled Babe when she had possession. Babe missed on her first throw but scored on her second. The Cyclones led by three.

But then Doll gained possession and scored her second field goal of the night. The Cyclones led by one and less than a minute was left to play.

With the ball back on Vick's side of the court, she made a valiant effort and intercepted a botched pass from Cyclone forward Gypsy Butcher. Lucille caught the midcourt pass from Vick and sent it on to Coral who couldn't get a shot so passed it off to Doll. This time, the Cyclones didn't foul Doll. But they didn't let her near the basket, either. Time ticked away. The All-American Cyclone guards wouldn't give an inch. It looked like Dallas would win.

In the final forty seconds, Doll sent a strong pass to Lucille, who was near midcourt. Lucille caught the pass and pivoted to shoot. When the ball left her hands, she was sure she would miss. Except on this night the ball had a mind of its own. It made a perfect arc and shot down through the basket. Seconds later, the final buzzer signaled the end of the game. The Cardinals won by a single point, 22–21. Dallas fans sat stunned. The OPC crowd went wild.

BY THE TIME the caravan got back to Durant, pulled into Graham-Jackson Hall's parking lot that evening, and dropped off the victorious Cardinals, they were all famished except for Vick, who said she didn't feel well and went to bed early. Aunt Lucy opened up the cafeteria's kitchen, found the bread, and made roast beef sandwiches with leftover potato salad on the side. They wolfed down the food so fast that Aunt Lucy had to warn them not to choke. Then she offered up a treat: she invited the whole team to her room where they could spend an hour listening to the radio.

Every girl yelped with pleasure. OPC didn't allow radios in the students' dorm rooms, and few of them could ever afford one anyway. When they had all found a place sitting on the floor or on the bed, Aunt Lucy clicked on her favorite station that she listened to almost every night, KWKH and W. K. "Old Man" Henderson's radio show. Anyone who owned a radio had listened to Henderson, with his southern drawl and his "Hello, world! Hello, you lil' ole North American continent. This is KWKH at Shreveport, Lou-ee-see-ana, and it's W. K. Henderson talking to you. Don't go 'way." At night, he pilfered radio air space that boosted the power on his station from five hundred watts during the day to almost fifty thousand watts at night.

People from across the country tuned in to hear him lambast the Department of Commerce, rail against the growing horror of chain stores, and chew out President Hoover. He had a way of taking his listeners into his confidence, of talking to them like they were his best friends. His swearing on air, along with the questionable methods his engineers used to boost radio power, had gotten him in trouble with the Federal Radio Commission, and he would often complain about a lawsuit pending against him.

During his show, he would read a few of the hundreds of telegrams he received daily from his listeners, and then he would comment on the news of the day. Children were starving. The safeguarding of the nutrition of children was fundamental to the future of this great nation, especially in this era of unemployment and depression. Yet President Hoover kept saying that even though the Dow Jones was plummeting, these industrial flurries had no effect on the soundness of American business. Recovery was just around the corner! Henderson would call Hoover "a half-assed Englishman," a "hairbrained ninny-compoop," or a "cross between a jackass and a skunk."

The swear words made Aunt Lucy blush, but all the girls had fun listening to Henderson's bluster.

AFTER DROPPING OFF his players at their dormitory, Babb had taken time to thank those who had driven with the Cardinals to Dallas, pat them on the backs, and guarantee that their enthusiasm had contributed to the victory. Cardinal fans left for home feeling that they were a part of something wonderful.

Babb arrived back at the Hotchkins' home where he boarded during the school year, and found Atha and Mrs. Hotchkin waiting for him in the drawing room. Atha was wearing a pretty flowered dress, and the room smelled like her honeyed perfume. She looked older because she wore glasses, but Atha was the same age as Doll, nineteen. Age didn't matter to Babb; she lit up his life. It was no wonder that his brothers thought that she looked like whistle bait. After Mrs. Hotchkin said she'd go and make some coffee, Atha reminded Babb that she hadn't seen or heard from him in two weeks. She didn't know if he was alive or dead. Babb apologized but reminded her that he had explained that during basketball season he might not be around as much.

When Mrs. Hotchkin reappeared with the coffee mugs, she helped Babb describe the Cardinals' victory over Dallas. After they finished, Atha asked them to turn on the radio so she could listen to "Old Man" Henderson on KWKH. Henderson was just introducing Reverend Dodd, a Baptist minister who held radio revival services at nine o'clock almost every night. They sat through the sermon until Henderson came back on and started reading the telegrams from fans requesting music and asking why he swore so much.

Atha stayed until almost 11 p.m. until Mrs. Hotchkin finally stood up, yawned, and said it was way past her bedtime. Since they were losing their chaperone for the evening, Babb drove Atha home.

THAT NIGHT, LUCILLE had trouble falling asleep. Her worry-brain kept churning up images from the game with the Cyclones. After taking the final shot in the last seconds, she was so convinced that she had missed she had closed her eyes and didn't even see the ball swish through. Only the groans from Dallas fans had signaled that her shot was good. Coral grabbed her hands and wrapped her arms around her shoulders. Other teammates congratulated her, but she took their thanks in a growing state of confusion. Hours later, she still felt muddled. Every time she pictured the last seconds of today's game, it was Doll making the winning shot, not her. Everything felt like a dream. Maybe she couldn't fall asleep because she was already dreaming.

The next morning was Sunday and everyone showed up on time for church except for Vick. During the night, her fever had spiked to 104 degrees, and Aunt Lucy checked her into the city hospital. Her teammates wanted to pay her a visit after church, but Babb said "absolutely not." Vick had caught the flu and could be very contagious. With the final games of the season against two tough teams, Tulsa Business College and the Wichita Thurstons, coming up in the next several days, the Cardinals couldn't risk a flu epidemic. Aunt Lucy assured the girls that Vick was feeling much better this morning after receiving lots of fluids and would be back on her feet in a few days.

Due to lack of sleep, Lucille struggled to keep her eyes open during the church sermon. Dr. Hotchkin wasn't preaching, and the younger minster just wasn't that inspiring. Afterward, she and Coral walked back to the dorm and decided to beg coffee from Aunt Lucy, who brewed it in her room even though it was against the rules to have small appliances in the dormitory. Aunt Lucy had helped make those rules, and she said that it gave her a special privilege to break them. When Coral and Lucille arrived with their mugs in hand, she didn't hear them at first. She was sitting in her armchair reading the new edition of the *Literary Digest* magazine. Coral cleared her throat, and that's when Aunt Lucy noticed them and started telling about the famous people who had died. She loved to read the fine obituaries about the rich and famous printed in the magazine.

They spent several minutes complaining about the growing crime rate in this country before Aunt Lucy saw their mugs and realized that they wanted coffee.

Just as they were getting ready to leave, the dorm mother jumped up, handed Lucille her magazine, and told them they'd find something particularly interesting inside. Aunt Lucy shooed them out of her room before they could ask her what it was.

Back in their own room upstairs, they paged through the magazine until coming to an article titled "Rival Queens of Basketball." They stopped reading after the first paragraph and scrambled to find their teammates— everyone had to see this.

They discovered La Homa and Teny in the bathroom scrubbing

uncooked oatmeal and honey off their faces. Flecks of the mixture were scattered on the porcelain sinks and the black-and-white tiled floor. La Homa had designed the facial concoction herself, allowing it to sit on her face fifteen minutes before rinsing it off. She never used soap, only cold cream at night. Her complexion was so smooth and unblemished that other schoolmates demanded the recipe. Soon the entire girls' dormitory was washing valuable food down the drain.

Lucille and Coral let them dry their faces and then dragged them into their room, promising a big surprise. Teny and La Homa sat on Coral's bed while Lucille told them to listen carefully. Then she pulled out the *Literary Digest* and began reading.

"The damsels of Dallas are basketball queens of the world."

After Lucille read the first line out loud, Teny moaned. La Homa asked if they were kidding. Everyone talked at once, causing Lera and Vera to barge in and see what was causing the ruckus. Coral explained that the two teams they had beaten this year, the Shoe Shops and Golden Cyclones, had gotten a big write-up in a national magazine. That piqued their curiosity, and they settled in next to Teny and La Homa. Coral said it looked like children's story hour at the library.

Lucille continued reading.

"Four times in four years, a team of slim, pretty Dallas girls has marched off with the championship in national AAU basketball tournaments. Twice in that time, a pair of Dallas teams met in the finals. At least a dozen Dallas girls have enjoyed official All-America basketball recognition, one young woman five straight years. One of their best players is probably the greatest female athlete in the world. Her name is Mildred Didrikson, but Dallas fans call her Babe. AAU records list the Babe as American champion and record-holder in the 80-meter hurdles, 12 seconds; javelin throw, 133 feet 5½ inches; and baseball throw, 296 feet 3 inches."

Lera added that she had heard that Babe took the long jump, too.

"Dances, dates, and talkies mean nothing to the lives of these girl athletes, since they spend long evening hours in arduous drills and practice.

The supreme reward lies in the near-hysterical allegiance tendered by thousands of Dallas basketball fans."

Lucille went on reading the two pages of accolades for the Slipper Girls and the Golden Cyclones that mentioned every player's name, told if she was pretty (but not if she wasn't), and described her particular greatness at basketball. Pictures of both teams and then a single photograph of Babe adorned the first two pages.

Once Lucille finished, Lera strode across the room, opened the window, and shouted out that the Cardinals were the greatest basketball team on earth. Vera started singing OPC's school song. Teny giggled, and Coral asked Lucille if she could read the article for herself. Handing the magazine to Coral, Lucille walked over and nudged Lera and Vera out of the way because they were letting in the cold and closed her dorm window. They didn't want to end up like Vick, she said. And so what if a national magazine saw fit to write about the comings and goings of certain famous Dallas basketball players that the Cardinals had recently clobbered on the court? It didn't mean a thing even if sportswriters thought that they were just students at a little church school. Maybe the sportswriters knew what they were doing, had anyone thought of that? Lucille pointed out that the Cyclones had made it to the finals four years in a row. None of those present, herself included, had ever been to a national tournament. They shouldn't get too arrogant.

Lucille's reasoning was more certain than even she realized. With the Cyclones, the Cardinals were up against wealthy and experienced foes when it came to McCombs and Employers Casualty Insurance Company. They hated losing. And McCombs had proved himself to be a wily expert at public relations. That article from *Literary Digest* ended up being reprinted in newspapers across the country with headlines that read, "Dallas Dolls Dominate—Darned Regularly," "Dallas Damsels Dominate Cage Tourneys," and "Dallas Damsels are Queens of the Basketball Universe."

They were indeed.

THE *DURANT DAILY DEMOCRAT* ran its own stories about the local heroines, describing how the eyes of the basketball world had been focused on Durant's own Cardinals as they went, doped to lose, into the second game in a week with the national champion Cyclones. "Behind most of the way, Coach Babb's girls put up a fight such as has never before been seen on a Southwestern court, and they came home to the acclaim of homefolks, whose hearts and cheers followed them to Dallas."

Durant's citizens had gone basketball crazy.

According to the 1930 census, Durant was the twenty-second-largest city in Oklahoma. But to those who lived there, the diverse culture, colorful history, and progressive ideas made them feel like they belonged to a metropolis. Even during these hard economic times, everyone stuck together. Right away, they understood what it meant to house a girls' basketball team that beat Babe Didrikson and the Golden Cyclones—twice! If the Cardinals kept winning, there would be national publicity that would raise the town's profile, too. It wasn't merely that the Cardinals had won but also the business-like way they did it that impressed their fans. No bluster or bragging; no showing off, intentional roughness, or other bursts of emotion. They won fair and square. And, if the occasion should arise, they would be good losers, too. Babb had gotten them so focused on being present each second, paying attention to every play as it unfolded, nothing seemed to rattle them when they were on court.

Babb, meanwhile, was taking full advantage of the good feelings toward the Cardinals. First on his agenda was obtaining dependable transportation to the national championship. As newfound celebrities, Babb and the Cardinals were getting invitations every day to attend meetings at local community associations like the Lions Club and chamber of commerce, along with its affiliate, the Young Men's Business Association. It gave the Cardinals a reason, besides church, to dress up.

While at the Lions Club, the entire team sang songs and shouted a few of their school cheers. Then Doll gave a speech. As the team captain, she was tasked with explaining the secret behind the Cardinals' great victories.

Both Toka Lee and Babb had warned her not to make it all about "give Doll the ball." Doll assured them that she wasn't that self-absorbed. She had something else prepared. Being a thriving member of the dramatic club, and perfectly comfortable with an audience, Doll felt right at home giving a speech.

She began by thanking the club members for the delicious luncheon. Then she dragged out the mobile chalkboard hidden behind the piano, causing a few whispers among the gentlemen about her being a perfect little teacher.

"Goals which the Cardinals seek to attain," said Doll, "comprise five letters that spell success on the basketball court of life." She wrote the letters *G, O, A, L,* and *S* vertically on the chalkboard and then explained her statement in this way: "*G* stands for grit, which keeps a team fighting until the final whistle. *O* is for obedience to the coach's orders and is necessary for team spirit and play. *A* is for the aim to win national championships. *L* is for loyalty to the school and the team. *S* is for service to the team, the school, and the coach."

Doll finished by saying, "The Cardinals are determined to win the national title to bring honor to their school, their town, and their state."

During the enthusiastic applause from the Lions Club members, she curtsied and strode back to her seat. Her teammates, of course, had heard the speech before, just not from Doll. They were Babb's words from the second or third day of practice, and he gave it every year for the new girls' benefit and to remind the returning players what they were in for.

Babb spoke last. He rose from his seat and struck the tone of a college professor turned statesman: sincere, well spoken, concerned, but unwilling to compromise when it came to his students and players. He expressed appreciation for the spirit of community that the Lions Club embraced. He said that the Cardinals would not exist as a winning team without the generous support of the Durant civic clubs. Then he introduced the eighteen members of his squad including Vick, who had just gotten over the flu. Even though he could ramble on like a preacher, he was careful not to take the spotlight away from the players. He worked behind the scenes, catching a potential benefactor after church services, on a chance meeting, or just after a basketball home game. He approached people off guard and then charmed them into thinking that everything was their idea. That's how he got a few Durant car dealers to donate automobiles for travel to the national championship. And he always thanked them by letting them know how they saved the day, making them feel like heroes.

But hovering like a shadow below anyone's awareness was the dire financial circumstances of OPC itself. Even Babb didn't know how bad it was.

Six years before, in 1926, the school's financial future seemed very secure. Besides a strong enrollment, the school received over twenty thousand dollars in gifts that helped pay off all outstanding debts. That same year, Dr. Hotchkin had stood before the Board of the Women of the Presbyterian Church at their annual meeting in Montreat, North Carolina, and presented a request for an endowment. The board granted the request and made fifty thousand dollars available to the school in the name of the much beloved missionary Mary Semple Hotchkin. The dedication ceremony was an important event that brought the whole Presbyterian Church Mission Agency to the OPC campus.

Those funds paid off bills and put OPC in the black for two years. The school's board of trustees initiated a move to generate more capital from the general education board, but that application fell through.

In 1928, Dr. Hotchkin developed general ill health diagnosed as hypertension that possibly included arteriosclerosis. After making an excellent report to the board of trustees, he asked that they consider his resignation. Despite his request, the board renominated him to the position, and he accepted. With the money from the endowment, he hired an additional Bible teacher and sponsored more visiting lectureships. In his report to the board in 1930, Dr. Hotchkin said that student life had a distinctly religious tone that led to moral and spiritual uplift. Of course there was the basketball team, but the glee club had also won national recognition. He juxtaposed this vivid description of a school life that benefited young women, including those with Indian blood who attended on scholarship, to issue a warning about growing financial troubles. "'The struggle is a hard one. There is distress financially, and this distress is common to all business, but have we not succeeded in the primary undertaking. . . . Have we not proven Isaiah 32:2 and become 'streams of water in a dry place?'"

Dr. Hotchkin's plea led to a discussion about combining academic instruction with Southeastern State Teachers College, but nothing came of it that year. And his growing heart problems left him exhausted with little energy left over to act as chief administrator or to fund-raise for the school.

Two days after Vick left the Durant Hospital, Mrs. Hotchkin brought in her husband with a bad case of the flu, high fever, sore throat, and dehydration. By the end of the week, he was feeling better and asked his wife to have Babb visit him. He had some news for the coach that couldn't wait. When Babb arrived, he found Mrs. Hotchkin seated in the waiting room. He said he was glad Dr. Hotchkin was feeling better, and she nodded, saying that his fever was down.

She looked pale and while she spoke to Babb opened her purse and pulled out a small green bottle of camphor. She screwed off the lid, poured several drops into a handkerchief, carefully resealed the bottle, and then held the handkerchief next to her nose. The sharp odor caused her face to resume its natural, rosy color. Just as Mrs. Hotchkin was putting away the bottle, a nurse bustled into the waiting room, her rayon hose making sandpaper sounds as she walked. She reported that the reverend was awake and waiting to see Babb.

When Babb entered Dr. Hotchkin's room, he found the reverend sitting up in bed and sipping water through a straw. Startled by Dr. Hotchkin's feeble looks, Babb hid his reaction by gently teasing that the reverend looked darn good for an old man and then relaxed into the chair next to his bed.

Dr. Hotchkin smiled, but said he couldn't do small talk right now. He reached out and gripped Babb's wrist. Babb leaned in to listen closely.

Times are bad, Hotchkin said, and the church may not be able to fund OPC next year. He had missed the General Assembly meeting because of his illness, and the news from that meeting was not good. They would still help out with the lower grades, but the junior college might have to share courses with Southeastern College, or close its doors.

The whole situation would not be resolved until this October at the next General Assembly meeting. Dr. Hotchkin hoped he could make it, but if he couldn't, he might need Babb to go in his place.

Babb couldn't speak. He had known the school was cutting back on expenses, just like everyone else. It was hard times every day for most people. He'd always just assumed that Dr. Hotchkin, who loved and nurtured OPC like his own child, would always take care of things. Everyone had read about Dr. Hotchkin's fund-raising miracles in the *Polished Pebbles*. OPC's newsletter had printed excerpts from his forceful speeches to the General Assembly that contained words like *grace, kingdom come, faith*, and *goodwill*. No one had been able to refuse Dr. Hotchkin anything when he was healthy.

Babb asked Dr. Hotchkin what he planned to do, and the reverend relaxed back into his pillow, exhaustion turning his skin light gray. He said that he was going to ask the board of trustees to employ someone to take over campus affairs so that he could focus on fund-raising. But that wouldn't happen until next year. In the meantime, he had to save the school. He couldn't help with funding the Cardinals, and neither would the Presbyterian Church. There was no money.

Babb understood the dire warning in Dr. Hotchkin's words. Fortunately, this year the chamber of commerce and the Lions Club were joining other small businesses to contribute to his basketball team. Their next game was at home against Tulsa Business College, and their final away game was this Saturday against the Thurstons in Wichita, Kansas.

Babb told Dr. Hotchkin to rest assured that he was already handling his end of the fund-raising. He asked him not to worry about the Cardinals and to get well soon. But as he left the hospital, his mind was already conjuring new ways to find additional money to pay for the weeklong national tournament. It would take all his energy and focus and everyone would have to work doubly hard.

Most of all, they had to keep winning.

THURSDAY NIGHT, THEY defeated the Tulsa Business College team on their home court, 38 to 28. Then the Saturday matchup against the Wichita Thurstons would be their final game of the season before the AAU National Tournament. A win would give them twenty-four straight victories. Fortunately, Vick was fully recovered. The Thurstons would be up against a healthy Cardinal team.

At Friday morning practice, Babb held light drills and kept switching players and positions. Everyone felt lighthearted and ready for the game tomorrow night in Wichita. Especially Lucille. When she watched Vick jog onto the court and receive Babb's blessing to return to full practice, she felt like a burden had been lifted.

They were getting ready to scrimmage, and Lucille met Vera at center court to jump for the ball and start the game. Buena, acting as referee, tossed the ball for the jump. Lucille caught the tip and sent the ball to La Homa. Right in front of her, Vera, who came down hard after her jump, landed wrong, twisted her ankle sideways, and dropped to the ground.

"Vera's down," Lucille yelled.

Vera stayed down, and by the time Babb pulled off her shoe and sock, her ankle looked like a melon. He asked Lucille to help Vera to stand. Once she was up, she hung her arms around Lera and Lucille's shoulders, and the two tallest girls helped Vera hop to the sidelines. Babb told her to elevate her leg and keep the ice he gave her on the injury until the doctor arrived.

Vera remained calm and followed Babb's every instruction.

Lera, on the other hand, was frantic. "Why don't you all do something," she moaned. "Can't you see her leg is broken?"

Babb assured Lera that Vera's leg was not broken.

But Lera, in her panic, couldn't stand still. She kept circling her sister, pausing, and then getting a pained expression on her face. She watched as Babb walked to the gymnasium office to call the doctor.

"What did he say?" Lera cried when Babb returned.

"To keep doing what we've been doing."

"It's feeling better," Vera said.

But Lera started moaning again, and Vick said, "Lera, if you don't stop making a spectacle of yourself, Mr. Babb will have to cart you off to the asylum for deluded people up the road a ways."

Bo-Peep shouted, "I'll be happy to drive," and even Coral joined in by saying that she would call ahead to make sure they had extra beds.

Lera gaped at them like they were the ones who were going crazy, but when she saw the tears pouring down her teammates' faces from the laughter, and that Vera's ankle was already getting better from the ice, she plopped down on the court and began shaking with laughter, too.

THE WICHITA THURSTONS represented the Thurston Garment Factory, and its players were often referred to as the Garment Workers. They had placed second in the nation last year behind the Cyclones at the national tournament. This year, they edged past the national champions to win that matchup, and now they were claiming to be the number one team in women's basketball. Sportswriters, who described the Cardinals as having "high ambition," gave Wichita, with three All-American forwards, the edge. Everyone agreed that this would be a preview of the national championship.

The game against the Thurstons was on a doubleheader bill that also featured two top men's teams, the Henrys Clothiers of Wichita and the Oklahoma City Hupps. Since both teams were undefeated, the Cardinal-Thurston game was attracting more attention from sportswriters than the men's game, even though that matchup represented an historic rivalry—The Henrys hadn't beaten the Hupps on their home court in three years.

All eighteen players, including Vera, who had promised to keep icing her ankle while she watched the game, made the three-hundred-mile trip north to Wichita in three cars—Babb's Ford, Mrs. Hotchkin's sedan, and another sedan on loan from a local car dealer. With Dr. Hotchkin feeling much better, Mrs. Hotchkin was able to perform one of her favorite duties and act as chaperone for the game.

After checking in at the motor hotel, they drove to the Wichita Forum where the AAU women's basketball national championship tournament was held in 1929. The night began with snow flurries. At 5 p.m., just when Wichita workers were hurrying home, sleet pelted down like needles of ice. By 6 p.m., streets had become a little slick. Still, a rowdy crowd showed up expecting to see their Thurstons demolish the Cardinals.

Wichita got off to a flying start and led, 8–1, after five minutes when Myrtle Brockett flashed three pretty baskets. Showing their appreciation for the home team, the crowd kept booing the Cardinals every time they got the ball.

Lucille seemed a little rattled by the noise at first. But then she remembered one of Babb's recommendations when playing against a rowdy home team. "Put your blinkers on," he liked to say, referring to the gear placed on horses' heads to hold their vision straight down the road. Lucille imagined her own mental blinkers, and soon she, Coral, and Doll found their rhythm and rallied with two points each. By the end of the first quarter, the score stood at 8–7.

In the second quarter, Wichita held the lead, now at 13–10, only to have the Cardinals speed up the game and tie it all up at fifteen apiece by the half.

At the jump off, Lucille won the ball easily, batting it right into Coral's hands. She scored. But Wichita gained possession and decided not to let go. The other side of the court, with Vick, Toka Lee, Teny, and Allene as a substitute, became a battlefield. Wichita kept stealing the ball back and had possession for most of the third quarter. Lucille, watching from her side of the court, began to wonder if Vick was well enough to play. Babb should put in Bo-Peep, she thought. She felt helpless and pictured herself breaking the rules and racing past half-court to rescue her teammates.

But soon enough, the Cardinal guards tightened up any openings, and Wichita led by only one at the end of the third quarter, 20–19.

The fourth quarter began with Wichita's coach, Irvin Van Blarcom, sending in a secret weapon, All-American Jo Fetcho, making their fans stand up and cheer. Everyone had thought that she was injured. The Thurstons slowly inched ahead as Fetcho caged a setup. But the Cardinal guards held Fetcho to that one goal. And when Babb sent in La Homa, the fastest girl on the team, the Cardinal offense sped up, too. In turn, Vick, Teny, and Toka Lee made sure that every Thurston forward had a bad night. They played the final minutes of the game in slow motion.

La Homa and Lucille made two goals each to put the Cardinals ahead. Doll sank two free throws, and then La Homa clinched it with a brilliant shot as she evaded two Thurston guards and got in for a layup.

The final score was 27–23. The Cardinals had forged ahead so quickly in the final minutes, the home crowd didn't realize the extent of their loss until the buzzer sounded the end of the game. Dead silence ensued.

Afterward, Babb kept the Cardinals' celebration to a minimum. Instead, they put on their red warm-up suits, filed into the stands, and stayed to watch the men's game. Since Mrs. Hotchkin didn't bring the usual ham sandwiches for a ringside picnic, Lucille's mouth started to water from the smell of chili and onions. She wasn't the only one. Toka Lee waved over a vendor, and soon, every Cardinal was chewing on a hot dog.

Before the men's game got started, Babb announced a big change in the location of this year's AAU national tournament. Dallas decided against holding it at Fair Park again because the AAU wanted 60 percent of the receipts. The Salesmanship Club, sponsor of the Dallas event, said that the AAU's part in the success of the tourney didn't warrant more than a fifty-fifty split. The AAU disagreed. The Lion's Club in Shreveport, Louisiana, offered to sponsor the tournament and agreed with the sixty-forty split. So this year the team would be traveling east for the national championship.

Bo-Peep and Buena pointed out that Shreveport would be a more neutral territory for every team who wanted to beat Dallas.

Coral suggested that the real reason Dallas reneged on its agreement was that the team didn't want to take the chance that the Cardinals would beat them again on their home court.

Mr. Babb laughed and said that he hadn't thought of that. But the idea did seem quite possible.

When the referee tossed the ball in the air to start the men's game, everyone grew quiet and finished their hot dogs while watching the play and rooting for Oklahoma City. The Henrys started out fast, racing up and down the court, dribbling like demons. The men had ten players instead of the twelve required for women, allowing them a freer and faster game. Fewer guards meant less shot blocking and increased scoring. By halftime, Wichita had a 27–16 lead. The Hupps were completely outclassed.

About halfway through the third quarter, an Oklahoma City player found some room and scored three quick baskets in a row. The Cardinals leaped up and cheered the great effort.

"Who is that number six playing for Oklahoma City?" La Homa said, referring to the player who had just scored.

"Bart Carlton," Babb said. "His stats are some of the best in the league."

Bart was a college basketball star now making a name for himself in the AAU.

La Homa was still standing and cheering for Bart after everyone else had sat back down. Before she joined them, she turned and announced loud enough for the whole team to hear, "I'm going to marry that man."

Doll and Toka Lee, sitting closest to La Homa, grabbed each other and laughed. Teny told La Homa to stop blocking the view and sit back down. Lera and Vera said that they would start planning her wedding shower. Everyone else just snickered, but La Homa was deadly serious.

Seeing the frown on her teammate's face, Lucille asked how she had arrived at that decision. But La Homa never got a chance to answer. Just then the entire crowd moaned and Babb jumped to his feet. Lucille and the rest of the Cardinals focused their attention back on the game, and saw the center from Wichita and an Oklahoma City forward were circling around each other like boxers in a ring, fingers curled into fists. Even the noisy crowd could hear the curse words flying out of their mouths. The Wichita center was a good three inches taller than the stocky Oklahoma City forward, but he didn't back down. Instead, the smaller man swung a right upward hook that caught the taller man square in the jaw. The Wichita center dropped like a rock. Scores of angry Kansas fans sped onto the court. The referees attempted to hold them back, blaring their whistles.

"Take your seats, take your seats," the game announcer roared into his microphone.

"They're going to strangle that poor Oklahoma City boy," Vick shouted. La Homa covered her eyes. "I can't watch."

Babb, whose face had gone red with anger because of the unruly fans who were threatening all of the Oklahoma City players, yelled with relief that the police had arrived.

Six policemen carrying nightsticks hurried onto the gymnasium floor, drawing the attention of the rioting crowd members. The policemen quickly dispatched the most threatening fans; the rest eventually took their seats. The injured player was carried off the court by the team's medical crew. The Kansas crowd cheered his recovery. The Oklahoma City player who had landed the punch was led away by police. A referee then called a technical foul on Oklahoma City, further pleasing the onlookers.

The next morning, the newspapers would nickname the two players involved as "Towering" Tom Picknell of Wichita and "One Punch Spike" Leonard from Oklahoma City. When the fight occurred, Wichita was leading, 39–22.

Worn out by the excitement, everyone settled back and watched Wichita kill Oklahoma City, 53–40.

But the nasty encounter had shaken Babb. He couldn't help but imagine his own team being threatened by a raucous crowd. The AAU always hired extra policemen, just in case, but Babb felt that violence only served to reinforce the claims of the Women's Division and other female physical educators that girls shouldn't play basketball. Parents usually wanted their daughters to participate in a game that helped them learn about life. But if those same parents had been in attendance tonight and witnessed the brawl on court, they might decide that basketball was too rough for their daughter. Other families after hearing about their experience could decide the same thing until there were no girls left to play. The Women's Division would win and the downfall of women's basketball would be inevitable.

CHAPTER 12

Next Stop, Shreveport

oach Babb hated it when any AAU team lived up to the Women's Division's predictions about the dangers of athletic competition. If the economic depression didn't bankrupt OPC and bring an end to the Cardinals, then the women physical educators would, if given the chance. Babb saw this firsthand because he served on the AAU Rules Committee.

Part of the rules committee's job was to communicate with the organizations that oversaw women's basketball: the Women's Division of the NAAF (Hoover's organization), the Women's Section on Athletics of the APEA and the CWB. The rules committee had less to do with Hoover's Women's Division—a policy-making and publicity organization for women's sports in general (that just happened to hate basketball more than any other sport)—and was more involved with the CWB.

The CWB had been in charge of women's basketball for over thirty years. Shortly after the invention of basketball in 1891 by Naismith, Senda Berenson, a physical educator at Smith College, changed the rules to encourage teamwork and control roughness, since most of the young women were playing in long skirts and Victorian clothing. She divided the court into three sections, and players couldn't step outside of their assigned section. A single player could hold the ball for no more than three seconds. Other rules applied but remained fluid over the following decades. As players became more skillful, everyone agreed that the rules should change to make the game more challenging—within reason. The women physical educators who issued these rules changed them often and published them on a yearly basis, giving those in charge the highest authority over women's basketball.

The CWB had published the yearly *Official Basketball Guide* since 1901. Then something happened that upset the CWB's careful rule-making process: the AAU showed up.

After the 1931 AAU national tournament in Dallas, several coaches and officials petitioned the AAU, which followed the rules set forth in the *Basketball Guide*, to have their own set of rules that combined the best features of the boys' and girls' games. They understood that the girls' game needed to become more exciting, or it would start losing fans. But developing its own set of rules would shatter any relationship, contentious or otherwise, with the women physical educators. Still, the coaches and players within the AAU demanded some action, so Lyman Bingham, head of AAU Women's Basketball, wrote to the CWB's chairwoman, Eline von Borries. His letter stated that the AAU would be willing to cooperate with the women's rules committee in the publishing of a joint rulebook "provided they could get together on the rules."

Getting together was the hard part.

Babb, in his daily routine as coach and professor, and his love of debate and public speaking, made him a vital member of the rules committee. He had attended many meetings that had left him weary and angry, even though he believed in the CWB's basic tenets, "for the good of those who play." Once in a large city, riding in a taxi down an avenue lined with expensive shops and restaurants, he saw mothers with nannies pushing baby carriages strolling down the streets. Every woman was wearing a hat that matched her fur coat. He'd never seen such carefree attitudes. Didn't they know how most people lived these days, barely getting by? Would they even care? Why did those women physical educators who came from neighborhoods like this want to take away the one thing that was improving their lives? If these physical educators had their way, his charges would never play competitive basketball again. Most of them would lose their scholarships and have to return home, giving up all hope of a college education that would lead to a better life.

These antagonistic feelings toward the PE ladies and their crusade against athletic competitions weren't unusual, and existed even within the ranks of the women's PE groups. Some PE members believed that if girls wanted competition, they should have it, and they *wanted* to form a coalition with the AAU. The CWB itself was made up of dedicated physical educators who never got paid, loved the game of basketball, and devoted their time and talent toward increasing the health and enjoyment of female players. They weren't opposed to changing rules so that the girls' game required more skill. The problem was using the rule changes to increase attendance at competitive events. The physical educators considered any athletic matchup viewed by a cheering crowd of people who had paid entrance fees to be evil, commercialized exploitation. The rhetoric coming from the Women's Division had gotten so contentious, the AAU had come to symbolize the mustache-twirling villain who tied young ladies to railroad tracks.

Still, the AAU was a powerful group. Von Borries arranged an official meeting between them and the CWB for late March 1932, directly after the AAU national tournament but before the national APEA meeting scheduled for mid-April.

The AAU wanted two major rule changes that incorporated men's basketball rules. The first would allow one guard, called a roving guard, to play up and down the full court. The second rule modification—guarding on any plane—would change the way the player with the ball could be guarded. As the rule currently stood, a guard's hands had to be kept within her opponent's vertical plane—her upright body—at all times. Guarding with one or both hands spread horizontally over the ball was considered overguarding and a foul. The AAU wanted to allow the players to use their arms to guard the ball in any way possible, like the men. The player with the ball would need to pass or shoot more quickly and would need to become more adept in the tactic of pivoting, bouncing, and passing.

Eventually, the CWB adopted the men's guarding rules for the 1932–33 season and published them in the guidebook. But the APEA, at its annual convention in April, voted against allowing the AAU membership a say in developing the official women's basketball rules. The CWB's main complaint was that the AAU did not have a woman as the head of its basketball division. The APEA did make some gestures toward closing the rift with the AAU by appointing members to the CWB who were more receptive toward competitive basketball and had ties to industrial firms, church recreation centers, and other groups that organized basketball games. Within months of this ruling, the AAU would hire Lillian Van Blarcom, the wife of Irvin Van Blarcom, coach of the Wichita Thurstons, to head up its women's basketball division.

Even though Babb had good reason to worry about repercussions from the near riot that had occurred in Wichita during the Henrys/Hupps matchup, he didn't need to be concerned this time. The ever-vigilant PE ladies at the Women's Division were too busy planning their final protest against the Los Angeles Olympic Games in July. In fact, as a "special project," they had been protesting these upcoming games, especially the women's track-and-field event, since 1929. That year, at its annual meeting held in New York, the Women's Division went on record opposing the participation of girls and women in the 1932 Olympic Games and included the following resolutions:

> Whereas, Competition in the Olympic Games would, among other things (1) entail the specialized training of a few, (2) offer opportunity for the exploitation of girls and women, and (3) offer opportunity for

possible overstrain in preparation for and during the Games themselves, be it Resolved, that the Women's Division of the National Amateur Athletic Federation go on record as disapproving of competition
for girls and women in the Olympic Games. . . . Whereas, The Wom-
en's Division is interested in promoting the ideal of Play for Play's sake,
of Play on a large scale, of Play and recreation properly safeguarded,
Whereas, It is interested in promoting types and programs of activities
suitable to girls as girls, be it Resolved, That the Women's Division or
whomever it shall designate shall ask for the opportunity of putting
on in Los Angeles during the Games (not as a part of the Olympic
program) a festival which might include singing, dancing, music, mass
sports and games, luncheons, conferences, banquets, demonstrations,
exhibitions, etc.

The Women's Division resolved to promote these resolutions far and wide
as often as possible.

Other organizations, including the National Board of the Young Wom-
en's Christian Associations of the United States of America, the National
Association of Directors of Physical Education for Women in Colleges and
Universities, and the Athletic Conference of American College Women,
later adopted these resolutions. Finally, in 1929, Ethel Perrin, chairwoman
of the division's executive committee, launched a nationwide crusade
against training to compete in the Los Angeles Olympics targeted at school
girls, college women, and "other girls," meaning those who played for the
AAU. Perrin's campaign raced full force into the limelight and received
newspaper coverage throughout the country.

The following year, the Women's Division sent a letter and petition to
Count Henri de Baillet-Latour, president of the International Olympic
Committee and copies to all 115 members of the National and International
Olympic Committees. They also sent copies to the International Council
of Women, Women's Pan-Pacific Conference, Sixth Pan-American Con-
gress on the Child, and the National Council of Women in the United

States. They included a quote from Pierre de Coubertin, founder of the modern Olympic Games, given in an International Olympic publication in 1928: "As to the admission of women to the Games, I remain strongly against it. It was against my will that they were admitted to a growing number of competitions."

Their resolution to sponsor the world's biggest play day at the same time as the Olympics fell flat and wouldn't take place. To keep their protest alive, the Women's Division planned to hold its annual meeting in Los Angeles the week before the start of the Olympics in July. But its years of opposition did not prevent women from competing. The AAU had joined with the American Olympic Committee to hold the Olympic trials for both men and women, and athletes across the country, including Babe Didrikson, tried out for a spot on the U.S. Olympic Team. When asked if the vocal opposition of the Women's Division would have any effect, the president of the American Olympic Committee responded, "There are tens of thousands of girls who demand the right of competitions, and they are going to get it."

THE FIRST DAY of March, the Cardinals played their last official game of the season at home against Lucas Funeral Home. The Fort Worth team did not have the reputation of being too tough. They had won some games, and lost a few. Nothing remarkable, and it wasn't even supposed to be close against the Cardinals. That's why the fans sat shocked into silence while OPC slogged through the first three quarters, trailing badly.

Lucille's flashy passing, Coral's quick pivots, and Doll's sharp aim had disappeared, replaced by an invisible force field that held back the offense and made for a tedious game. Fortunately, Toka Lee, Teny, and Vick kept the defense solid, preventing Lucas Funeral Home from running up the score. OPC's pep squad entertained the despondent crowd by teaching them cheers and yelling encouragements at the Cardinals.

At halftime, even though it looked like his team could lose its winning streak, Babb didn't seem too worried. More often than not, they had trailed at the half. To Babb, this game seemed like the others, and his Cardinals would do what they always did, come from behind and win.

But it seemed that his Cardinals had gotten complacent. They thought Lucas Funeral Home would be pushovers, and it took three full quarters before that shine wore off. Gaining momentum in the fourth quarter, the Cardinals finally pulled ahead to eke out a win, 21–18.

Too tired to do much studying after the game, Lucille, Toka Lee, La Homa, and a few others begged Aunt Lucy to let them listen to "Old Man" Henderson on the radio. That evening, the sometimes explosive announcer was exhausted, too. "Listen folks, this is KWKH, and it's W. K. Henderson talkin' to you. But I'm not gonna talk long. I'm sorta tired tonight," he said in his intimate manner. He played music instead. Besides his famous rants, he also played cowboy songs, Tin Pan Alley ballads, banjo ballads, and hymns on phonograph records requested by listeners who sent him letters and telegrams. Henderson loved New Orleans jazz and would sneak in recordings by Fletcher Henderson, Jelly Roll Morton, and Clarence Williams. He even commissioned a station theme song called "The KWKH Blues" recorded by a regional jazz band, Eddie and Sugar Lou's Hotel Tyler Orchestra.

The next day, none of the Cardinals pasted any newspaper write-ups about the game into their scrapbooks, not even Lucille, who saved everything, even movie tickets and locks of hair. The whole thing was best forgotten, like all bad memories.

With only a couple of weeks left before the national tournament, Babb told the *Durant Daily Democrat* that his team wouldn't play another game before leaving for Shreveport. Instead, he would put them through two daily sessions of strenuous practice, one held as usual early in the morning before breakfast, and the other at sporadic hours, usually in the evening. It all depended on the Southeastern men's practice schedule. Since the old bus had been unceremoniously retired, getting the Cardinals to both practice sessions became a logistical problem. Professor Scroggs, still wearing his fur coat because of the chill in the air, volunteered to drive team members in his Model A sedan every morning and evening. It took two trips back and forth to get everyone to the field house on time.

Because money was tight, Babb could select only ten girls for the Shreveport traveling squad. He kept hoping that more funds would turn up from generous businesses or even an ardent wealthy fan. But the economy was growing worse, and some people living on farms and ranches were talking about leaving Oklahoma altogether, seeking better opportunities out west. Finally, as a last resort, he asked Dr. Hotchkin if the OPC Board of Directors might change their minds about providing funds for the team. Dr. Hotchkin said they wouldn't, and then he gave Babb even worse news: he had decided to retire as president of OPC at the end of this year. Babb's heart sank. This bad news was in addition to rumors that some OPC instructors who were married and had a second income from their husbands were going to refuse a salary next year.

Babb needed his paycheck and had plans to ask Atha to marry him after the basketball season ended. But these were all matters that Babb couldn't think about right now. He put thoughts of the future out of his mind so that he could focus on the task at hand—cutting players from the squad that would travel to the national championship. Being a coach whose guiding principle was the idea that every player contributes to the team, the fact that not every player gets an equal reward for their performance irritated him. But it had to be done.

Two weeks before they were scheduled to leave, Babb called a team meeting. While the players sat and looked up at him with worried frowns, he explained the situation in a very factual manner—they could afford to take only ten players. This was the way things had to be, he told them. He would post the AAU national tournament roster outside Aunt Lucy's room at Graham-Jackson Hall by eight o'clock tomorrow morning.

The next day, by 7 a.m., every girl on the team stood waiting for the roster. Aunt Lucy used two hat pins to post the roster Babb had given her.

Those girls who knew they would be on the list—Doll, Toka Lee, Teny, Vick, Coral, and Lucille—stayed in the back while the others crowded around the list.

Vera Dunford
Toka Lee Fields
Doll Harris
Ernestine Lampson
La Homa Lassiter
Juanita Parks
Lucille Thurman
Hazel Vickers
Allene West
Coral Worley

Those who didn't make it left hurriedly. Ginny Hamilton had to be consoled by her older sister Alice, who had traveled with the team last year. Buena Harris decided she needed the time to study, anyway. Susie Lorance found Aunt Lucy, who offered the tearful girl some hot tea.

"Looks like you made it, Vera," Lucille said to the tall redhead standing next to her.

Vera's thick hair was curling uncombed into her green eyes, which were full of tears. She looked ready to slug someone.

"I'm going to see Mr. Babb." She turned on her heel and headed out of the dormitory and down the sidewalk to the administration building where Babb had an office.

"But you made the team." Lucille followed on her heels, trying to keep up, but Vera wouldn't stop.

When they arrived at Babb's office door, which was slightly ajar, Vera pushed it open. Babb was saying over the telephone, "Shreveport's less than two weeks away, for goodness' sake." Then he hung up, and the telephone receiver thumped back into its cradle. A second later, the phone jangled. Babb answered and politely turned down another challenge. Finally, he noticed Lucille and Vera standing in his doorway.

"We are being besieged," he said, motioning for them to come in.

His usual high spirits were on the floor. He looked worn out. Apparently, their close call with Lucas Funeral Home had made the Cardinals a target. During the last forty-eight hours, several teams the Cardinals had already beaten, including the Shoe Shops, Crescent College, and the Tulsa Business College, telephoned, wanting rematches. Babb said he felt like a seasoned gunfighter living in the Wild West.

"Huh?" Vera, caught up in her anger, wasn't paying attention.

"A gunfighter," Lucille repeated.

The Cardinals had developed a winning reputation, and now all the young guns wanted to provoke then into a fight.

"They are looking for a shortcut to notoriety," Babb said.

"Oh," Vera nodded. Babb had explained many times that he didn't believe in shortcuts.

Just then, the overhead light blinked on and off three times before flickering out. Frustrated, Babb stood up and jiggled the light switch to cure a short in the electrical line. No luck. He walked to the window behind his chair and raised the blinds, but the afternoon sun had passed to the other side of the building.

"At least the heat's working," he mumbled. "Now what can I do for you two?"

Vera faced Mr. Babb with her arms crossed. "I'm here to register a complaint."

He gestured for Vera to sit in the leather chair in front of his desk.

Vera uncrossed her arms and perched on the chair. Lucille planted herself near the doorway, listening. She could barely hold back her curiosity about what was causing Vera's tantrum.

"Mr. Babb, here's the deal," Vera said. "I'm on the travel roster for the national tournament, which is great. But you don't have Lera there. You know I can't go to Shreveport without Lera."

"There's only room for ten players," Babb said. His voice sounded irritated, and Lucille figured that he would stand by his rules, like always. He explained that he needed Vera as a substitute for Lucille at center position and that he made decisions based on what he thought would benefit the whole team. Sometimes things didn't always work out the way we wanted them, he told Vera.

"Yes, sir, I understand. But I just can't go without Lera. I can't, and that's that. I'd feel so bad that I got to go and she didn't. Even if I got the chance to play, I wouldn't be any good." Vera sounded tearful.

Babb said that he wished he could take every player, Buena Harris for one, who had the best grades of any girl on the team. "She knows that if it weren't for our lack of funds, she'd be able to go. Can't Lera understand that, too?"

Lera and Vera Dunford

"Lera understands just fine. It's me, not her. I can't go without her."

Babb leaned back in his chair and looked up at the ceiling. After several minutes, a smile flickered across his face.

"Can she drive?" he asked abruptly.

"What? Lera? Oh, yes! Better than me, better than anyone!"

"Lera can go as a driver." Babb was taking two cars for the team on loan from local car dealers. Dr. Hotchkin and his wife were coming along as chaperones, driving their own automobile loaded with equipment for the team. Babb needed a second driver, besides Bo-Peep, and that would give him an excuse to bring along both redheaded twins.

"I knew you'd figure out something!" Vera stood up and yelled. "You're not so mean." She clasped her hand over her mouth and muttered an apology.

But Babb wasn't the least bit upset. "A coach is not supposed to win popularity contests, Vera. Only games."

The phone rang again, and Lucille took that moment to scoot Vera out of Babb's office. As they were walking back to the dorm, Lucille put her arm through Vera's and asked in as friendly a manner as possible, "Can Lera really drive?"

"Anything—trucks, mowers, wagons, cars, even one of those low-to-the-ground race cars once. Not in a race. Just for fun. She's the best driver I know."

Well, that's one problem solved, for now, Lucille figured. But listening to all those phone calls Mr. Babb was getting from other teams, she was afraid they'd all be too exhausted from playing exhibition games by the time they got to the national tournament.

A few days later, Babb announced one exhibition contest before leaving for Shreveport. The Dallas Shoe Shops had claimed that it had been weeks since their last matchup, and they'd improved as a team. They were sure they could beat the Cardinals this time. Besides, at a dollar charged per ticket, money for Shreveport could add up fast.

Babb set up an interview with the *Durant Daily Democrat*, and using his best PR voice, he told the reporter that he had evolved a new scoring play that he would keep under wraps until a critical time at the national tournament. The reporter asked what it was, and Babb shook his head and said that it would remain a secret unless the Slipper girls were getting one over on the Cardinals. Then he wouldn't hesitate to use his secret weapon.

The crowd in attendance would also be entertained by Durant's 180th Infantry Band before the start of the game and between the halves. The 180th Infantry had been consolidated with the Seventh Infantry in 1917, and some members had been Choctaw code talkers, used for transmitting coded messages, during the world war. They were renowned statewide as an excellent marching band.

On the day of the game, Lucille felt more nervous before the jump-off than she had in weeks. Anxieties clutched at her insides, and beads of sweat rose on her forehead. Other teammates felt apprehensive, too. Could they pull this out after nearly losing to Lucas Funeral Home? But once the game started, things clicked right along. Doll performed well, hitting almost every basket. The Cardinals beat the Slipper Girls, 36–24.

A good crowd had turned out, but the receipts from the game still didn't cover what they needed for Shreveport; they remained short of funds to cover meals. "We still lack sufficient funds to get us through the week at the national tournament," a worried Babb told the *Durant Daily Democrat*.

Five days before the Cardinals were scheduled to leave for Shreveport, the Young Men's Business Alliance (YMBA) held a meeting and appointed a committee to figure out how to raise the rest of the necessary funds. Their accountant figured an exact amount of $225. The YMBA pledged $50. The Lions and Rotary Clubs said they would contribute, too. Committee members A. H. Ferguson, attorney, and J. T. Foote, local businessman and owner of the Durant Nursery Company, who both served on the OPC Board of the Directors, led the charge to collect the remaining dollars.

The news made headlines in the *Durant Daily Democrat*, declaring that the City of Durant would be sending their Cardinals to the tournament.

AT OPC, DAILY classes continued. Cardinal team members going to Shreveport had to finish schoolwork *before* leaving town and were so busy that they lived from hour to hour without enough time to even write home. The pep squad had gone poster crazy, and covered walls with colorful GO CARDINAL signs. Someone had drawn a picture that depicted Babb as a dog catcher running around with a net and trying to capture the elusive hound of victory at the national tournament. Every Cardinal put her signature on that poster. Home economic students at OPC held a pie supper, charging five cents for admission. Teachers instead of boys bid on the decorated boxes that contained fried chicken, potatoes, green beans, and a pie. The Cardinals received all proceeds from the auction, about eight dollars.

But the school's competitions didn't end at basketball. Buena Harris and other girls were preparing to participate in the yearly contest for the

Hymnology Scholarship, where two hundred dollars was divided among the three girls who had memorized the largest number of hymns. One-tenth of the enrollment of the high school department received membership in the State Honor Society. And five medals were awarded to those students who had the best housekeeping record. Lucille, needless to say, was not one of the recipients. She was, however, working to neatly pack her clothes for the trip to Shreveport.

Saving up the money she had earned all year at her part-time job, Lucille had put a trench-style raincoat in the new layaway program at J. C. Penney, and she had recently accumulated just enough money to pay off the remaining amount. She felt very stylish in her new black coat with soft knit collar, large buttons, gathered waist, tapered sleeves, and full skirt-effect bottom. With the few cents left over, she bought hair ribbons, but none were as pretty as the satin ones Doll always wore. She hurried to finish packing because she was also going to a party.

Ginny Hamilton had asked Lucille, Vick, Lera, Vera, La Homa, and Coral over for a going-away slumber party the night before they would be off to the national tournament on Monday. Mrs. Hamilton put sheets and blankets on the floor of her front room and laid down one rule—all girls must be asleep by midnight. She didn't want to incur Babb's fury at the sight of groggy girls the next morning. Ginny's older sister Alice joined them to tell stories since she had been to the national tournament last year in Dallas and had even competed in the beauty contest. But she had gotten the most fun out of marching in the enormous parade sponsored by the AAU. Hundreds of girls dressed in basketball uniforms that ranged from wool bloomers to satin shorts had trotted with their teams down the main street in Dallas. Newspapers took their pictures and two marching bands led the procession. The whole thing was like a holiday, she told them. Everyone working downtown had lined the streets and cheered them on.

"I heard there was more than one game going on at the same time," said Coral. Like a three-ring circus?

Vick asked about the sportswriters. Are the players allowed to talk to them?

Alice said that only one game was played at a time, but only a few minutes were allowed between games in the beginning, to keep everyone on schedule. Babb never let them talk to any reporters unless he had arranged the meeting. The team was always under close supervision.

Ginny sat listening to her sister's stories and didn't join in when her teammates started asking questions. Lucille put her arm around Ginny's shoulder, and said, "We'll miss you."

Ginny shook her head and said, "No you won't."

Every player sitting on the floor voiced their regret that Ginny wouldn't be at Shreveport. Finally, the praises encouraged her to start giggling because they all *looked* sincere. But she knew good and well that they would get caught up in winning, as they should, and forget that she existed.

Mrs. Hamilton interrupted with her lights-out call, and each girl snuggled into her own blanket on the hardwood floor and tried to sleep, despite the new adventure awaiting them in the morning.

MONDAY MORNING, THE girls were ready. They stood outside of Graham-Jackson Hall waiting for their rides, each with a single suitcase, though some were sharing because they weren't bringing many clothes. Just the uniforms and warm-up suits that had started to unravel around the edges.

Going a bit faster than was required, Bo-Peep and Lera pulled into the parking lot driving the loaner cars. Babb and the Hotchkins were already there making sure that everyone was accounted for. Just as they were stowing bags into open trunks, another car pulled up next to Babb, and several young men all dressed in spiffy suits hopped out. It was the boys from the YMBA arriving just in time with extra funds. Their leader, a freckled-faced redhead, handed Babb an envelope with $225 cash inside. Then he asked everyone for their attention because he had a surprise.

Two boys dragged out several bulky, cotton satchels. One looked inside and called out Doll's name. After a slight hesitation, she stepped forward, and the boy pulled something red and soft out of the bag and handed it to Doll. When she saw what it was, her face lit up with pure joy. Then, she stepped out of the way, and the YMBA began calling out every girl's name. Even those who weren't going to Shreveport had their names called.

The YMBA had paid for the specially made team cardigans and white wool skirts and red berets to match the sweaters. The substantial bright red sweaters, made from expensive wool, had two large patch pockets sewn onto the front just above the hem. Shiny white buttons cascaded down the front, and the letters PC (Presbyterian College) were embroidered in white over the heart. Without even leaving the parking lot, the girls already felt like champions.

CHAPTER 13

Brains, Beauty, and Ball Handling

Bright yellow ID tags pinned to lapels or dangling on shoestrings around the necks of more than two hundred young women fluttered and flew around downtown Shreveport like confetti. Accompanied by chaperones, they rode the trolley cars that stopped at the Strand Theatre, a twenty-five-hundred-seat opera house with velvet seats and glass chandeliers that stood a few blocks up from the Red River. When they weren't competing in a game or attending practice, athletes, dressed in their team colors, window-shopped on Texas Street and ate peanut butter and apple sandwiches in Princess Park near the state fairgrounds. The visitors quickly adapted to the bustle of downtown Shreveport, home to an astounding eight railway terminals.

Surrounded by cotton and rice fields carved out of the boggy cypress groves and pine forests, Shreveport, with its population of less than eighty thousand, was doing better than most. Geologists had discovered the town was nestled over vast deposits of petroleum. That's why there were so many rail stations. To distribute the refined product, the St. Louis Southwestern, the Illinois Central, Texas & Pacific, and Kansas City Southern, among others, had built their own terminals in downtown to transport the oil along with passengers. Tugboats and barges also moved these oil products from the inland port and down the Red River, to the Mississippi, and the rest of the world.

Grover C. Thames, president of the Lions Club and the chairman of the AAU tournament, was able to attract enthusiastic business sponsors that included Howards Odorless Cleaners, Slattery Building Hat Makers, and the Majestic Drug Store. Town officials devoted themselves to building interest in women's basketball. Days before the tournament, *Shreveport Times* sports columnist Flint Dupre wrote up a list of things he wouldn't care to do: sit on the ringside of the Schmeling-Walker fight; try to show Babe Ruth why he doesn't deserve as much money as he was paid last year; referee an ice hockey match; and get into an argument over girls' basketball teams. He described a supporter of the Chicago Taylor Trunks who wrote a letter to the editor claiming that the Trunks were the best girls' team in the country. A strong supporter of the Golden Cyclones wrote back and argued that the Trunks might be the best in Chicago, but he had seen them do stupid things like get a lead and then stall, stall, and continue to stall. He ended his letter by declaring that the Chicago team was entirely too slow and not in a class with the Golden Cyclones.

Apparently, tournament officials felt the same way. According to Bill Parker for the Associated Press, the Cyclones were seeded at No. 1. The other top teams were the Southern Kansas Stage Lines, previously known as the Wichita Thurstons, at No. 2, Crescent College, No.3, and OPC at No. 4. Of the twenty-two women's basketball teams invited to play in the 1932 AAU national tournament, most were from independent amateur clubs sponsored by business schools; insurance, telephone, soft drink, sign, and oil companies; banks, hospitals, and department stores. Three were from high schools and three were college teams, Oklahoma Presbyterian College, Crescent College, and Randolph College. No college team had ever won an AAU national basketball tournament.

On Monday, the first day of the tournament, when the Cardinals arrived at the Jefferson Hotel in downtown Shreveport the AAU representative was waiting with red velvet gift bags filled with free passes to the movie the-ater, restaurant discounts, other coupons, and a welcome letter. It felt like Christmas in March. Every player tore open the envelope with the letter and read it all the way through. Then they tucked it in their bags to save for their scrapbooks.

March 20, 1932

Dear Young Lady,

We are very happy to have you in Shreveport on the occasion of the National Basketball Tournament. You must have a good time. If you don't have a good time, I shall be greatly disappointed.

I hope you will get out of the hotel and walk around through the business district. Wear your team sweat suits on such occasions and help me get more customers to attend the games. You are all the picture of health and everywhere you go, folks will be impressed with your good looks. Parents who are afraid to permit their daughters to play sports will admire you as among the best athletes in America.

Attached hereto is a yellow tag—your identification tag. Please do not lose it. Wear it! It will get you into all games, picture shows, and it is also your meal ticket. The management of the Capitol, Majestic, and Strand Theaters will extend the courtesy of their theaters to you if you are wearing it.

Team trophies will be awarded to the winner and runner-up of the championship tournament and the winner of the consolation tour-nament. Gold basketball charms will be awarded to members of the championship team and the All-American team; silver basketballs will be given to the runner-up.

The Tournament Committee is responsible for your local

expenses, beginning at noon on Monday and ending when you are eliminated from the tournament. The Committee will not pay for telephone calls, either local or long distance, telegrams, pressing, or any other such expenses.

    Yours for a good time,

Grover C. Thames
Supervisor of Recreation, American Athletic Union

The Cardinals had drawn a bye and weren't scheduled to play until Tuesday. But they checked in and then hurried to the Louisiana State Fair Coliseum to have their picture taken with the other teams for the newspapers. Afterward, everyone found their rooms and settled in. The Hotchkins accounted for each girl at dinnertime and announced that roll call would take place every morning at six, one hour before breakfast.

After dinner, Babb called a meeting to review the schedule for the next day. They had a one-hour practice session at the coliseum first thing in the morning, and then the Cardinals were up against the Kansas Booster Girls at 10 p.m., the final game of the day. The Cyclones played the Shreveport Hospital Charity Nurses right before the Cardinals, at 9 p.m.

Using his deep, stern-sounding voice, the one that resembled a minister's while giving a hellfire sermon, Babb said that every girl must be in bed by ten tonight and must eat a substantial breakfast in the morning. If he found out that anyone had disobeyed these orders, well, there was still time to send her home and bring back a substitute. The week would be filled with constant activity, and he was depending on each player's good judgment.

Doll listened to her coach give orders. By now, she was used to him making sure no one got too excited about anything, even winning games. He liked level heads and no surprises. And that's what he usually got. He led the Cardinals like a military general, and she was second in command. During every game, when he spoke, the players snapped into action like crack soldiers, a routine that made fans and sportswriters shake their heads in amazement.

Winning games had made life a lot easier for Doll. Her teammates had quit giving her the side-eye and had finally gotten used to her drill-sergeant attitude. Everyone knew she was the star player. They admired her bracelet with dangling gold and silver basketball charms she had collected at tournaments since junior high school. Her favorite was the golden basketball she earned last year when the AAU elected her to its All-American team. After the Cardinal wins against the Cyclones this past February, the *Durant Daily Democrat* seemed starstruck in its article about Doll, describing her as the outstanding feminine goal shooter in the country. Out of the 1,119 points scored during the season, Doll had accounted for 461, and that topped the total scores of their opponents for the season by 58. The writer called her a "black haired, black eyed midget" but with appropriately shaped legs who performed "floor work without parallel among the teams of the United States."

The descriptions of her body made Doll cringe with self-consciousness. But then again, that's why she told herself to "think pretty, look pretty, be pretty." People judged women by how they looked, their grace and poise. As the Cardinals continued to become better known, the way newspapers reported on their games seemed to change. Before, a headline might have read "Cardinals Beat Houston Green Devils in Competitive Matchup;" now they read, "Pretty Cardinal Maidens Prepare for National Tournament." The better the female athlete, the more crucial it seemed to be that she was deemed attractive.

Lying in bed that night in the hotel room she was sharing with Toka Lee, Vick, and Coral, Doll didn't care about the politics of it all. And she didn't follow Babb's orders to forget about the game tomorrow—she just couldn't. When the lights were out and no one could see, she closed her eyes and prayed that she would play her best. More than anything, she wanted to keep winning.

• • •

THE NEXT MORNING, Doll got up at 5 a.m. and let Mrs. Hotchkin know that she was leaving early. She choked down a piece of toast and some coffee from the hotel diner, and then rushed three blocks to Shreveport's coliseum, the brick-and-mortar sports arena at the nearby state fairgrounds. Freckles sprinkled Doll's nose and cheeks in a bold pattern against her flushed skin. Her black hair, ruffled by the morning breeze, fell loose and wavy to her shoulders. She pulled her jacket snugly about her as protection from the chilly fog that rose from the nearby Red River.

Babb had asked her to meet him for an early-morning inspection of the court before their practice session. He never felt assured until he examined all the details and felt the air of a place, its energy.

When she entered the athletic complex, it was so quiet she thought she was the only one there. Then she spotted Babb, wearing a black suit that complemented his straight black hair, a starched white cotton shirt, and navy-blue silk tie. He looked just like he did when she met him for the very first time over two years ago. He was standing underneath the iron hoop at one end of the basketball court, enthralled by the large, empty stadium. As soon as Doll went to stand next to him, the arena began to wake up. Small noises grew louder as they echoed off the walls. Three men with oily mops applied varnish to the floors, which soon glowed in the hazy daylight streaming through the windows. Doll inhaled the pungent odor and felt at home.

Babb greeted her by asking if she thought the half-court line looked right.

Sure it did, she said after walking the line. Feeling a swift pat on her shoulder, Doll turned to find O. L. "Runt" Ramsey, coach of Southeastern College's men's team, wearing a referee's uniform and now shaking hands with Babb. They had become good friends after Babb had convinced him that girls could be skilled basketball players. Ramsey was the reason that the Cardinals had gained access to Southeastern's field house for practice and games. It turned out that he would be among the officiating staff this week. Babb had pulled some strings and gotten his friend the tournament job.

After they had walked the court, measured the goal height, and taken a practice shot from the free-throw line, Babb told Doll, "Tonight will be a smasher." His usually resonant-sounding voice seemed higher pitched and excited. Surprised, she grinned up at him. Precisely at eight, the rest of the team appeared, walking single file like fledgling geese with Mrs. Hotchkin in the lead and Dr. Hotchkin in the rear. Babb hurried his team out onto the court since they had only one hour. When the challenge arose, he told them, they would put into play what he had called their secret weapon in his interview with the *Durant Daily Democrat*. The team had spent just a few sessions practicing a new offensive move called a pick—a legal block set by a forward by putting her body in the way of a defender so that her teammate could take a shot or receive a pass. The men's team had started calling the move a screen.

After an hour of running drills and setting screens, the Cardinals were forced off the court when the next team arrived. Doll was pulling on her warm-ups and accidentally caught sight of charms from her bracelet lying on a red wool team cardigan that had been left on the bench. In her eagerness to retrieve her charms, Doll inadvertently snagged the sweater, creating a thick yarn jumble. Toka Lee noticed the injury to her new sweater right away. Normally, she would give Doll the benefit of the doubt. But this time, she raised the sweater up in Doll's face and showed her the damage. Close to tears, she insisted that Doll apologize.

When Doll saw why her friend was upset, she told her to get over it. Toka Lee resented Doll's arrogance and said that it was her Cherokee and Irish blood that made Doll so irritating.

Soon they were shouting.

Every Cardinal getting ready to leave stopped what they were doing and stared. The sight of those two arguing was as rare as snow in Shreveport. Babb and Dr. Hotchkin had already left for a meeting, but Mrs. Hotchkin intervened before the fight escalated. Doll apologized and offered to fix the ruptured threads back at the hotel. Mrs. Hotchkin made the two girls shake hands. On the walk back, everyone seemed on edge. Babb the psychology professor would have diagnosed it as "heightened awareness caused by too much adrenaline."

Doll took a deep breath and willed herself to relax. She hoped that since she was the team captain, others would follow her lead and focus on the task at hand. Everything they had worked toward was on the line.

AT 6 P.M., the coliseum sprang to life. Basketball fans breezed through the entry doors and grabbed empty seats to watch the evening's first match between Crescent College and the high school girls from Castor, Louisiana. Earlier in the day, the Houston Green Devils had beaten Monroe, Louisiana's Independents, 38–12. Games were scheduled every hour from 7 to 10 p.m. Some who missed eating dinner bought the fried ham sandwiches, called pig sandwiches, and sipped strong black coffee or gulped Dr Pepper and other syrupy soft drinks. Spectators read newspapers or perused souvenir AAU programs, checking team photographs and reading through rosters to see who looked like winners.

"No street shoes allowed on the court," an AAU security guard shouted over and over to wandering spectators. Sportswriters from Shreveport, Dallas, Chicago, and other towns and cities huddled at their courtside tables drinking coffee and smoking Camels. Doll recognized a few of them, including Johnny Lyons of the *Houston Post-Dispatch*.

The *thwat* of a dribble and a bounce, the squeal of sneakers, and the swish of baskets were the sounds of the players on the court tossing balls during warm-up practice.

Strolling through the bustle dressed in new red wool cardigans and white cotton sweatpants, the Cardinals—accompanied by the Hotchkins— arrived ready for a long night since their game was so late on the roster. Doll had fixed Toka Lee's sweater, and the area where the thread had been pulled now looked perfectly smooth. They were best friends again, as if nothing had happened, and both were up and ready to play.

Even though enthusiastic fans had showed up, the crowd seemed sparse, with vacant seats dotting the coliseum. Local sportswriter Otis Harris would take notice of the crowd size in his column the next day: "Shreveport appears not to have warmed up to the ceremony with the desired degree of heat, and an affair of this nature certainly warrants better attendance."

While waiting for their turn, the Cardinals watched familiar teams play their matchups. Crescent College beat the high school team from Castor, 38–26. Tulsa Business College topped Lynn's Business College from Shreveport, 31–28, and the Southern Kansas Stage Lines from Wichita obliterated Shreveport's Atlas Sign Company, 49–9.

At 9 p.m., the Golden Cyclones made their tournament debut against the Shreveport Charity Hospital Nurses. Numerous Dallas fans shouted with glee while the Cyclones demolished the local team so severely that the next day the *Shreveport Times* declared that it would take a great set of players to dethrone the current champions.

The Charity Nurses lost to the Cyclones, 32–8. In fact, every team from Louisiana lost that day, causing those rooting for home teams to become discouraged and leave early. By the time the Cardinals were ready to play, only a couple of hundred people remained in their seats, including Babe Didrikson and the rest of the Cyclones, who weren't there to root for OPC.

At the starting whistle, Lucille jumped center and won possession. Doll scored eight points just three minutes into the game. The Boosters looked asleep. After ten minutes, Babb benched most of the first string except for Lucille and Vick. Every Cardinal got to play against the Kansas team.

When Vera scored a quick two points, the Booster guards seemed worn out. Suddenly a guard who missed the rebound kicked the goal post hard out of frustration and then fell flat on her back, holding her right leg in the air and moaning. After the injured player was assisted off the court, the Cardinals increased their lead, and by halftime, the game had the feel of an easy win.

A few minutes after the start of the second half, the referee called a shooting foul on a Kansas guard. Her team had failed to complete a single goal during the entire game, while the Cardinals kept a steady stream of leather pouring through the hoop. A dozen Kansas fans started booing.

Someone tossed a paper cup half full of liquid onto the sidelines that splatted into a puddle. When no one appeared to clean it up, Babb looked agitated. He finally asked Mrs. Hotchkin to find a janitor. Babb didn't sit back down but started pacing in his slow, stiff-hipped fashion along the sidelines.

When the referee called another foul on Kansas, the Boosters' coach shouted an obscenity and leaped up from the bench. People sitting in the stands started shouting, too, causing the boy hawking Dr Peppers to stop walking up and down the coliseum steps. Even though prohibition had made liquor and beer illegal, Babb suspected that some in the crowd had found a bootlegger and were drunk. In his whole life, Babb had never downed a beer or tasted any form of alcoholic beverage due to his religious upbringing and his father threatening to skin his children alive if he ever caught them drinking.

The referee called a technical foul on the Kansas coach, and the shouting match resumed. Loud boos erupted. Kansas fans barked at the referee, too. This rowdy behavior continued for several minutes until Babb lost *his* temper. Being a disciplinarian and a perfectionist, he hated it when others couldn't control themselves. He trudged across the court to confront the other coach and covertly check his breath for alcohol. When Babb reached the two arguing men, he stepped between them and put a hand on the other coach's shoulder.

Babb leaned over and said, "We are wasting time here."

The Kansas coach, who did not have liquor on his breath, accused Babb of paying off the referee. Anger surged up his spine, and Babb wanted to start shouting, too. But his players needed to finish the game and get some rest tonight.

Instead of giving into anger, Babb growled at the coach, "Your family here tonight?"

The coach's ruddy face turned pale. He stopped shouting, stepped back, and gazed up into onlookers' faces.

"Can we get started?" Babb said to the referee, who quickly nodded.

The Kansas coach accepted the holding foul assigned to his player and the technical foul assigned to him. A few minutes later, the Cardinals finished off the Boosters, 61–4. They didn't get back to their rooms until midnight.

EARLY THE NEXT morning, Babb was walking from his room to the elevator, when a hotel maid rushed up to him. He had asked her if she would mind checking on his players when she made her rounds at night. She didn't know their names, but she knew what they looked like. When she told Babb that one girl didn't make it to her room, the description fit Vick.

Walking into the hotel restaurant the following morning, Babb was furious. Instead of taking Vick aside, he stood at her table where she was eating breakfast with La Homa, Lera, and Vera and asked her where she was last night. "After all this school has done for you," he said, his voice low and angry.

Vick had no idea what he was talking about.

Disturbed by Babb's complaints, La Homa spoke up and said that since there was an extra bed in her room with Lera and Vera, Vick had stayed with them.

When Babb said that if La Homa was covering for Vick, she would go home, too, Vick hopped out of her chair and dragged Mrs. Hotchkin over from where she was sitting at another table.

"Will you believe her?" Vick said, gesturing toward Mrs. Hotchkin.

Once Mrs. Hotchkin understood Babb's accusation, she verified that Vick had asked permission from her last night to stay in a different room. It had been so late, and Mrs. Hotchkin was very tired, so she gave her approval and then went to bed without informing Babb.

Without apologizing, Babb left Vick's table to sit with the Hotchkins.

Vick sat fuming. She'd always known Babb didn't like her, and now her feelings had been proven correct. But Lera told Vick that she shouldn't be too angry at Mr. Babb. Since Vick officially roomed with Doll, the team captain had probably put the idea into his head.

Even though Doll and Vick weren't friends, they weren't enemies, either. Vick didn't believe that Doll would betray her. Nonetheless, after breakfast, she confronted Doll in their hotel room. Doll looked confused. When Vick realized that she had jumped to the wrong conclusion, just like Babb had done with her, she apologized to Doll and asked her to forget the whole thing.

AT 10 A.M., the free-throwing contest sponsored by the AAU opened the day's events at the coliseum. Each team sent two representatives. Doll and Coral lined up with the other competitors that included Babe Didrikson to see who could make the most shots. Each player was allowed twenty-five tries, and the top five women with the highest number of baskets would move on to the finals, scheduled for Thursday night. It required skill and focus. That's why Doll knew she would win.

The participants advanced in alphabetical order according to their last names. Their teammates sat in the bleachers ready to cheer. First up was Myrtle Brockett, forward of the Southern Kansas Stage Lines.

Brockett nailed twenty-four shots out of twenty-five. That set the standard for the morning competition. The next girl completed twenty. The next, fourteen. Babe could only score nineteen, a sad number that made her wince. Doll, whose turn came shortly after Babe's, felt on top of her game. Toka Lee, Bo-Peep, Lucille, Teny, and all the other Cardinals, including Mrs. Hotchkin, who never missed a Cardinal competition of any kind, applauded loudly from the sidelines when Doll's first basket whisked through. After making ten in a row, she tilted her chin upward as confidence energized her performance. She took the shot, expecting the ball to shoot through the net. When it bounced off the rim instead, shock waves surged through her body. She couldn't believe she missed. But then she missed again. And again. Her final score was seventeen. Two less than Babe. Determined to get over her disappointment, she threw all her hope into Coral's chances, who would be going last since her name was Worley.

Coral's ability to concentrate was uncanny. It was her confidence that waivered sometimes, but today she made the first five baskets so quickly, Lucille stood on her feet and Vick put her fingers to her lips and gave one of her shrill whistles that echoed off the walls. When she was done, she found she had made twenty-three out of twenty-five. Coral finished second that day and would compete in the finals on Thursday night.

IN ADDITION TO the basketball games, the other competition held on Wednesday was for the most beautiful girls.

After tomboy Babe Didrikson's rise in popularity, high school physical educators started posting signs on bulletin boards that read, DON'T BE A MUSCLE MOLL. Those who sponsored girls' athletic competitions felt compelled to calm this public anxiety. Shreveport newspapers ran a Girls in Athletics column that reassured its readers that "everywhere these players go folks are impressed with their beauty. They are all the picture of health and typical American girls. Parents who fear to permit their daughters to go in for athletics should look over these groups of young women who are among the best athletes in America."

The AAU encouraged women's basketball teams to recruit and train highly skilled female athletes. Only the best players and teams would attract crowds. At the same time, the AAU had to uphold society's image of the feminine ideal—a woman who was poised, graceful, and beautiful. Because of the onslaught from the Women's Division and the public's nagging idea that working-class female athletes were mannish, AAU leaders staged an event during the national tournament that would exhibit their players' feminine charms—a beauty contest!

Each team selected its prettiest player to compete. Some girls considered it like a sideshow that provided certain types of entertainment. Usually, athletes didn't care about the beauty pageant as long as they could keep playing basketball. The Cardinals' only championship at an AAU-sponsored tournament occurred in 1930 when team captain Verna Montgomery won the beauty contest and made headlines as the Cardinals' "Brunette Beauty Queen."

The AAU claimed that the judges were anonymous, but everyone knew they were the sportswriters. Many of these newspapermen were true admirers of women's basketball and acted out of a genuine desire to report on the progress of certain teams. But that wasn't always the case. Sometimes they made snide remarks about players' looks or how their uniforms fit. In one article printed in the *Hutchinson News*, the middle-aged writer was the Kansas secretary of the state's boxing authority and considered himself an expert in all sports. He wrote, "Girls' basketball must have some merits altho [*sic*] I, for one, have never discovered them. It will be played, however, and fusses over the (shape of the uniforms meant) nothing to anybody. . . . But all this to one side, if a genuine improvement in the girls' sport is sought why doesn't someone with power to act insist the ladies go to the showers and take their baths after the game is over? I never knew a girls' tournament in which most of the players didn't put their suits on in the morning and wear them until everything was over at night."

How many boys took showers during a sporting tournament, and who would care about that? Only young women needed to smell good after playing basketball. Perhaps the teams didn't take showers because they couldn't afford another team outfit to change into, or maybe, since all facilities had been built for men, there weren't even showers available. This sportswriter apparently didn't think to ask.

THE CARDINALS' GAME on Wednesday was scheduled immediately after the beauty contest at 8 p.m. against Tulsa Business College. By the afternoon, they still hadn't decided who would compete. Lucille, Vick, and Bo-Peep encouraged La Homa because she was truly beautiful. But La Homa was a first-string substitute who didn't want any distractions when it came time to play against Tulsa. Others encouraged Lera or Vera because they were tall and striking with their red hair.

Vera said that she'd be happy to do it because she was prettier than Lera.

Lucille and La Homa giggled. Vick rolled her eyes.

Lera stretched her neck to show off her profile and said that Vera's pockmarked complexion would never make her a beauty.

Vera said that she had never had a pimple in her life.

Lera held up a fist and said that she'd provide her with a giant pimple right in the middle of her eye, and that's when Lucille interrupted. Since the twins looked just alike and were equally beautiful, it was too bad that they both couldn't compete.

By game time that night, the Cardinals didn't have anyone willing to enter the contest. Two other teams didn't, either, so nineteen girls would participate.

Five minutes after Southern Kansas Stage Lines beat the Houston Green Devils, 32–23, two men scurried to set up a microphone at center court. They rolled an upright piano onto the sidelines near an exit. Nineteen beauty contestants gathered on the court's sidelines, wearing their basketball uniforms and shoes. Chatting and laughing, they were helping each other with last-minute touches of lipstick and rouge. Contestants included five girls from Shreveport: Clarice Ratcliff, Nehi Bottling Company; Theresa McKeithan, Charity Hospital Nurses; Jewell Baggett, Meadows Draughon's Business College; Opal Hill, Lynn's Business College; and Helen Chapman of the Atlas Signs Company. Jewell Baggett slipped off her uniform top to reveal a white tight-fitting tank-style leotard underneath.

The lights dimmed. A large spotlight gleamed onto the court. The contestant from the Green Devils, who had just lost to the Stage Lines, complained that she smelled like mildewed laundry and wouldn't have a chance.

"Welcome ladies and gentlemen to the event you've all been waiting for—the Amateur Athletic Union's parade of basketball beauties," an announcer's voice boomed over the loudspeakers. Audience members clapped their approval. The contestants scrambled to form a line.

"Are you ready to meet tonight's all-star beauties?" the announcer thundered. The crowd screamed, "Yes!" A piano player strummed several dramatic chords, *dum dum da.*

Each girl walked up to a microphone set on center stage, announced her name, and then smiled at where she thought the anonymous judges might be hiding. Wolf whistles and yelps peppered the air. A much bigger crowd had shown up tonight at the coliseum. After each contestant introduced herself, the stadium lights brightened and the contestants circled the court, swaying and strutting in single file so that the judges could get a good look at them. After several minutes, the announcer's voice said that the judges were ready to proclaim the winner. The piano player halted his music so that those in the crowd could hear the names. Team members watching began shouting for their teammates to win, and the contestants scrambled to form a straight line.

Third runner-up was Dot Purdy of the Jacksonville, Florida Pirates.

"Dot, Dot, Dot," the crowd chanted as she rushed forward.

Second runner-up was Jewel Baggett from Shreveport. The crowd stood up and cheered because a local girl had finally won a prize. The spotlight caused her tank-style leotard to become see-through, and more wolf whistles punctured the air.

The announcer proclaimed the new reigning queen of basketball to be Miss Imogen Lockett representing Crescent College in Eureka Springs, Arkansas. Grover C. Thames, sponsor of the tournament, placed a dozen roses in her arms and a star-burst crown on her head. She also received a fur-lined cape, a scepter, and the largest trophy of the tournament. She posed to get her picture taken for tomorrow's newspapers.

The two men hurried back onto the court, removed the microphone, and scooted away the piano away.

At 8:20 p.m., the Cardinals opened play against Tulsa, and it was a slow offensive for both teams during the first half. At halftime, the Cardinals had a 12–8 lead. During the third quarter, OPC pulled further ahead, and Babb began sending in substitutes. Bo-Peep replaced Toka Lee but went in too fast for an intercepted pass, fell, and injured her ankle. Babb sent in Lera as her replacement. Everyone got to play, and the Cardinals sailed into the Thursday semifinals by beating Tulsa, 28–19.

THE NEXT DAY at lunch, a few hours before their semifinals game against the Southern Kansas Stage Lines, Vick and Coral were sitting across from Doll at the hotel restaurant eating tuna salad drenched in mayonnaise. Doll couldn't stand mayonnaise because of the smell—it reminded her of rotten eggs. Toka Lee, next to Doll, had started writing postcards to her parents. Doll was explaining how Shreveport's sportswriters had embraced Kansas City as their favorite since every team from Louisiana had been losing.

Toka Lee looked up from her writing and asked if Doll was suggesting that the crowd would be with Kansas City tonight and not with OPC.

Looking very serious, Doll said, "I'm saying, be prepared."

While she was talking, shrill voices sounded from across the hotel restaurant near the entrance. The voices grew louder, and everyone crooked their necks to see who was being so rude.

Wearing tennis shoes, blue jeans, and a blue work shirt, "Texas Tomboy" Babe Didrikson, as she was recently labeled by the press, loped across the restaurant and out the side door followed by two young men, obviously reporters, one wearing thick, black-rimmed glasses and a camera on a strap around his neck. Babe was always doing something to grab attention, playing her harmonica while standing on her head, challenging anyone big and tough to a fistfight. Once, she told reporters that she could run faster than a horse and buggy but never got a chance to prove it. In three months, she would be representing the United States in the Los Angeles Olympics.

Babe wasn't too friendly with the other players, and no one got to know her very well off the court. Most of the teams, including the Cyclones, were staying at the Jefferson Hotel, and the athletes from different cities mingled when they had time. However, coaches and chaperones kept strict watch, and hard practice schedules prevented players from making too many friends.

Doll watched Babe traipse by along with her entourage. She knew from past experience that the popular athlete wasn't any better at basketball than most of the Cardinals, yet she got all the fanfare. Once finished with their meals, Doll and the other Cardinals headed upstairs to change into their uniforms. They had a practice session scheduled for 2 p.m., and then the rest of the day would be spent watching their competition, including Babe and the Cyclones, work out at the coliseum.

THURSDAY NIGHT, A bustling crowd showed up for the semi-finals, where the Cardinals would take on the Southern Kansas Stage Lines, and the Golden Cyclones would battle Crescent College. The Cardinals' game was scheduled to start directly after the finals of the free-throwing contest.

Five girls, including Coral, lined up to be judged this night—not for how they looked but for their actual skill at basketball. This time, the spotlights didn't snap on, and under the same glaring lights as a basketball game, each player made fifty shots. Coral stood last in line. Just before her turn, Susie Tugwell from Lynn's Business College in Shreveport made forty-seven out of fifty. She had the whole stadium on their feet rooting for the hometown girl. When Coral was up, she missed her first shot and then her second. She missed ten in a row before she made a basket. But then, with her teammates on their feet shouting encouragements, she made every basket after that except for the last. Coral ended up in a three-way tie for third with thirty-eight baskets. Hoping to make a name for herself separate from Doll's reputation, she felt discouraged. Tugwell's score set a new AAU record, and the sportswriters reported that she was the "Queen of the Goal Makers."

By game time, the Cardinals were facing a thunderstorm of screaming Kansas and Louisiana fans. The Stage Lines felt confident against the Cardinals, and their followers were ready to watch them destroy OPC's winning streak. Dr. and Mrs. Hotchkin sitting with the Oklahoma contingent, now at about two hundred, all shouted approval when the red-clad Cardinals raced on court.

Babb called them into a huddle and calmly outlined how they should focus on each move so that any distractions, like the unruly crowd, would disappear. They clapped all at once and jogged to their places on court. At the starting whistle, Lucille made a perfect jump and sent the ball straight to Coral, who scored in the first thirty seconds. Dr. Hotchkin and the other Oklahoma fans jumped to their feet and shouted praise. Throughout the first quarter, the Cardinals played flawless basketball. By halftime, they were leading, 24–14.

During the break, even Mr. Babb seemed thrilled by the fast pace set by his team. "Keep scaring up the dust," he said.

They breezed through the third quarter, ahead by twelve points. Kansas's fans sat dejected, and those from Louisiana who might be swayed began to root for the Cardinals.

When the fourth quarter began, the Cardinals' offense started freezing out the guards, keeping the ball outside and away from them. Since there was no set time limit for ball possession in both men and women's basketball, Coral, Doll, and Lucille decided to stall, and they played a game of keep-away for as long as the guards would let them. Kansas tried fouling Doll but couldn't get in close enough. Until the final three minutes.

With the flick of a wrist, momentum changed, just like the wind abruptly switching directions. This time, it was Kansas who came from behind. The coliseum shook with the crowd's approval as they gained possession and kept it, making eight points in quick succession and coming within two goals of tying up the score. The Kansas guards started playing an aggressive game, knocking Coral off her feet. Flustered by the sudden roughness, she missed her free throw.

In the final minutes, Doll was fouled four times and made six free-throw baskets. Worst of all, while leaping to catch a wild pass from Teny, she felt a sharp pinprick, under her kneecap after landing hard on her heels. She ignored the pain, but Babb knew something was wrong and pulled her from the final seconds of the game. He made her elevate her knee until the tournament doctor made an examination. Doll didn't know what to expect. She felt scared, and it made her angry.

Vick, Teny, and Toka Lee did their best to keep from fouling out.

All of the Cardinals would be swallowing aspirin and nursing bruises tonight. Babb prayed that no one else would be injured.

When the buzzer finally sounded, signaling the end of the game, the scoreboard read 44–36, in favor of the Cardinals. The players shook hands with their opponents and didn't have much time to celebrate their big win. They were all anxious to watch the Cyclones battle Crescent College. Who would they play for the national championship?

While her teammates were finding their seats, Doll met with the doctor. He didn't find any swelling but told her to wrap her knee for the game tomorrow. She should be prepared to remove herself from the game if the pain got worse. For now, it was just a little sore, but she was worried. She understood that they would have to play smarter and be a lot better to win the national championship.

IN THE SECOND semifinals matchup, the Cyclones were having a hard time with Crescent College. Tied after the first quarter, the Cyclones inched ahead, and by halftime the score was 17–12. When Babb motioned for Doll to leave her seat, she hesitated. Her knee felt stiff, and the third quarter was about to start. But she followed her coach while he signaled for Lucille, Coral, and Vick to join them, and then he led them out of the arena to meet a man dressed in a three-piece, tweed suit who turned out to be Grover C. Thames. He had arranged for a few of the players to appear tonight on KWKH, "Old Man" Henderson's radio show, heard across the nation. Upon hearing the news, the girls grinned at each other and gave quiet cheers while following Thames. They couldn't wait to shake hands with their favorite radio star.

Henderson himself was one of the wealthiest men in Shreveport. Owner and president of the Henderson Iron Works and Supply Company specializing in oil-drilling equipment, Henderson caught the radio bug in 1922, and by 1926 turned his six-thousand-acre country estate north of Shreveport into a broadcasting compound complete with power plant, thousand-watt transmitter, studios, and offices for technical personnel and visiting guests. Operating at less than one thousand watts during the day, Henderson aired his show at night when atmospheric conditions allowed his signal to expand to fifty thousand watts and could be heard across the United States.

Thames drove the group a few blocks into the downtown area, where they ended up at one of KWKH's remote broadcast studios. Once inside, they noticed that the whole place smelled like a coffee factory. A vase filled with red roses sat in the entryway, and tins labeled "Hello World Coffee" with Henderson's picture on the front were stacked behind the front desk.

Just a moment, please, the receptionist said when Thames told her who they were. "You expectin' Cardinals?" she said into the phone. She hung up and began searching noisily for something in her desk drawer. Still searching in her desk, she yelled, "Aha" and pulled out a piece of Wrigley's Spearmint gum. She unwrapped and popped it into her mouth and then asked everyone to follow her through a door and down a hallway where they could look through a glass and see the radio show host sitting at a desk in a large studio and talking into a microphone. A red light was flashing ON AIR over the door. Suddenly, the red light above the studio door stopped flashing, and the receptionist pushed open the oversized, soundproof studio door.

Henderson was a bald man with wire-rimmed glasses. When he stood up to shake hands, Doll noticed that the top of his head reached only a few inches above hers. He smelled sweetly spicy, like cinnamon and orange marmalade. When the record he had playing reached the end, he swiftly removed the needle, leaned into the microphone, and announced that he was now surrounded by feminine charm. The Oklahoma Presbyterian College Cardinals from Durant were shooting to be America's basketball champions at the AAU women's tournament here in Shreveport.

Henderson signaled for Doll, Vick, and Lucille to speak, and they managed a loud "hello" from their seats. Sipping coffee from a mug, he said that one thing was certain, tomorrow's game would be a doozy! He motioned for Vick to say her name and the position she played. Vick stuck her face close to the microphone, almost the size of her head, and shouted out her response. Henderson laughed and said that she had knocked a few listeners off their seats. She didn't have to shout.

Lucille spoke next, and when she stood up and walked to the micro-phone, Henderson raised his eyebrows and said that he knew a thing or two about basketball and that she must play center position since she was taller than most men.

When Lucille said, "Yes, sir," she had a frog in her throat. Henderson told her to speak up a bit, and Lucille announced that she wasn't the tallest on her team. Lera and Vera Dunford were six feet tall.

Lucille had been talking with Henderson for several minutes, and Doll was starting to get a little nervous. She'd never talked over the radio and hoped her voice would sound okay. Just then, the station owner motioned for her to stand up, and he called her the cutest little athlete he'd ever seen. When he went on about her freckles, Babb interrupted and said that she was one of the best forwards in America who could score twenty points in a game. Doll told him where she was from and that her favorite subjects were math and English.

Finally, Henderson directed his attention at Babb and asked him about his secret to coaching girls' basketball. Babb said it was very simple. They were the hardest-working, best-conditioned, and most united team in the competition. They had won by learning how to pace themselves, play a quick, consistent game, and be patient and wait.

That struck Henderson as amusing. He had watched a girls' game once and it didn't look like they did much waiting around. Babb laughed and said that he understood how it might sound funny. What he meant to say was that every player was always on alert. "I believe basketball isn't just what is, but what might be."

Babb said, "Basketball is passing, flow, and creativity. Wait and see how the play unfolds, and then react without expectations. In other words, let the plays develop while meeting your opponents head on. It takes a lot of heart, and that's how we'll win."

Henderson slapped Mr. Babb on the back and told him that for a quiet guy, he sure did like to talk!

To finish up, Henderson asked for a school song. By now, all the Cardinals were used to singing in public, and since Coral had the best voice, she led her teammates in one of their favorites titled "There's a School." It was published in the OPC school booklet given to every student.

THERE'S A SCHOOL

There's a school far out on the Prairie
Where the western winds caress;
There's a school 'tis known so far and wide
Which we'll always love the best
And the Sun sets bright behind it
To rise another day
With a glorious, flaming dawning
On the garnet and the gray.

There's a school far out on the prairie
Where the gentle moonbeams fall;
And a team 'tis known so far and wide
For it plays good basketball
And the lusty cheers resounding
Through the corridors all day
Announce another triumph
For the garnet and the gray.

There's a school far out on the prairie
Where the loyal maidens dwell
'Tis a school of happy knowledge
'Tis enshrined in our hearts as well
And our tender love surrounds it
As we while the golden day:
And we pledge our hearts with gladness
To the garnet and the gray.

Chorus
Oklahoma Presbyterian College
Our hearts are thine always
As we sing thy praise forever
Oh, the garnet and the gray!

The Cardinals' time on air lasted fifteen minutes. When they were leaving the studio, they met some familiar faces walking down the hallway—Coach McCombs of the Cyclones and three of his best players, Ruby Mansfield, captain; Lucy Stratton, guard; and, of course, Babe Didrikson. During the Cardinals' time on the air, Thames had driven back to the coliseum and picked up a few of the Cyclones just after they defeated Crescent College.

Doll glanced over at Babe as she walked by and caught her eye. Babe quickly looked away, but Doll knew what she was thinking. The outcome tomorrow night depended on them. Whoever had the better game, her team would win.

It was all up to Doll, and that suited her just fine.

CHAPTER 14

A Team That Won't Be Beat Can't Be Beat

March 25, 1932

The next morning, a few Cardinals lingered at their table in the hotel restaurant after finishing breakfast. They were restless and for good reason—it was the most important day of their lives. Lucille pulled at the raspberry-colored thread, loosening it from the sleeve hem of her wool OPC team sweater. La Homa kept flicking the rubber band she wore around her wrist to remind her not to eat sweets. Coral sipped her coffee, and Vick read the article beneath the headlines in the morning edition of the *Shreveport Times* that announced the team's matchup with the Cyclones tonight in large bold type. The piece very generally described the results of yesterday's games, including the Cardinals' victory over the Southern Kansas Stage Lines. But the column right next to it by Helen Carney, Shreveport tennis star, was the reason Lucille kept worrying that thread. The headline read, "Girl Developed on Given Chance in Various Sports—Golden Cyclones' Star Never Recognized Until Senior School Year." It was all about how, two years ago, the Cyclones' coach, McCombs, "discovered" a bashful sixteen-year-old school girl without "any particular hopes or ambitions" and turned her into a sports prodigy. But at the end of the article, the coach reassured everyone that he "did not make Babe what she is. She made herself."

When Vick finished reading and put down the newspaper, she said that most people would want to read the overly flattering article about Babe Didrikson and not pay much attention to yesterday's recap about the Cardinals because the writing just sat there, dry as cut hay. No matter how many games they had won or interviews they'd given to fancy radio announcers, it wasn't enough. The Cardinals would always be the little church-school girls. Young, inexperienced, and lucky but with flashes of talent. Even reliable Johnny Lyons, who had announced the Cardinals' brilliance in his *Houston Post-Dispatch* sports column way back in December, didn't write anything now that disputed the common wisdom about the young Oklahoma team—that they had played hard and fast games during the week, but inexperience combined with fatigue would lead to defeat. Take Mesquite, Texas, for example. The young team had clashed with Randolph College in the consolation bracket last night. Poor Mesquite failed to make a single basket in the first half and scored only six points in the second, leaving the final at 34–6. The point spread shouldn't have been that big. Mesquite had played well the first two days of the tournament, but last night, they looked just plain worn out.

According to the sportswriters, the Cardinals could easily end up like Mesquite. The Cardinals had little depth with only four substitutes. One of them, Bo-Peep, was injured. Worst of all, their star player was injured, too. The fate of the OPC team seemed certain. But that was two days ago. The sportswriters and those other educated men who made predictions didn't know that Doll's knee seemed to be fine this morning. Lucille's ankles appeared sturdy. Toka Lee promised not to foul out again. Vick never seemed to get tired, even after hours of practice, and Teny had been getting plenty of sleep. They were the best-conditioned team at the tournament. But no one knew any of that because no one regularly reported on the church-school girls.

The harder question to answer was not if the *sportswriters* thought that the Cardinals could win but if the *Cardinals* believed it themselves. Deep down, Lucille didn't think so. In fact, every win this season had come as a surprise to her. That's why she always got so nervous before a game. Because the outcome wasn't assured. Oh yes, everyone acted with such confidence in front of Mr. Babb, but underneath it all, in the very center of their hearts, they had doubts. Sure, they had won every game this season, including against the Cyclones, but the AAU tournament officials had seeded them to finish only fourth and the Cyclones first. These educated men must know something, right?

Lucille noticed that the hem on her sweater had started to unravel. To prevent the destruction of her treasured team sweater, she promised herself that she would stop worrying. The upcoming practice session at the gym would help.

The four Cardinals left the restaurant to get ready for the light workout Babb had scheduled, mostly shooting free throws and running passing drills. Some players' parents were arriving at the bus station this after-noon, including La Homa's mother, most of Lucille's family except for two brothers who stayed home to run the farm, Teny's mother, and Toka Lee's older sister, a high school basketball coach. The Dunford twins' redheaded older brother had skipped college classes at Oklahoma City University to watch the tournament. Doll's parents couldn't get away from the farm, but everyone she knew, including Mr. Daily, her high school basketball coach, had sent telegrams wishing her well.

Back home in Durant, there was fevered interest for news about the Cardinals. Each day of the tournament, the *Durant Daily Democrat*, using the AP wire, had reported on wins, injuries, and gossip telephoned in from Dr. Hotchkin—about Doll's favorite breakfast item (hash browns with ketchup) or Coral's secret for shooting free throws. By the night of the tournament finals, the *Durant Daily Democrat*, in an effort to keep up with demand and not draw the ire of Durant's citizens, set up two telephones at Boyet-Long Drug Store to deliver the scores to fans. The newspaper received reports from the Coliseum via news-agency teletype, and would call Boyet-Long with the updates. Those manning the phones expected at least four hundred calls that evening.

The drugstore planned to stay open past its 7 p.m. closing time so that those Cardinal players like the Hamilton sisters, Ginny and Alice, and Buena Harris who had to stay behind could get the news first.

BY 6 P.M., the sun was setting in Shreveport. Three games were scheduled tonight: at 7 p.m., Randolph College and Lynn's Business College would play a consolation game to get the crowd warmed up; at 8 p.m., the Southern Kansas Stage Lines would meet the Crescent College to decide the third- and fourth-place finishers; and the championship game would start at 9 p.m.

Lights from the coliseum shone like beacons above the parking lot, piercing through the unseasonable fog that had risen from the nearby Red River. Fortunately, it wasn't raining. Shreveport was known for rain, hail, and even tornadoes that time of year. The featured matchup between the Cardinals and the Cyclones had drawn a capacity crowd of almost four thousand. Every one of them must have been eating popcorn because the warm, buttery smell filled the air as the Cardinals waited to take the court. Finally, it was their turn.

Lucille stood with her team gazing out at the noisy throng. Just one year ago, as a senior at her tiny Union Valley high school, she was playing outdoors on a dirt court. Since then, she'd competed in thirty games as a Cardinal, but she'd never seen anything like this. She hoped her ankles would hold up and that her stage fright wouldn't paralyze her. But then she thought of her mother and father watching her from their seats in that noisy crowd. This was the first time her father was seeing her play with the Cardinals. Finally it hit her—after all the success she saw this year with the Cardinals, she might finally live up to her dad's expectations. She might just be that basketball star.

Next to her, Teny gave a startled jump when the master of ceremonies bellowed a cheerful welcome over the loudspeakers to the boisterous crowd. Coral and Vick seemed unruffled, like always. Toka Lee trotted up to join them after making sure her sister was sitting on the team bench near Mrs. Hotchkin.

Doll was clutching a Western Union telegram from her former Cement High School coach, Mr. Daily, and her teammates. "Every Bulldog heart beats for you," it read. She had no doubts. Texas teams had won the national tournament five years in a row. Just like the great football competition between the University of Oklahoma Sooners and the University of Texas Longhorns that had been fought since 1900, seven years before Oklahoma statehood, the Cardinals would be battling for Oklahoma glory. In fact, OU had lost to UT for the last six years in a row. If the Cardinals could beat the Cyclones tonight, history would be made with an Oklahoma winner.

After reading through the message one more time, Doll put it protectively into the pocket of her warm-ups.

The booming voice of the master of ceremonies began introducing the Cardinals' starting lineup: Coral Worley, Hazel Vickers, Ernestine Lampson, Toka Lee Fields, Doll Harris, and Lucille Thurman. Next came the Golden Cyclones: Babe Didrikson, Ruby Mansfield, Isla Rhea, Lucille Stratton, Agnes Robertson, and Alberta Peace. Lithe Babe Didrikson, the "Texas Tornado," circled the coliseum arena floor in a preemptive victory lap while everyone else warmed up. Already she was skillfully drawing in the crowd's sympathies. It was no secret that Babe was an expert at intimidating her opponents. In last year's national tournament, she scored thirty points in two games and hit a late shot to beat Wichita in the finals, 28–26. Upon retelling that story over and over, Babe would inflate the points she scored sometimes by five or ten. No one ever questioned her enthusiasm.

Babb called his team together and gave final instructions. Yes, they had beaten the Cyclones before. But this was not that game. Pay attention. Be ready for everything. Know where your teammates are, count on them, and never grandstand—the same words he delivered before every game. And tonight, like always, Babb would stay out of the limelight, a quiet, almost stoic presence who trusted his team to win. For Babb, watching the players move the game forward was like seeing how the pieces could solve their own puzzle. Every choice counted. Every player had to be her own coach because the rules in girls' basketball outlawed coaching from the sidelines.

Dr. Hotchkin stood near his wife, Maria, who was dressed in OPC colors, a bright red skirt, white silk blouse, and red pumps. Dr. Hotchkin and his wife were deep in conversation with the Cardinal substitutes, Bo-Peep, nursing a sprained ankle, and La Homa, Lera, and Vera, still invigorated after warming up with the team. Suddenly the restless crowd stopped clapping and stomping and began to cheer. That meant the referee had started toward the jump circle. Everyone fixed their attention on center court.

Even though he didn't believe that God ever took sides, Dr. Hotchkin whispered a prayer asking for a little help anyway.

When Lucille stepped onto center court, the crowd's cheering became a roar. She and Ruby Mansfield, the Cyclone center, prepared to jump for the ball, feet spread wide, knees bent, arms out. Lucille couldn't help but notice Ruby's bright red nail polish that matched her name. The whistle trilled as the referee tossed up the ball between the centers. Split-second timing allowed Mansfield to tip the ball into the hands of a Cyclone forward who took the shot. Arching up and up, and then downward, it swished through the net. The battle for the championship had begun.

The Cyclones drove hard during the first eight-minute quarter. Babe, a relentless rebounder, sank four baskets in a row. At the end of the first quarter, when the teams switched goals, the Cyclones led 12–4.

At Boyet-Long Drug Store in Durant, a small crowd of avid fans huddled together in the little restaurant near the dispensary. The report of the first-quarter score was met with the sounds of Dr Peppers and cherry Cokes being slurped through straws while the phones rang constantly. Frowns, grimaces, and long, sour looks reflected in the enormous mirror that hung over the soda fountain. Ginny and Alice both wished they were at the coliseum to support their teammates and not stuck sitting on the plastic-covered soda fountain stools. But instead of complaining, they closed their eyes and anticipated that Lucille would win the jump and the next report would be a good one.

At that moment, Lucille was taking her position for the second quarter jump-off. She sank low, her eyes on the ball. A wheezing, whistle sound came not from the referee's bright, shiny whistle but from his runny nose. Lucille blinked, calming her nerves and forcing herself to focus. The real whistle sounded. She leaped. Her fingertips found the rough leather first, and pushed it toward Doll. She pivoted, squared off with the goal, and sent the ball flying. It floated through the net for two points. The floor shook as the crowd applauded.

Throughout the second quarter, Vick strode the court like Hercules. She outjumped the Cyclones' forward and tapped the ball to Toka Lee, who passed down court to Doll. The three forwards kept the ball in constant motion and out of reach of the Cyclone guards, whipping it around until the right shot appeared. Lucille faked an overhead pass and sent a bounce pass straight through a maze of Cyclone arms and legs to Coral, who scored on a breaking jump shot.

Doll attracted the Cyclone defense like flies to honey. When she had all three of them gathered around her, she made several sharp, explosive cuts, and sent the ball to Lucille, who was standing in the keyhole area under the basket with no one defending her. She stretched for a layup and knew the ball would go in just from the feel of it.

The Cardinals attacked quickly, moving the ball back and forth across the floor like a ping pong ball. The Cyclones defense, made awkward by the sheer speed of competition, committed several fouls, resulting in a free-throw standoff. Doll won that competition hands down. Big guards couldn't help but reach in for the ball and foul her. They knew she was a dangerous sharpshooter. They suspected she'd be less accurate on the free-throw line than in play, but they were wrong. Doll's form was perfect. She squared her shoulders to the goal, staggered her right foot in front of her left, took three deep breaths, and smiled. Even after she sent the ball sailing, flowing like water, her eyes remained on her goal and her arms stayed upright in dramatic follow-through until the ball fell through the net as smooth as marble.

In the second quarter alone, she made eight free throws in eight tries.

The Cardinal guards, Vick, Teny, and Toka Lee, put relentless pressure on the Cyclones during the second quarter. Teny, who had ended up with the job of guarding Babe, found that she could outjump the famous athlete to grab the rebound. Mansfield, the Cyclones' big center, telegraphed her intention to heave the ball by making a soft grunting sound deep in her throat. Since she was Vick's girl to guard, Vick began yelling "shoot" every time the center grunted, stopping her in her tracks. Little Toka Lee used her speed like a runaway freight train. She could drop-step faster than her opponent could pivot, and she kept the Cyclone forward moving everywhere but toward the goal. The forward became so upset at her inability to get past Toka Lee that she kept charging the goal and drawing fouls. By halftime, she had three fouls on her and was sitting on the bench. The news was bad for the Cyclones because they had just lost one of their best shot makers.

By halftime, the Cardinals had a 19–16 lead.

During the ten-minute break, a reporter asked Babe how she felt about being outscored by a pint-sized whirlwind like Doll Harris. The question caught her off guard, and for the first time, she was speechless. When she finally found her voice, she told the reporter, "This game ain't finished yet."

After receiving the halftime report at the Boyet-Long Drug Store, the place lit up with buzzing conversation. A phone rang every second, it seemed, and Mrs. Hamilton, Ginny and Alice's mother, was recruited to help answer. All three Cardinal players, Buena, Alice, and Ginny, finishing their second round of soft drinks, nervously tapped their feet against the tiled floor. They knew Babb was giving his halftime talk, and they hoped it was a good one.

Coach Babb gathered his players around him. He shook their hands, congratulating them on their speed and consistency during second quarter play. He admired their relaxed command of the game.

"Just remember, play against the game, not the team," he said. And then he said something not expected. "Now close your eyes."

Every Cardinal did.

"Picture your best moves. Whatever they are, they aren't your best moves anymore. They're common, everyday moves. Picture what you have to do to win." After a few seconds of silence, he told them to open their eyes. Across from Lucille, Vick was grinning like the Cheshire cat. Doll looked indomitable, and even ice-queen Coral seemed changed by Babb's words.

Teamwork wins games, he reminded them again before letting them go because the second half was about to start.

Lucille walked to center court for the third-quarter jump off. Mansfield stalked into position opposite Lucille. None of the Cyclones liked being on the losing end of this back-and-forth game. Mansfield hunched in closer to Lucille, trying to intimidate the much younger player. Lucille didn't pay attention. By this point in the game, she'd gotten her nerves in check and now her only goal was to connect with the ball. Even so, she missed the jump.

During the third quarter, the Cyclones regained the lead. Babe took control. Her teammates kept feeding her the ball, and she would make the shot. After she hit a perfect layup, her arms went straight up in a victory salute, and her fans roared. Her skillful display had paid off. At the end of the third quarter, the Dallas Golden Cyclones were ahead by seven points. The fans were on their feet for the rest of the night.

The standing crowd grew stone silent as the two centers met for the fourth quarter opening tip-off. This time, Lucille's fingertips caught the ball first. She launched it to Coral, who passed off to Doll. Lucille flew down the court and caught the pass from Doll for a running layup. When the Cyclones drove for the goal, Teny stole the ball and sent it speeding crosscourt and right into Doll's hands. Doll was immediately fouled and then sank both free throws.

Again, the Cardinal defense prevented the Cyclones from scoring. Vick stuck to Stratton like chewing gum and, laying claim to the ball, tried to wrestle it away from the bigger girl. Instead of calling a foul on Vick, the referee declared the struggle a stalemate and ordered a jump-off. Vick put Stratton off balance, and even though she was four inches shorter than the Cyclone center, she won the jump. But the Cyclone guards stole the ball back anyway and scored. They now led, 27–26. Then, after a sloppy pass down court, the ball spun loose, causing gold Cyclone suits to meet Cardinal red in a brawling mix-up. Vick dove for the ball and came up with it. The crowd shouted approval. She passed it crosscourt to Coral who shot it back to Lucille, standing in her favorite keyhole position. Flexing her knees, she bounced the ball against the backboard and into the basket. The Cardinals led by one.

With four minutes left to play, the Cyclones took possession and did the only thing they could. They slowed down the game, completing several passes before being fouled. Babe made two points at the free-throw line, and the score was 30–29, Cyclones.

Two minutes remained. Doll called a time-out and then limped to the sidelines. Was she reinjured? The crowd grew quiet. Babb looked at her with elevated eyebrows, and she shrugged. Just like against Wichita, when the momentum needed changing, Doll used her skills learned in the dramatic club at school and put on an act. Babb rubbed her knee to keep up the ruse and then whispered, "Crank it up." She shook out her leg, bent down and touched her toes, stood back up, and nodded at Babb. When she ran back on court, she wasn't limping. The crowd cheered.

"Crank it up," Doll told Coral and Lucille.

In an instant, Coral scored.

A second later, the ball returned to the Cardinals' forwards without a counterscore from the Cyclones. Lucille fired in another two points. The Cardinals led, 33–30. The fans were screaming. Everyone loved the comeback Cardinals.

The Cyclones shook their heads, bewildered by the Cardinals' successive field goals. Forgetting that they were in a game that required skilled footwork and fast handoffs, they passed the ball around like schoolkids on recess. Twice the Cyclones got open to shoot, and twice the ball rolled around the rim of the basket and then dropped outside. The next instant, out of nowhere, Babe squirmed into position and hit a stunning, impossible shot. Suddenly her team, with minutes left, was back in the game.

Ignoring the tumultuous crowd, Toka Lee snatched the rebound and passed it off to Vick, who heaved it straight across the court to Doll. This time, her defender didn't commit a foul. Doll gave a sharp pass to Lucille, who sent the ball to Coral, and they continued the passing game until seconds were left. Then Lucille, stretching up to her full height, sank a perfect field shot. The Cyclones scrambled to take the ball back down court. Just as Babe touched the basketball, the final gun fired.

Sixteen-year-old Lucille gazed at the bellowing crowd and then at the scoreboard that read 35–32. Everyone seemed to be moving in silent, slow motion. She could barely hear the uproar. Her eyes were stinging with tears as she watched Toka Lee and Doll jump into each other's arms. Dr. Hotchkin pumped Babb's hand up and down, and Maria Hotchkin gave him a tight hug. All at once, it had come down to this moment, and they were in it.

Back in Durant, a telephone jangled at Boyet-Long Drug Store. Eight people jumped to answer, but Mrs. Hamilton reached the receiver first. She listened for a couple of minutes, hung up the receiver, and then proceeded to torture the others by not saying a word. After a few seconds, she couldn't hold the news any longer. When they heard the final score, Ginny, Alice, and Buena leaped out of the soda-fountain chairs, spilling their third round of drinks across the sparkling white counter. No one raced to clean it up. But the phone lines wouldn't stop ringing. It seemed as if the whole town had decided to call. Who won? By how much? When are they coming home? At the end of the night, after things had quieted down, those manning the phones calculated that they'd received over one thousand calls in two hours.

At the Shreveport Coliseum, the Cardinals ran to their coach and circled their arms around him. Babb's usually stern face and quiet manner were replaced with an impossibly broad grin and bright eyes. Lucille still couldn't believe that it was her own team receiving this thunderous applause, the Cardinals that had won it all.

Fifteen minutes later, AAU officials set up a display of trophies for the top three teams, silver and gold basketball charms for the top teams' players, and pins for the soon-to-be-named All-Americans on a wooden table facing a microphone in mid-court. The officials presented the third-place trophy to the Southern Kansas Stage Lines and the second-place trophy to the Cyclones. The Cardinals, dressed in their warm-up pants and new red-wool OPC sweaters, received their AAU national championship trophy. Sitting atop a black, circular base, the art deco–style trophy, about three feet tall, showed two bronze women, apparently playing at center position, standing on tiptoes facing each other and reaching high for the bronze basketball right at their fingertips. Every team member, even those not on the traveling squad, would receive golden basketball charms. As the team's captain, Doll accepted a dozen red roses. She blushed when the AAU official handed her the flowers. Crowd members hooted and hollered their approval as Doll turned and waved at the fans.

The Cardinals gathered around Babb, who held their first-place trophy in both arms. Each player stole a moment staring at a prize no other Oklahoma women's basketball team or any women's college team had ever won. They all seemed bewitched. No one was listening to the final announcements of the evening, that is, until someone called Doll's name.

The announcer had to repeat her name.

Doll handed her roses to Toka Lee and sauntered out to receive her All-American award for the second year in a row. But the second announcement caught her by surprise. Doll was named captain of the 1932 AAU All-American team.

Lucille watched her teammate step into the spotlight. She'd never thought in a million years that she'd be here, and certainly not as a national champion. She began to rerun the game in her mind—the missed opening tip, the Cardinals' expert teamwork, Babe's crowd-pleasing moves, the

At the national championship in Shreveport. Babe Didrikson is second from left in the top row; the four All-American Cardinals are in the front row. Front row left to right: *Coral Worley, Lucille Thurman, Hazel Vickers, and Doll Harris.*

momentum leaving the Cyclones and the Cardinals regaining it again and again. Then the memory of her sinking the final game basket and securing the win for her team —she'd forgotten about it completely.

"Lucille . . ." She felt a hand on her arm and looked up into Babb's eyes.

"It's your turn."

"What?"

"They've called your name. You're an All-American."

Lucille shook her head. Babb nodded yes. He gave her arm a little tug. She stood up. He gave her a push. She saw seven other women standing before her, all world-class players, including Doll Harris and Babe Didrikson. She walked up to the announcer who handed her the tiny gold pin and the embroidered All-American patch with the AAU red, white, and, blue logo, and she started to cry.

"Hazel Vickers," the announcer called, then: "Coral Worley."

Lucille's heart leaped upon hearing her best friend's name. Her tears ceased. Suddenly she was back home in Cookietown, the smell of eggs and bacon sizzling, buttermilk biscuits fresh out of the oven, coffee boiled thick and strong, the comforting mumble of her mother and father talking quietly together before calling the family to breakfast. Lucille shivered. She didn't feel like an All-American. She felt like the country girl she was.

"Ladies and gentlemen," the announcer thundered into the microphone, "here they are—the Amateur Athletic Association's 1932 All-Americans."

CHAPTER 15

A Hometown Welcome

Aunt Lucy fidgeted, trying to adjust her corset while standing on the corner of Broadway and Jackson Street in Hugo, Oklahoma. The undergarment was bunching along the sides because she had dressed in a hurry this morning. A hundred others had gathered along the Jackson Street walkways, and every one of them had stopped by and greeted her with a bright "hello."

Last night, after the Cardinals won the championship, Babb and Dr. Hotchkin had spent hours in a clandestine huddle with other supporters and on the telephone with Aunt Lucy making arrangements for a parade down Main Street when the Cardinals arrived back in Durant. It would be a big surprise. Aunt Lucy's job was to gather the players left behind—Buena, Alice, Ginny, Susie, and Allene—and get them to Hugo by 10:30 a.m. where they would meet up with the others on their way back from Shreveport. Named after French novelist Victor Hugo, the town stood fifty miles east of Durant along Highway 70 and would serve as a staging area before the parade.

With her girls gathered around, Aunt Lucy stood waiting in front of the corner drugstore, as instructed by her brother over the phone early this morning. Twenty members of a marching band sat in the back of an open-air military truck parked nearby. Everyone waited, stretching their necks and looking for the first appearance of the three cars carrying the national champions, due to arrive any minute.

Those passing through town on their way to other cities saw the crowd and stopped their cars. When they heard what the festivity was all about, most decided to take the day off and head to Durant.

After what seemed like hours but was only minutes, someone with a bullhorn assigned to stand watch at the edge of town spotted Babb's roadster speeding along in the distance. He called out to another man posted closer to town, and he in turn informed the crowd. Cheers erupted, and with their instruments glinting in the sun, the band started playing "Boomer Sooner."

Babb arrived first. Without hesitating, he sprang out of his car and waved over the other drivers, Bo-Peep and Lera, who brought their automobiles to a jolting halt. Car doors opened all at once, and squeals erupted when the second-string players, plus a fluttering Aunt Lucy, poured across the sidewalk to greet the road-weary champions. While they hugged and chattered in excited, breathless words, others joined in, and soon the gathering was a celebration. When the Hotchkins pulled up, Dr. Hotchkin said that he hated to break up the fun, but there was a parade waiting for them back home in Durant. It was time to get a move on.

After changing into their bright red uniforms, the Cardinals piled into the three matching convertible Cadillac Fleetwoods provided by a local bank president. Securing her hair with one of her trademark ribbons, Doll sat next to Toka Lee in the front seat. Bo-Peep, Alice, and Buena scrunched together in the back. The remaining twelve Cardinals distributed themselves among the other two deep burgundy, luxury automobiles with whitewalled tires, shiny chrome headlights, and hood ornaments that looked like flying angels. Pulling out onto the highway, they followed the truck

Homecoming, fall 1932. The Cardinals pose with members of OPC's pep squad. Coral Worley is standing at the highest point. The three girls facing the camera below her are (left to right) *Doll Harris, Hazel Vickers, and Lucille Thurman. Virginia Hamilton is standing, dressed in her uniform, next to the car door. Sitting on the hood,* left to right: *Buena Harris, Irene Williams, La Homa Lassiter (behind Irene), unknown.*

carrying the band, now playing "Hot Time in the Old Town Tonight." Babb and Aunt Lucy rode with the Hotchkins.

Lucille sat next to Coral in the front seat of the second Cadillac. She felt giddy riding in the convertible and feeling the wind thrash her ears. Finally, when the car entered Durant and the highway turned into Main Street, Lucille and everyone else sat wide-eyed and severely impressed. Like a dream, everything seemed too perfect to be true.

Three other marching bands were waiting to join in along with horseback riders showing off their best gear, automobiles carrying town dignitaries including the mayor, and an OPC float featuring cheerleaders and the pep squad. Declaring an official holiday, businesses on Main Street closed shop so that employees could enjoy themselves. This was not a normal, peaceful parade like those celebrating Thanksgiving Day or a college homecoming. It was a carnival, with the sugary smell of cotton candy and snow cones thick in the air.

From bootblacks to bankers, newsboys, kids, and older folks, an ocean of people stood on both sides of the street, all jostling each other to get a better look at the famous athletes. Big, little, poor, rich, old, young, ignorant, and educated, they had come from miles around, including neighboring Texas and Arkansas. Applause, cheers, whistles, cries of "welcome home heroes" sounded like sweet, boisterous music along with the marching bands. Numerous crowd members waved flags and held homemade signs that read, WE LOVE YOU, CARDS, PRIDE OF OKLAHOMA, and OUR GIRLS ARE UNBEATABLE.

Rolls of tickertape, springing from the throng, soared overhead like joyful snakes, trailing across the parade route in colorful waves. Someone rich was throwing Indian head nickels. One plopped into Lucille's lap. Another hit Coral's ear. She handed it to Lucille, who stuck the coins into her pocket.

The other players grinned and waved, shook hands with those that ran up to the cars, and yelled at friends spotted in the crowd. Several excited fans, mostly young girls, jogged along with the Cadillacs and begged autographs from the national champions.

When Lera and Vera, sitting in the backseat of Lucille's car, spotted their brother Orvis in the crowd, a tall, freckle-faced college man with carrot-colored hair, the twins leaped up and screamed. La Homa, who was sitting in between them, had to grab Vera's arm to keep her from toppling out of the backseat.

When the cars finally reached the end of Main Street, they turned left toward Campus Park at Southeastern State Teachers College, where giant magnolia trees grew in thick groves. A reception area had been set up where the players were able to talk with fans, sign more autographs, and be interviewed by reporters from as far away as Oklahoma City and Dallas.

Lucille was asked to tell the story of the Cardinals' big win over and over, and each time Babe Didrikson became more wicked and Lucille more heroic. By the end of the day, her throat was sore, but she felt ecstatic. This was how life should be.

TWO WEEKS LATER, Doll ought to have been studying for final exams. Instead, she was sitting on her bed and pasting keepsakes into her scrapbook. The Associated Press had named her the best female basketball player in America. Last year, Babe Didrikson won that honor. Doll's picture appeared on the front page of the sports section with the following caption underneath:

> Doll Harris, new queen of the country's girl basketball players, is shown above with the cup awarded the Oklahoma Presbyterian College Cardinals . . . Doll led the Cardinals to victory in the finals over the Golden Cyclones of Dallas, Tex. She was named captain of the All-American team.

Since the parade, she had received Western Union telegrams, postcards, and letters, some containing newspaper articles about the Cardinals. Some of the letters and postcards were from fans. One came from a man in Connecticut and said that if she was ever in Hartford to give him a call.

"A Listener" from Detroit wrote on a postcard: "Hello Ollie [*sic*]: Just listened to your broadcast from KWKH. More power to the girls from Oklahoma Presbyterian College."

Other letters asked for her autograph and included return postage.

And some letters came from her relatives. "Piss Aunt" Pauline wrote, "I'd have given three farms in Arkansas to have seen [the championship] game."

It took all her willpower to put away her book of memories and start studying. In two weeks, she and her teammates would be leaving school for summer vacation. They all had big plans.

• • •

THE SUMMER OF 1932, Amelia Earhart became the first woman to fly solo across the Atlantic. She took off from Newfoundland and fifteen hours later landed in an Irish sheep pasture. For her record-breaking efforts, New York City held a welcome-home ticker-tape parade, and President Hoover honored her with a celebration at the White House.

Babe Didrikson astounded the world with her track-and-field performance at the Olympic Games in Los Angeles. She won two gold medals, in the javelin and hurdles, and a silver in the high jump. Sportswriters labeled her the greatest female athlete of all time.

Meanwhile, Vick was working in the fields with her father, eliminating the thick-growing sunflowers and morning glories that were threatening to strangle his thriving cotton crop. She carried a cumbersome hoe down each row, chopping at the tangled weeds. Every second row, she stopped to file a sharp edge back onto the hoe, getting runny cuts on her hands in the process. She wrapped her wounds in a ragweed cloth to stop the bleeding and prevent infection and then continued to work. Her father paid her one dollar a day, and by the end of summer she had earned enough money to cover her school expenses and purchase new Converse high-topped shoes.

Every morning, Lera and Vera were up before daylight, feeding the livestock on their father's ranch. First, they fed the chickens and guineas and gathered their eggs. When the sun was just peeking over the horizon, they scattered corn and soybean meal on the ground for hundreds of noisy turkeys. Near midmorning, they loaded up their father's battered Ford truck with hay and drove down the bumpy, rutted dirt road that wound throughout the cow pastures. Lera always drove while Vera sat in the back and pitched out the hay.

La Homa spent the summer in her mother's kitchen, hulling peas, shucking corn, and boiling tomatoes and peaches to loosen their peelings for canning. She often ate the sweet corn raw because it tasted like candy. Every morning in July, she gathered a gallon of blackberries and made two batches of sugary jam, which she planned to give to her friends at Christmas.

Lucille also worked on her parents' farm, milking their seven cows morning and evening. On weekends, Coral would visit. Lucille's neighbor owned quarter horses and gave permission to the two college girls to exercise them. Coral could ride anything, even green-broke colts. She would touch the skittish horse on his soft, warm nose, run her hand down its neck, and then leap on its back, and they would race across the pasture.

Doll spent June at Toka Lee's home in Pryor, Oklahoma, near Tulsa, where they held a two-week basketball clinic for high school girls. Fifty girls from around the county paid five dollars apiece to attend.

Doll left Pryor for her hometown in July. She took the bus from Tulsa to Chickasha, where her older sister, Verdie, picked her up in their father's old Model T. It often backfired at stop signs, spewing oily black smoke.

During their nineteen-mile drive home, Doll told Verdie that it was high time that she took control of her life. She was going to change her name officially to Doll, leaving the dreaded Velma Bell behind forever.

"Good for you." Verdie smiled.

Babb married Atha Segroves at her parents' house in Ardmore. Afterward, they spent their honeymoon in Chickasha visiting Babb's older brother John and his wife, Sadie, along with other relatives and friends. They spent the rest of the summer in Mangum, where Babb's brother Ray lived. Even though Babb's siblings welcomed Atha into their family, they whispered to each other that she had "big shoes to fill" when they compared her to Babb's beloved first wife, Mata.

The next fall, after school started, Babb got a phone call that caused Atha to chirp with excitement. The world-famous Babe Didrikson wanted to come to Durant, play for the Cardinals, and attend college. Babb told her that she could come by anytime and check out his psychology class to get a real taste of college life. She would have to study hard if she wanted to catch up with the other students.

Babe Didrikson arrived in Durant without fanfare, stayed for a brief tour, and left just as quietly. She never came back. Rumors spread that Babb had told her that she wouldn't be given any special treatment and

DURANT HAS EYES ON THAT NATIONAL CHAMPIONSHIP

From left to right: *Hazel Vickers, Ernestine Lampson, Lucille Thurman, Coral Worley, Toka Lee Fields. Doll Harris is holding the basketball.*

that she would have to compete against Doll, Lucille, and Coral for a spot on the first string. That alone was supposed to have sent her packing. Later that year, Babe lost her amateur standing and was suspended from competition by the AAU because she had helped a Dallas automobile dealer with his summer sales and posed in photographs that appeared in newspaper ads. She never played competitive basketball again. But this setback didn't stop her. She went on to become a sensation on the golf course and the leading female player of the 1940s and '50s.

At the start of the new basketball season, Lloyd Gregory, the renowned sports editor of the *Houston Post-Dispatch*, wrote about the Cardinals in his column called Looking 'Em Over, saying that the girls on the Presbyterian squad are as "pretty and attractive a group as you'll see anywhere. And their speed and grace are amazing." When he asked Babb to describe his players, Babb said, "They are just a bunch of country girls who like to play basketball." Every girl, he said, worked her way through college by washing dishes, sweeping, or waiting tables. "They are a fine group of girls."

To Babb, all that mattered was helping his players learn to rule themselves on the basketball court and in real life. Secretly, though, he dreamed of glory and what great heights the Cardinals would attain. There was no telling.

Epilogue

August 25, 2003

At the Special Events Center in the National Cowboy and Western Heritage Museum in Oklahoma City, those who knew the Cardinals all started to find each other. Eighty-nine-year-old Virginia Hamilton Childers, who looked regal wearing a black evening dress with dollops of turquoise and pink, still lived in Durant and had traveled with her daughter to receive tonight's award. Other OPC Cardinal family members had come from Texas, Arkansas, and Hawaii.

The Oklahoma Sports Hall of Fame was holding its annual awards ceremony to induct new members. Everyone was keeping an eye out for the actor Dennis Weaver, famous for *Gunsmoke*, *McCloud*, and the movie *Duel*. He would introduce John Jacobs, track coach at the University of Oklahoma from 1922 to 1968. Weaver had been one of his star athletes. Other inductees included Dale McNamara, a pioneer in women's collegiate golf; Kenny Monday, the Olympic wrestler; and Sean O'Grady, world champion boxer. The Oklahoma Sports Hall of Fame was also honoring the Oklahoma Presbyterian College Cardinals basketball team from Durant, Oklahoma, as its first Team of Legend.

1958 Cardinal reunion. The former players are sitting on the steps of OPC's administration building. Back row left to right: *Gwen Hamilton, Ernestine Lampson, Alice Hamilton, La Homa Lassiter, Lucille Thurman, unknown;* front row left to right: *Juanita Parks, Virginia Hamilton, unknown, unknown.*

Getting ready to find her assigned seat before the ceremony, Virginia was chatting with Lera Dunford Chadwick, Thelma Worley Smith, and La Celia Henderson, La Homa Lassiter Carlton's daughter. La Homa didn't feel well and had stayed at home in Houston. Bo-Peep's daughters, Ann Wright and Carol Jean Shook, introduced themselves and joined in the conversation. Wright, a former U.S. Army colonel who had just retired from the State Department, was organizing a breakfast celebration for all the Cardinal relatives the next morning.

Minutes later, Doll's older sister, Verdie, arrived. Although she attended the event in a wheelchair, she stood up to shake hands. She was there to represent Doll, who had passed away just two years earlier. Taking on the job of team historian, Virginia had organized a few reunions over the years. None of the Cardinals had seen each other since their fifty-year reunion in Durant in 1983. Lucille, Vick, Coral, Teny, and the Dunford twins had always shown up, usually with their husbands. Doll and Toka Lee were the only players who never came.

After Doll had graduated from OPC in 1933, she accepted a position as the girls' athletic director and basketball coach at Pasadena High School near Houston, Texas. When she discovered that an assistant's position was available, she recommended Toka Lee, and the two best friends moved to Texas where they both became very popular teachers and mentors. They remained good friends throughout their lives.

Doll Harris Forrest on the bleachers of the sports field named after her, 1991

Doll married Bill Forrest in 1935. In 1950, they moved from Pasadena to Deer Park, another Houston suburb, where Doll continued her teaching career. A year later, Texas sportswriters named Doll, along with Babe Didrikson, as one of the best Texas women basketball players. In 1999, Oklahoma sportswriters recognized Doll by including her in the All Century Women's College basketball team. Doll retired from teaching in 1978. Expressing its gratitude for her valuable contribution, Deer Park Schools named a new athletic field after her.

After leaving OPC, Lera, Vera, and Vick had joined a brand-new professional women's basketball team in Cassville, Missouri, called the

All-American World Champion Girls' Basketball Club. One evening, for fun, all the team members dyed their hair to match Lera and Vera's bright red color. Their red hair was so popular, the team's name was changed to the All-American World Champion Redheads. Vick retired from the Redheads in 1939 to coach high school basketball in Oklahoma. When World War II began, she informed her school superintendent that she was going to California to build airplanes at Lockheed, to help the war effort. She stayed out west, got married, and was a schoolteacher for many years.

La Homa started teaching high school in 1935 in Mangum, her hometown. That didn't last long. Bart Carlton—the same handsome basketball player for Oklahoma City whom she had swooned over when the Cardinals had watched his team lose in that contentious game against Wichita—asked her to marry him, and they settled in Tulsa. They had met by chance in 1934. Bart continued playing basketball and was considered one of the best players in the AAU.

Lera Dunford Chadwick and Vera Dunford Hatcher, 2003

After graduation, Coral Worley joined Doll and Toka Lee in Pasadena, Texas, teaching school and coaching basketball. She also played for Babb, who had been hired by the Moody Club in Galveston, Texas, to coach its basketball team, the Anicos. Coral left Texas in 1937 and returned to her hometown, Cache. There, she worked as a teacher until the beginning of World War II, when she joined the civil service, serving in Ohio and California. When the war ended, she accepted a position as

FORMER TEAMMATES MEET AS RIVALS

TWO OLD TEAMMATES, now rivals in the women's national basketball tournament, greeted each other warmly at the Allis last night as they were quartered in preparation for the championship play. Doll Harris, left, former captain and all-national star of the Durant Cardinals, now with Pasadena, is shown with Lucille Thurman, present captain of the Cardinals, defending their title, representing Oklahoma City university.

From left to right: *Doll Harris and Lucille Thurman, 1934*

treasurer of Reynolds Army Hospital in Fort Sill, Oklahoma, so that she could be near her sister, Thelma. Coral died in 1987.

Out of all the Cardinal players, Lucille stuck with basketball the longest. She played for the Lion Oil basketball team, and then moved to Little Rock, Arkansas, and joined the Lewis and Norwood Flyers, a top AAU team. She was elected to the All-American team every year until she retired in 1939. Her statistics proved her to be one of the most outstanding female basketball players in the 1930s. Lucille married James Berry in April 1939. She died in 1990 and was survived by her husband, a son, a daughter, and two grandchildren. She was among the first women inducted into the Helms Athletic Hall of Fame in Los Angeles and was the first woman admitted into the Arkansas Athletes Roll of Honor Hall of Fame.

Now, at the Oklahoma Sports Hall of Fame ceremony, the whole team would finally receive acclaim. After attendees took their seats, the house lights darkened and the master of ceremonies introduced Lynne Draper, founder of the Jim Thorpe Association and creator of football's Jim Thorpe Award. He briefly told the audience about the new award being initiated tonight that would honor an outstanding sports team.

Brent Skarky, sports anchor for KOCO, the ABC affiliate in Oklahoma

City, then presented his video about the Oklahoma Presbyterian College Cardinals, a scrappy team from a tiny girls' junior college, and their victories achieved under the dire circumstances of the Dust Bowl and Great Depression: between March 1931 and March 1934, the Cardinals won eighty-nine consecutive games, including two consecutive Women's National AAU Basketball Championships. In June 1933, they beat the world-champion Canadians, the Edmonton Commercial Graduates, three in a row, playing in Edmonton. They represented North America in the Women's World Games held in 1934 in London, England. Lucille proudly carried the American flag in the opening ceremonies.

After the introduction, the house lights came up, and every player's name was called to receive her award. Except for Virginia and Lera, who were the only team members present, family members accepted the trophy that had the sports hall of fame logo engraved in crystal. The base contained the names of all the Cardinals along with the designation that would go down in history: Team of Legend.

In the midst of America's worst drought and financial depression, Babb had found college scholarships for all his players. Then he performed the perfect screen—in basketball terms—that opened up a path to victory: he placed himself in the way of poverty, discrimination, and politics so that all his players could gain an education, earn recognition, and play a sport they loved. In turn, every Cardinal stepped out of her comfort zone and

Virginia Hamilton Childers with the author, 2002

embraced adventure. They became coaches and teachers, respected community leaders, and mothers.

Soon after she was married, Lucille received a letter from a school principal who insisted that basketball was too strenuous for growing girls. She replied that, on the contrary, it helped girls develop "clean habits; the know-how of taking a loss and the thrills of winning; the stamina and stick-to-itiveness necessary to become a success at any job; the control of temper; and the ability to think and plan." For Lucille, her teammates, and the other young women who challenged society's norms to pursue their dreams, basketball had given them not only confidence and drive but also the tools to succeed. And these farm girls, who at one time never thought of lives beyond the cotton fields, got to be heroes.

Acknowledgments

WHEN I DECIDED TO investigate the history of my great uncle, Sam Babb, and the OPC Cardinals, I asked my parents, Jerry and Lee Reeder, for help. This book could not have been written without their expertise, enthusiasm, and support. We set out driving down I-35 toward Durant, Oklahoma, in the middle of a terrible drought. Somehow the dire weather seemed fitting. We ended up in the Durant Public Library on Main Street, and when it looked like we were going to come up empty-handed, Mother asked a very nice librarian if she knew about the OPC Cardinals.

"Of course," she said.

She picked up the telephone and called Virginia Hamilton Childers, who invited us to her home not far from the library. Defying the hot, dry weather, beautiful prize-winning irises of all colors lined her drive and spread throughout her yard. She asked us in right away. It turned out that Virginia was the only Cardinal who had stayed in Durant, and she organized the former team's reunions. She also had become the team's chronicler, having written articles for the newspaper and local history books about the Cardinals and OPC. She gave us generous access to her own scrapbook, brimming with newspaper articles, letters, and other memorabilia. With Virginia's help, we contacted the Dunford twins, La Homa Lassiter, and Hazel Vickers, along with the families of Lucille Thurman, Doll Harris, Toka Lee Fields, and Buena Harris.

Oklahoma Presbyterian College closed its doors in 1966. During our visit to Durant, we discovered that in 1975 Chief David Gardner located the headquarters of the Choctaw Nation in the former OPC buildings, which seemed fitting. The history and grounds have been well preserved, and the headquarters still resides in the redbrick buildings.

Telling this story depended on the heartfelt sharing of many family histories. Lucille Thurman Berry's daughter, Cindy, sent her mother's unpublished autobiography and stories Lucille had written about her time with the Cardinals. In addition, I am indebted to other Cardinal players and family members who generously offered memories, letters, and scrapbooks: Hazel Vickers Cone; La Homa Lassiter Carlton and her daughter, La Celia Carlton Henderson; Lera Dunford Chadwick; Vera Dunford Hatcher; and Margaret Seaton, who shared knowledge of her friend and mentor, Doll Harris. Also: James A. Berry, David Chadwick, Dennis and Betty Chadwick, Patsy Morris, John H. Murphy, Wanda Roberts, Deanna Shelton, Carol Jean Shook, Mary Skaggs, Shirley Smith, Thelma Worley Smith, and Carol White.

Thank you to W. Lynne Draper for his encouragement and recognition of the Cardinals as a Team of Legend awarded by the Oklahoma Sports Hall of Fame. My aunt, Jann Byford, a tall girl who played half-court ball in high school, read my manuscript early on and made sure that I got the technical parts of playing by girls' rules right. And I couldn't have gotten by without help and encouragement from my sister, Rosalind Reeder, and my husband, Andy Newberg.

I also wish to thank the Galveston Moody Club, Oklahoma City University Library Archives and Special Collections, Bill Welge and the Oklahoma Historical Society Newspaper Archives, the Shreve Memorial Library (Shreveport, Louisiana), Presbyterian Historical Society, University of Oklahoma Archives, and the Wichita Public Library Archives. Jeffrey Monseau, college archivist at Springfield College, searched the American Alliance for Health, Physical Education, Recreation and Dance Collection and found information vital to this story.

The writing of this story started out more than a decade ago. Liz and Ric Satriano read everything that I wrote and gave me invaluable criticism.

I would also like to thank Denise Vega for her thorough critique sessions early on. John Glassie provided invaluable writing and storytelling expertise.

A very special thanks goes to my amazing agent, Mackenzie Brady, who quickly saw the potential of this story. She guided me in the rewriting of my proposal and read through my manuscript drafts, helping me to bring the narrative voice to life.

I am also very grateful to my editor at Algonquin Books, Andra Miller. Her clear recommendations and detailed edits showed that she adored the adventurous young women in the story as much as I did. In addition, I am indebted to my awesome copy editor, Jude Grant.

Finally, I want to thank my grandmother, Lydia Babb Thomas. As a result of her diligent research and subsequent letter-writing campaign, her favorite brother, Sam, was posthumously inducted into the Oklahoma Athletic Hall of Fame in 1978. Years later, not long before she died at the age of ninety-one, she handed me a worn, yellowed folder stuffed with old newspaper articles, letters, and photographs of Sam and the Cardinals.

"For safekeeping," she said. "You might want to tell their story."

Notes

MUCH OF THE MATERIAL in this book about my great-uncle, Sam Babb, comes from family history and stories passed down to subsequent generations from his many siblings, including my grandmother. In addition, dialogue and personal stories depicted throughout were drawn from scrapbooks compiled by Doll Harris, Lucille Thurman, and Virginia Hamilton, which were stuffed with memorabilia from almost every game, including all of the road trips. Unfortunately, many of the scrapbook materials, particularly newspaper articles, were somewhat haphazardly clipped and did not contain author names, dates, pages, and in some cases it was impossible to determine even which newspaper an article came from. Moreover, the extensive newspaper archives for the *Durant Daily Democrat* located at the Oklahoma Historical Society did not include papers from March 8, 1930, to December 23, 1932. The only record of the months I needed was in the scrapbook clippings. While I have tried to provide complete publication information in the notes, it has not always been possible, and sometimes articles are cited simply by title alone. Ellipses in article titles indicate omissions from where the original articles were torn.

Lucille loved to write and kept several diaries during her time at school; her unpublished autobiography, "The Way the Ball Bounces! Or Swish Went the Net! Or My Name Is in the Hall of Fame," was a valuable resource. In addition, she wrote a twelve-page story about her time with Babb, "About Sam F. Babb, Coach of the Cardinals," sent to my grandmother and the Oklahoma Athletic Hall of Fame in 1978. In 2001 and 2002, I was fortunate to conduct personal interviews with Virginia Hamilton Childers,

Thelma Worley Smith (Coral's sister), Hazel Vickers Cone, La Homa Lassiter Carlton, Lera Dunford Chadwick, and Vera Dunford Hatcher.

Chapter 1

The matchup between Cement and Fletcher, as well as the description of Doll's family life, was gleaned from her scrapbook and saved writings from her senior yearbook, which also included letters from classmates and her report card. Scrapbook newspaper clippings titled "Coach Daily Sums Up Year's Basketball Play," 1930, and "Nine-Year Trail of Bulldog Teams Given" were also in the scrapbook. In addition, the Cement Museum and Jesse James Visitor Center provided a wealth of local color, photographs, and general information about the town before and during the Great Depression. A letter to Doll from Coach Daily described how he had arranged her meeting with Babb, and I assembled her conversation with Babb about OPC from interviews with other players who had the same experience, including Hazel Vickers Cone and La Homa Lassiter Carlton.

The description of western Oklahoma during the Depression, including the squirrel-hunting story, came from my father, who grew up on a farm near Duncan, Oklahoma, in the 1930s and '40s. General descriptions of the drought and Depression in western Oklahoma is vividly portrayed in Kenneth E. Hendrickson Jr., ed., *Hard Times in Oklahoma: The Depression Years* (Oklahoma City: Oklahoma Historical Society, 1983); and Pat Bellmon, "The Passing of Grit: Observations of a Farm Girl, Now a Spectator on the Land," in *The Culture of Oklahoma*, ed. Howard F. Stein and Robert F. Hill (Norman, Oklahoma, 1993), 186–97.

Chapter 2

The description of Babb's car and his driving ability came from interviews with former players and from John H. Murphy's memory of riding in his roadster after Babb moved to Galveston. Sue Harris Conway, the sister of OPC Cardinal Buena Harris, commented about Babb looking like a rich man in a phone interview in 2003.

The Cement area attracted many outlaws, and the Cement Museum and Jesse James Visitor Center offers stories and local color about that history. You can find more information about the outlaw gold hidden in the Keechi Hills on the NewsOK website, http://ndepth.newsok.com/treasurehunters (accessed January 19, 2014), and on other sites about treasure hunting.

My description of Doll and her family life is drawn from her scrapbooks and letters.

The lives of sharecroppers and tenant farmers during the Depression went from bad to worse, and I based my descriptions on Donald W. Whisenhunt, "We've Got the Hoover Blues: Oklahoma Transiency in the Days of the Great Depression," in *Hard Times in Oklahoma: The Depression Years*, ed. Kenneth E. Hendrickson Jr. (Oklahoma City: Oklahoma Historical Society, 1983), 101–14; and the website of the Oklahoma Historical Society, Encyclopedia of Oklahoma History and Culture, "Tenant Farming and Sharecropping," http://www.okhistory .org/publications/enc/entry.php?entry=TE009 (accessed February 11, 2014).

Babb's life on the farm and the description of how he lost his leg was based on my family's history and stories passed down from my grandmother and other relatives. My description of Babb's teaching comes from his thesis written in 1922 for his master's of science in education, titled "A Local Survey of the Arapaho Public Schools," a bound copy of which I found in the Bizzell Memorial Library at the University of Oklahoma.

Buster McElhaney, the prolific editor of the *Arapaho (OK) Bee*, was the main source for the story of Babb's journey from superintendent to basketball coach in stories published on January 7, 1921; July 29, 1921; December 30, 1921; August 4, 1922; October 20, 1922; October 27, 1922; January 26, 1923; February 2, 1923; March 16, 1923; August 10, 1923; and August 31, 1923.

My brief description of the beginning of women's basketball and the rules developed for women was derived from three main sources: Linda Ford, *Lady Hoopsters: A History of Women's Basketball in America* (Northampton, MA: Half Moon Books, 1999), 18–39; Betty Spears, "Senda Berenson Abbott—New Woman: New Sport," in *A Century of Women's Basketball: From Frailty to Final Four*, ed. Joan S. Hult and Marianna Trekell (Reston, VA: American Alliance for Health, Physical Education, Recreation and Dance, 1991), 19–35; and Susan K. Cahn, *Coming on Strong: Gender and Sexuality in Twentieth-Century Women's Sport* (Cambridge, MA: Harvard University Press, 1994), 83–87. I developed the overview of basketball rules for girls from the famous Byng, Oklahoma, girls' basketball coach during the 1930s and '40s, Bertha Frank Teague, and her book, *Basketball for Girls* (New York: Ronald Press, 1962). Teague sat on the 1978 committee that chose to induct Babb posthumously into the Oklahoma Athletic Hall of Fame.

The winning of the sportsmanship trophy was documented in "Cardinals Awarded N.A.A.U. Sportsmanship Trophy," *Polished Pebbles*, March 1931. I discovered this OPC student publication in Doll's scrapbook.

Chapter 3

Every player interviewed had clear memories of the frigid predawn basketball practice sessions at Southeastern State's field house and contributed to the scene about getting out of bed and getting ready for practice, including descriptions of Aunt Lucy, the old crank-start bus, and the tiny Buzzard's Roost gym. I also drew information from Jim Schneider, "Inducted into Women's Hall of Fame—Conway Woman, All-American Basketball Star, Gets Honor," *Log Cabin Democrat* (Conway, AR), November 26, 1966, 3.

Lucille Thurman's friendship with Coral Worley was described during the interview with Coral's sister, Thelma. OPC instructor Anne Semple's *Ties That Bind: The Story of Oklahoma Presbyterian College* (n.p., n.d., ca. 1957), provided invaluable information about the school.

I gleaned descriptions of Durant from Henry MacCreary, *Queen of Three Valleys: A Story of Durant* (Durant, OK: Democrat Printing, 1946). Information about Durant's economy, including pecans, was obtained from James C. Milligan, L. David Norris, and Ann Vanmeter, *Durant 1872–1990* (Durant, OK: Bryan County Heritage Association, 1990), 52–58.

Babb's coaching style was described in Lucille's writings and in "Victor Murdock Learns How Babb Can Direct Winning Cage Team," *Wichita (KS) Eagle*, after the 1933 AAU tournament.

I obtained the information about federal drought money in C. Roger Lambert "Dust, Farmers, and the Federal Government," in *Hard Times in Oklahoma: The Depression Years*, ed. Kenneth E. Hendrickson Jr. (Oklahoma City: Oklahoma Historical Society, 1983), 68. Information about farm foreclosure and exodus from Oklahoma can be found on the website of the Oklahoma Historical Society, Encyclopedia of Oklahoma History and Culture, "Okie Migrations," http://www.okhistory.org/publications/enc/entry.php?entry=OK008 (accessed February 21, 2014), and under "Great Depression," http://www.okhistory.org/publications/enc/entry.php?entry=GR014 (accessed February 21, 2014).

Chapter 4

The chapter title is a quote from Bertha Teague, *Basketball for Girls* (New York: Ronald Press, 1962), 66.

My description of Durant's Market Square was derived from James C. Milligan, L. David Norris, and Ann Vanmeter, *Durant 1872–1990* (Durant, OK: Bryan

County Heritage Association, 1990), 53–56; and Donovin Arleigh Sprague, *Images of America: Durant* (Charleston, SC: Arcadia Publishing, 2013), 18. My personal visit to downtown Durant; the Downtown Durant Walking Tour (see http:// downtowndurantwalkingtour.wordpress.com [accessed March 6, 2014]); Sprague, *Images of America*, 35, 55–56; and Milligan et al., *Durant 1872–1990*, helped guide me through the town during Doll's run. The Bryan Hotel, visiting dignitaries, and "Pretty Boy" Floyd's visits were described in the USGenWeb Project Oklahoma Archives, Bryan County History, County Seat—Durant, "Historic Bryan Hotel," http://files.usgwarchives.net/ok/bryan/history/towns/bryanhot.txt (accessed March 6, 2014).

The description of the Cardinals' Lions Club luncheon was pasted into the scrapbook provided by Virginia Hamilton Childers from an unknown newspaper; the article was titled "Girls Team of O. P. College Are Honored." Doll's scrapbook contained a clipping of the words to the OPC song. The description of Graham-Jackson Hall comes from my own observation and Ann Semple, *Ties That Bind: The Story of Oklahoma Presbyterian College* (n.p., n.d., ca. 1957), 36.

I found the letter from Toka Lee to Doll in Doll's scrapbook. Letters from Coach Daily and fellow high school students provided most of the background for my portrayal of Doll's childhood.

Statistics about the health of Oklahoma children during the Depression came from D. Clayton Brown, "Hard Times for Children: Disease and Sickness during the Great Depression," in *Hard Times in Oklahoma: The Depression Years*, ed. Kenneth E. Hendrickson (Oklahoma City: Oklahoma Historical Society, 1983), 62–65.

The story about how Doll got her name was described by Verdie Harris Hodges, Doll's older sister. Other insights into Doll's personality were assembled from interviews with her former students and good friends, Margaret Seaton and Joyce Rice. The 1935 article "Doll Harris Says Arkansas Club Will Win Tournament," pasted into her scrapbook from an unknown Texas newspaper, also provided insight into Doll's character.

Chapter 5

When I visited with Virginia at her home in Durant, she explained how she had hunted mushrooms in secret places. The story about Hotchkin's run-in with the train came from *Polished Pebbles*.

Babb's relationship with Hotchkin seemed like father and son, according to those I interviewed and other sources, including clippings from *Polished Pebbles*. Other information about Babb's personality came from family stories. I generalized the contents of Babb's athletic reports from an "Athletic Report" submitted by Babb to the OPC Board of Trustees, May 12, 1931.

I found information about Hotchkin's wonderful sermons, including how he would talk about his mother sometimes, in clipping from unknown newspaper in Doll's scrapbook titled "College at Durant Founded a Century Ago by Missionary: Grandfather of Dr. Hotchkin, Present Head, One of First Whites in Southwest, was Indians' Friend." I was fortunate to find that the Hotchkin family had compiled a marvelous website with family history and scanned letters that helped me tell their incredible history. This website, Descendants of John Hotchkin of Guilford, CT, included information on the following family members: Ebenezer J. Hotchkin, http://hotchkinfamilyhistory.com/p183.htm#i142 (accessed March 10, 2014); Ebenezer Hotchkin, DD, http://hotchkinfamilyhistory.com /p183.htm#i1293 (accessed March 10, 2014); Mary Jane Semple, http://hotchkin familyhistory.com/p335.htm#i1292 (accessed March 10, 2014); Henry W. Hotchkin, http://hotchkinfamilyhistory.com/p192.htm#i1236 (accessed March 10, 2014); and Remembrance of Mary Semple Hotchkin by her and Ebenezer Hotchkin, http://hotchkinfamilyhistory.com/p192.htm#i1236 (accessed March 10, 2014). I also found information about Mary Hotchkin in Gladys Titzck Rhoads and Nancy Titzck Anderson, *McIntire: Defender of Faith and Freedom* (n.p.: Xulon Press, 2012), 572.

The history of Durant, Bryan County, and OPC was gleaned from the US-GenWeb Project, Oklahoma Archives, Bryan County History, County Seat—Durant, "Durant City History," http://files.usgwarchives.net/ok/bryan/history /towns/durant2.txt (accessed March 6, 2014); Virginia Hamilton Childers, "History of the Oklahoma Presbyterian College Cardinal National and North American Basketball Championship Teams," in *Bryan County Genealogy Library, Bryan County History* (Durant, OK: Bryan County Heritage Association, 1983), 68–76; and Clara Nash and Erma L. Taylor, "Bryan Co., OK; Oklahoma and Bryan County History," http://files.usgwarchives.net/ok/bryan/history/bchlhist.txt (accessed March 6, 2014).

Growing up in Oklahoma, I had read stories and visited museum exhibits about the Trail of Tears. I found additional facts and information about that dark part of our nation's history in the following: Len Green, "Choctaw Removal Was Really a 'Trail of Tears,'" http://www.choctawnation.com/history/choctaw -nation-history/ (accessed March 10, 2014); the website of the Oklahoma Historical

Society, Encyclopedia of Oklahoma History and Culture, "American Indians," http://www.okhistory.org/publications/enc/entry.php?entry=AM010 (accessed March 4, 2014); Natalie Morrison Denison, "Missions and Missionaries of the Presbyterian Church, U.S., among the Choctaws 1866–1907," *Oklahoma Historical Society's Chronicles of Oklahoma*, http://revfrankhughesjr.org/images/v024p426 .pdf (accessed March 4, 2014); and Luther B. Hill, A.B., with the assistance of local authorities, *A History of the State of Oklahoma* (Chicago: Lewis Publishing, 1909), 447–48.

Additional information about Durant's early days came from Henry MacCreary, *Queen of Three Valleys: A Story of Durant* (Durant, OK: Democrat Printing, 1946), 1–51, 94–99.

The story about the squabble that ended up with the dynamiting of a home in the public square near Main Street came from the *Indian Chieftain* (Vinita, Indian Territory [OK]), March 3, 1898, 4.

Chapter 6

The description of practice sessions was compiled from my personal interviews with players and also Lucille's writings. A January 15, 1979, letter from John Murphy (friend to Babb and Teny's husband) to John Clift, a reporter for the *Denison (TX) Herald*, talked about Babb's coaching.

During my interviews with the players, they all mentioned Babb's psychology class. I found descriptions of how the subject of psychology was perceived in "Keen Interest Shown in Talk on Psychology," *Warren (PA) Times Mirror*, November 4, 1930, 8; and "Woman's Department Club Hears Dr. W. F. Book of Psychology Department of Indiana U.," *Kokomo (IN) Tribune*, January 18, 1930, 6. La Homa vividly recounted how she asked Babb about being a lady, as well as how she almost didn't go to college because of a mighty hail storm.

To write about the history of women's basketball during the early 1930s, I immersed myself in articles from books, newspapers, and professional journals. My overview of the early oversight of women's athletics was compiled from Joan S. Hult, "The Governance of Athletics for Girls and Women: Leadership by Women Physical Educators, 1899–1948," in *A Century of Women's Basketball: From Frailty to Final Four*, ed. Joan S. Hult and Marianna Trekell (Reston, VA: American Alliance for Health, Physical Education, Recreation and Dance, 1991), 53–82; Reet Howell, ed., *Her Story in Sport: A Historical Anthology of Women in Sports* (West Point, NY: Leisure Press, 1982), 432–36; and George P. Edmonston Jr., "Up Close and Personal: Before Title IX," OSU Alumni History and Traditions, http://www.osualum.com/s/359/index.aspx?sid=359&gid=1&pgid=475 (accessed March 12, 2014).

I found information on the social mores and medical notions about girls playing sports in Howell, *Her Story in Sport*, 244–55 and 437–55 (including the menstruation study by Arnold); The *Encyclopaedia of Sports Medicine: An IOC Medical Commission Publication, Women in Sport*, ed. Barbara L. Drinkwater (New York: John Wiley, 2008), 10–11; Ellen W. Gerber, Jan Felshin, Pearl Berlin, and Waneen Wyrick, eds, *American Women in Sport* (Reading, MA: Addison-Wesley, 1974), 189–209; Ford, *Lady Hoopsters: A History of Women's Basketball in America* (Northampton, MA: Half Moon Books, 1999), 43–62; and Allen Guttman, *Women in Sports: A History* (New York: Columbia University Press, 1991), 135–53. These sources also contained general information about Trilling. I found a fantastic resource about Trilling and the Women's Division in Chris Hartman, "'Health and Fun Shall Walk Hand in Hand': The First 100 Years of Women's Athletics at the University of Wisconsin—Madison," UW–Madison Libraries Archives & Oral History, http://archives.library.wisc.edu/uw-archives/exhibits/athletics/athletics10bt.html (accessed February 26, 2014). See in particular the article's subsections "Blanche Trilling and the Evils of Competition," and 'The Effects of "Play for Play's Sake.'" Trilling's quote about having a sound constitution was also pulled from this resource. "Names," *Capital Times* (Madison, WI), May 24, 1930, 4, reported on Trilling's nameless dancers. Additional information about Trilling came from "Safeguarding Girls' Athletics; College Dean Tells How," *Brooklyn (NY) Daily Eagle*, March 7, 1927, 8; "Athletes, Not Champions, Is Women's Goal: Miss Blanche Trilling Works Out Athletics for All," *Capital Times* (Madison, WI), November 1, 1929, 37; "Game for Every Girl Is Slogan in U. Athletics," *Capital Times* (Madison, WI), March 19, 1930, 3; and "Woman Sports Director Foresees New Era," *Piqua (OH) Daily Call*, May 13, 1932, 12.

General information about the AAU's influence on women's sports came from sources cited above. I obtained more specific information about the AAU and its contentious relationship with the Women's Division in "Women Stars Enter for A.A.U. Athletics with Real Records," *Harrisburg (PA) Telegraph*, November 7, 1931, 4; "Prout Again Chosen as Head of A.A.U.: To Direct Women's Sport," *New York Times*, November 22, 1922, 25; Archives of the National Amateur Athletic Federation, AAHPERD Collection, Springfield College, Springfield, MA, including: Letter from L. Di Benedetto, AAU secretary-treasurer, to Grace Davies, member of the Women's National Basketball Committee, February 16, 1933; letter from Eline von Borries, CWB chairman, to J. Lyman Bingham, assistant to the AAU president, February 16, 1933; letter from Dorothy Folsom, active member of the Illinois Women's Athletic Club of Chicago and the AAU, to von Borries, November 6, 1932; Memorandum of Activities of Women's Athletic Editorial Committee, National Convention of the APEA, April 20–23, 1932; and Associated Press, "Women to Compete in 1932 Olympics: Action of Executive Board Unimportant: President of American Committee Says Girls Are Going to Get Competition They Are Asking for," *Monroe (LA) News-Star*, February 7, 1929, 10.

I found descriptions of Mrs. Hoover's leadership of the Women's Division of the NAAF in Howell, *Her Story in Sport*, 246–47, and her likable demeanor in Sue McNamara, "Mrs. Hoover Chucks Pomposity and Lives as Any Carefree Wife," *Vernon (TX) Daily Record*, November 23, 1929, 5. The most complete resource on the Women's Division, Hoover's oversight, and its prominent members, including Trilling and quotes from her speeches, was Women's Division, National Amateur Athletic Federation, comp. and ed., *Women and Athletics* (New York: A. S. Barnes, 1930). I obtained the quote from Hoover about women's inability to pioneer themselves from p. 69. Contributors included Mrs. Herbert Hoover, Ethel Perrin, Blanche M. Trilling, John R. Tunis, and Agnes R. Wayman; Alice Allene Sefton, *The Women's Division: National Amateur Athletic Federation* (Stanford, CA: Stanford University Press, 1941). This book was dedicated to Lou Henry Hoover. A flustered Women's Division representative commented on the nation's laziness in "Inner Resources," *Bismarck (ND) Tribune*, April 13, 1931, 4.

John R. Tunis, "Women and the Sport Business," *Harper's Magazine*, July 1, 1929, 211–21, was an eyebrow-raising read; and Jerome Holtzman, ed., *No Cheering in the Press Box*, (New York: Henry Holt, 1974), 260–72, provided additional information on Tunis.

The following articles also contributed to specific ideas put forth in the writing of this chapter: "Champion Girl Sprinter Ran for Train: Now Runs with Men at Northwestern," *Ames (IA) Daily Tribune*, April 9, 1931, 3; "Girl Athletes Insist Love of Sport Exists, Brand Olympic Critics 'Bluenoses,'" *Brooklyn (NY) Daily Eagle*, January 4, 1929, 13; "Woman Runner Falls Senseless during Race: Doctor Calls X-Country Competition Harmful to Members of Fair Sex," *Brooklyn (NY) Daily Eagle*, April 21, 1931, 28; "Marks Broken by Texas Girl," *Brownsville (TX) Herald*, July 26, 1931, 24; "Women's Division Speaking on College Campuses" [notice], *Lincoln (NE) Star*, April 23, 1933, 32; "Decries Women Taking Part Publicly in Sports Programs," *Manitowoc (WI) Herald-Times*, April 2, 1931, 7; Lock Morton, Miami Athletic Director, "Morton Muses over Many Rule Changes

Pending in Oklahoma: Eight-Semester Rule, Age Limit, Girl Tournaments and Team Management . . . , *Miami (OK) Daily News-Record*, January 16, 1931, 5; Dr. Morris Fishbein, Editor, Journal of the American Medical Association and of Hygeia, the Health Magazine, "Practical Health Problems: Basketball Menace [*sic*] Girls' Health," *Lubbock (TX) Morning Avalanche*, December 18, 1930, 3; "Basketball Tourneys for Girls Condemned," *New York Times*, April 7, 1930, 32; "Co-Ed Sprinter Gets Varsity Coach's Help," *Ogden (UT) Standard-Examiner*, April 2, 1931, 12; Arthur Dean, "Your Boy and Your Girl: "Girls and Basketball," Your Boy and Your Girl [column], *Olean (NY) Evening Times*, November 19, 1931, 7; "Experts Say Interschool Games of Basketball Menace Girls' Health," *Times Herald* (Olean, NY); December 23, 1930, 11; and "Athletics for Girls: Abstract from Report of Advisory Committee from the School Journal," *Wellsboro (PA) Gazette*, November 23, 1927, 7.

Chapter 7

Lucille's personal writings provided the basis for this chapter. Additional information about OPC came from Anne Semple, *Ties That Bind: The Story of Oklahoma Presbyterian College* (n.p., n.d., ca. 1957), 25–50; Virginia Hamilton Childers, *Bryan County Genealogy Library*, Bryan County History (Durant, OK: Bryan County Heritage Association, 1983), 68–79; and "To Aunt Lucy," *Polished Pebbles*, December 1931, 4. Description of play based on girls' rules was enhanced by reading Bertha Frank Teague, *Basketball for Girls* (New York: Ronald Press, 1962), 163–72; and Handley Cross, "Six Girls and a Basket," *Sport Story Magazine*, March 15, 1939, 46–52. The final scene with Lucille and the others eating candy before bed was constructed from Lucille's writings and interviews with the other players. They were still wondering how Babb had lost his leg when I met them decades later.

Chapter 8

The Christmas barnstorm was chronicled in articles from the *Durant (OK) Daily Democrat* and the *Houston Post* pasted into personal scrapbooks from Doll, Lucille, and Virginia Hamilton Childers. Information about Alice Humbarger was available in the *Bismarck (ND) Tribune*, December 26, 1931, 10, and the *Sandusky (OH) Register*, December 30, 1931, 6.

I accessed the Texas State Historical Association's *Handbook of Texas* online, "East Texas Oilfield," at http://www.tshaonline.org/handbook/online/articles /doe01 (accessed March 3, 2014). I traveled across 1930s Texas roads via the Texas State Library and Archives Division, Official Map of the Highway System of Texas, 1936, https://www.tsl.texas.gov/cgi-bin/aris/maps/maplookup.php?mapnum =6193 (accessed March 3, 2014). The *Durant (OK) Daily Democrat* inspired readers with its coverage of the road trip: "Cardinals' Basketball Christmas Schedule"; "Let's Get behind the Cardinals and Give Them a Boost"; "O.P.C. Cardinals Win First Game on Trip by 29 to 5 Score"; Cardinals Take Fast Game from Houston 6"; Cardinals Again Win from Houston Green Devils by 39–16 Score."

Player scrapbooks contained the write-ups about OPC's big defeat of the Green Devils in these Johnny Lyons's articles in the *Houston Post-Dispatch*: "Green Devils Will Play Durant Team at Reagan Tonight"; "Green Devils Are Defeated"; and "Durant Girls Show Speed in Texas Win."

Chapter 9

The *Durant (OK) Daily Democrat* continued its fine coverage of the Cardinal games: "Cardinals Defeat Jasper Independents 111 to 4 as They Continue Onslaught," December 31, 1931, 1; "Cardinals Add 59–12 Victory over Texaco Team at Port Arthur," December 31, 1931, 2; "Cardinals Make Fine Record on Road Trip," January 7, 1932, 2. "Carinals [*sic*] Win 15th and Last Game on Trip Defeating Athens 41–20," January 14, 1932, 6; "Conquering Cardinals Given Royal Reception."

Information about Doll and Babb's relationship (along with Doll's friendship with Toka Lee) was constructed from personal interviews and Doll's keepsakes. Rumor had it that Babb and Doll's high school coach, Mr. Daily, were writing a book about coaching girls' basketball, but I never found any manuscript. Toka Lee and Doll stayed good friends throughout their lives and passed away within six months of each other.

Fortunately, the Women's Division was prolific when it came to public relations. "The function of the Women's Division was not to conduct or organize any activities or to supervise the projects carried on in the field. It was interested rather in planting ideas which other could bring to fruition," quoted in Alice Allene Sefton, *The Women's Division: National Amateur Athletic Federation: Sixteen Years of Progress in Athletics for Girls and Women, 1923–1939*, (Stanford, CA: Stanford University Press, 1941), 1–8. See also the section attributed to Ethel Bowers titled

"Travel and Gate Receipts," 24–26; Sefton's discussion of conferences, 29–40; field work, 40; publications, 41–43; and publicity, 51–55.

Other information for this chapter was gleaned from *Women and Athletics, compiled and edited by the Women's Division, National Amateur Athletic Federation* (New York: A. S. Barnes, 1930). Many of its chapters discussed the inevitable failure of men who coached women and the bad influence of gate receipts. See "Competition," 39–41 (no author available); Agnes R. Wayman, "Play Problems of Girls," 42–44, a published speech that Wayman was said to have given in every state. Additional information about the state of college athletics came from "Raps Intercollegiate Athletics for Women," *Ludington (MI) Daily News*, April 1, 1931, 6. I found details about the nickname injunction in "It's Babe to You: Texas Girl Athlete Insists Name Is Birthright," *Journal News* (Hamilton, OH), December 15, 1931, 25.

When I visited the Crescent Hotel in Eureka Springs, Arkansas, it had been thoroughly modernized (but still advertised its hauntings). The following sources helped me accurately re-create the old Crescent Hotel and the women's college it housed: "Crescent College and Conservatory," *Encyclopedia of Arkansas History and Culture*, http://www.encyclopediaofarkansas.net/encyclopedia/entry-detail.aspx?entryID=5618 (accessed May 28, 2014); "Crescent College and Conservancy for Women," Lost Womyn's Space, June 1, 2011, http://lostwomynsspace.blogspot.com/2011/06/crescent-college-and-conservancy-for.html; Beth Campbell, The Very Idea! [daily column], *Springfield (MO) Leader*, July 28, 1930, 10. Campbell compared Eureka Springs to Switzerland in a travel piece.

I read about Arkansas basketball and Quinnie Hamm in "From the UCA Archives: A brief history of women's basketball," *Log Cabin Democrat* (Conway, AR) at http://thecabin.net/sports/college/2011-11-13/uca-archives-brief-history-women's-basketball#.VGe4v95NLoe; and "One of Country's Best Court Clubs Here January 27: The Famous Crescent College Comets of Eureka Springs with Quinnie Hamm, Captain, to Appear on Gentry Court," *Journal-Advance* (Gentry, AR) January 22, 1931, 1. Bo-Peep's heroic effort while driving down the hill came alive with each recounting from players. The Dunford twins loved to joke about Babb and how strict he was, which led to their emotional reaction to his demand that they stay in Durant and practice instead of going home for the remainder of the break. To Vick, Babb's stern demands were no joke. But they all enjoyed the party he gave them before they left for home. Babb drove west to Mangum so often that the *Polished Pebbles* published a column advising him to "run a bus," since he dropped off his players along the way.

Chapter 10

Information about Colbert's Ferry is from the website of the Oklahoma Historical Society, Encyclopedia of Oklahoma History and Culture, http://digital.library .okstate.edu/encyclopedia/entries/c/coo18.html (accessed May 28, 2014). I reconstructed each contentious move made by Texas's and Oklahoma's governors in the Red River Bridge War with the help of the following sources: "Bridge Controversy Is Hot: Murray's Action Expected to Bring Bridge Controversy to Some Early Solution," *Corsicana (TX) Daily Sun*, Jul 17, 1931, 1. "Bridge Controversy Is Hot: Texas and Oklahoma at Outs over Opening Red River Crossings," *Corsicana (TX) Daily Sun*, July 17, 1931, 1; "Battle Rages over Bridges at Red River," *The Jacksonville (IL) Daily Journal*, July 18, 1931, 1. "Battle between Texas, Oklahoma Rages Once More," *Times Herald* (Olean, NY), July 21, 1931, 9; "Free Bridge Is Opened Today: Barriers Removed from Texas Side of Structure Quickly," *Corsicana (TX) Daily Sun*, July 24, 1931, 3. "Martial Law Being Enforced in Oklahoma," *Delphos (OH) Daily Herald*, July 24, 1931, 1. "Murray Defies Federal Order Opening Bridge," *Iola Register (KS)*, July 25, 1931, 1: "Murray Extends Martial Law Zone of River Bridge Dispute; Returns to Capital," *The Taylor (TX) Daily Press*, July 27, 1931, 1; "Durant Boosters Here Wednesday with Brass Band," *Indian Journal* (Eufala, OK), July 30, 1931, 1; "National Affairs: The Red River War," *Time*, August 3, 1931, http://content.time.com/time/magazine/article/0,9171,846934,00.html.

Will Rogers' humor was a great comfort to many during the Depression. His collection of telegrams can be found at James M. Smallwood and Steven K. Gragert, eds., *Will Rogers' Daily Telegrams*, vol. 2, *The Hoover Years 1929–1931* (Stillwater: Oklahoma University Press, 1978), http://www.willrogers.com/papers/daily /DT-Vol-2.pdf (accessed March 10, 2014).

Polished Pebbles had a brief description of OPC's celebration of its basketball wins on the road. I assembled Doll's thoughts on her looks from her scrapbook. She also loved to dance. In later life, when high schools quit having girls' basketball teams in the 1950s, she taught science and coached the dance team pep squad that ended up winning a national championship (of course). The conversation about her between her teammates was gleaned from my interviews. In addition to Doll's scrapbooks and memorabilia, information included also came from interviews with Margaret Seaton and Joyce Rice, Doll's personal friends.

I got to know the famous Didrikson and the Golden Cyclones by reading Linda Ford, "Babe Didrikson & the Golden Cyclones," in *Lady Hoopsters: A History of Women's Basketball in America* (Northampton, MA: Half Moon Books,

1999), 70–72; Roxanne M. Albertson, "Basketball Texas Style, 1910–1933: School to Industrial League Competition," in Joan S. Hult and Marianna Trekell, eds., *A Century of Women's Basketball: From Frailty to Final Four* (Reston, VA: American Alliance for Health, Physical Education, Recreation and Dance, 1991), 155–66, esp. 160–64; Susan E. Cayleff, *Babe: The Life and Legend of Babe Didrikson Zaharias* (Champaign: University of Illinois Press, 1995), 50–77; and Bill Parker, "Babe Didrikson Dominates the Women's Olympic Track Squad," *Miami (OK) Daily News-Record*, January 18, 1932, 5. Cyclone AAU victories in 1931 were described in "Sport Notes by Paul Moore," *Corsicana (TX) Daily Sun*, March 30, 1931, 9; "Strong Teams to Play at Girls' Dallas Tourney," *Pampa (TX) Daily News*, February 7, 1932, 4. Sun Oilers beat OPC at Dallas tournament: "Wichita Girls Win in Quarter Finals," *Albuquerque Journal*, March 27, 1931, 3.

The following provided enormous insight into the exciting matchup between the Cardinals and the Cyclones: *Collegian*, vol. 2, nos. 14–16, January 14 and 21, February 11, 1932. Scrapbook clippings from the *Durant (OK) Daily Democrat*: "THOSE CARDINALS!"; "Doll Harris Stars in O.P.C. Threat"; and "Cardinals Defeat National Champs 33 to 28 to Take 21st Straight Game." Other clippings include "Durant Girls Beat Champs," *Daily Oklahoman* (Oklahoma City), February 11, 1932, 11; "Oklahoma Presbyterian Girls to Enter Tourney," *The Daily Ardmoriete* (Ardmore, OK), February 16, 1932.

Chapter 11

The rematch against the Cyclones was described in an undated scrapbook clipping titled "Cardinals off to Meet Golden Cyclones Again," from an unknown newspaper; and "Cyclones Face Strong Durant Sextet at Fair Park Court Saturday Night" and "Cardinals Come from Behind to Defeat Cyclones by 22–21 Score," both from the *Dallas Morning News*.

I discovered how KWKH, with Henderson at its helm, was like a fifty-thousand-watt beacon during the Depression with Margery Land May, "Hello-World Henderson" *Independent Record* (Helena, MT), April 7, 1929, 19; Robert Mack, "Henderson Asks for More Power," *Harrisburg (PA) Telegraph*, April 8, 1930, 2; "'Hello-World' Henderson Has Broadcast Way to Popularity with Many Thousands," *Tipton (IN) Tribune*, February 8, 1930, 7; Faded Signals: A Celebration of Broadcast History in Pictures and Sounds, http://fadedsignals.com/post /38588182990/kwkh-signed-on-the-air-in-1926-from-shreveport (accessed June 19, 2014); Clifford J. Doerksen, "Chapter 5: That Doggone Radio Man," excerpt from *American Babel: Rogue Radio Broadcasters of the Jazz Age*, American Radioworks: Hearing America, A Century of Music on the Radio, http://american radioworks.publicradio.org/features/radio/e1.html (accessed June 19, 2014).

My scene between Babb and Atha grew from family history (more like gossip) but seemed fitting. By this time, most of the players had a keen interest in team publicity. I constructed the scene in which they read about the Cyclones from interview notes as well as the following sources: "Rival Queens of Basketball," *Literary Digest*, March 13, 1932. The other newspapers that published this article were "Dallas Damsels Dominate Girls Cage Tourneys," *Courier News* (Blytheville, AR), February 10, 1932, 6; "Damsels Dominate Down in Dear Old Dallas," *Reading (PA) Times*, March 10, 1932, 11; "Dallas Dolls Dominate Darned Regularly," *Santa Cruz (CA) Evening News*, February 20, 1932, 1–3.

Newspaper clipping from Doll's scrapbook titled "O.P.C. Cardinals Guests of Lions Club Help Entertainment" told about her speech to the businessmen. Also, scrapbook clippings from the *Durant (OK) Daily Democrat*: "THOSE CARDINALS!" "Doll Harris Stars in O.P.C. Threat" and "Cardinals Defeat National Champs 33 to 28 to Take 21st Straight Game" describe the Cardinals' vibrant reputation throughout Durant.

The scenes at OPC and about Hotchkin's illness grew from player scrapbooks, personal interviews, and Lucille's personal writings, *Collegian*, vol. 2, nos. 14–16, January 14 and 21, February 11, 1932; and Anne Semple, *Ties That Bind: The Story of Oklahoma Presbyterian College* (n.d., ca. 1957), 45–50, who described the school's financial woes that led to Babb taking on even more fund-raising responsibility.

The scene where Vera sprained her ankle was a wonderfully funny moment during my interviews with Lera and Vera. La Homa recounted the nasty fight on court between the men's teams when she first caught sight of the man she would eventually marry. The Wichita matchup was also described in Doll's scrapbook clippings from the *Wichita (KS) Eagle*: "Nation's Outstanding Girls Teams Will Play in Feat . . . : Only Meeting between Clubs of Season Scheduled Here"; "Fist Fight Provides Wild Scene in Wichita Victory; Durant Beats Thurstons"; and "Henrys Lose Fight Decision but Wallop Hupp Cagers." The announcement that the national championship was being moved from Dallas to Shreveport was taken from a scrapbook clipping from the *Dallas Morning News* with a partial title that read "Dallas Salesmanship Club Turns Down National; Local People Balk at Giving Bulk of Receipts to A.A.U. Meet Is Moved to Shreveport."

Chapter 12

Babb fought for women to play a better game of basketball throughout his life. His thoughts depicted in this chapter were gleaned from an article that appeared in the *Edmonton (AB) Journal* around June 13, 1933, titled "Would Blacklist Edmonton as Basketball Centre." OPC had just beaten the famous Edmonton Grads in a best three out of five matchup, and outraged Edmonton fans raced onto the court, similar to what happened in Wichita. The entire article quoted Babb.

To wade through the maze of rule changes in the early days of women's basketball, I was guided by Susan K. Cahn, *Coming on Strong: Gender and Sexuality in Twentieth-Century Women's Sport* (Cambridge, MA: Harvard University Press, 1994), 94; and Joanna Davenport, "The Tides of Change in Women's Basketball Rules," in *A Century of Women's Basketball: From Frailty to Final Four*, ed. Joan S. Hult and Marianna Trekell (Reston, VA: American Alliance for Health, Physical Education, Recreation and Dance, 1991), 83–108, esp. 86–89, 94–101.

Specific information about the relationship between the AAU and the CWB came from several sources, including letter from L. Di Benedetto, AAU secretary-treasurer, to Grace Davies, member of the Women's National Basketball Committee, February 16, 1933; letter from Eline von Borries, CWB chairman, to J. Lyman Bingham, assistant to the AAU president, April 28, 1931; letter from Dorothy Folsom, active member of the Illinois Women's Athletic Club of Chicago and the AAU, to von Borries, November 6, 1931; and a report on the changing women's rules, "AAU Rules Changes: Committee on Women's Basketball Report to A.P.E.A. Council," Cleveland, 1934. Robert W. Ikard wrote about Mrs. Van Blarcom in *Just for Fun: The Story of AAU Women's Basketball* (Fayetteville: University of Arkansas Press, 2005), 43 and 132.

The section on the Women's Division and its boycott of the Olympic games draws from Associated Press, "Women's Division and the Olympic Games: Opposes Women's Entry into Next Olympic Games," *Freeport (IL) Journal-Standard*, January 4, 1929, 14; "Women's Body Raps Olympics," *The San Bernardino (CA) Sun*, May 30, 1930, 15; "Mable Lee Says Women Athletes Striving for an Athletic Democracy," *Lincoln (NE) Evening Journal*, July 23, 1932, 8; and Alice Allene Sefton, *The Women's Division: National Amateur Athletic Federation* (Stanford, CA: Stanford University Press, 1941), 55–58.

Information about the Cardinals' bumpy road to Shreveport and other preparations came from personal stories (especially from the Dunford twins and Virginia Hamilton) and these sources: *Bulletin of Oklahoma Presbyterian College for Girls*, 1932–1933 (copy obtained from player memorabilia); "Cardinals Settle Down to Strenuous Practice," *Durant (OK) Daily Democrat*, March 3, 1932, 4; "Cardinals Off for Shreveport for Tournament," *Durant (OK) Daily Democrat*, March 24, 1932; *Collegian*, no. 14. I also relied on scrapbook clippings from the *Durant (OK) Daily Democrat*: "Cardinals Are Guests of the Rotary Club," "Cardinals Will Be Sent to Tournament by City of Durant," "Cardinals Are Primed for Go with Dallas Six," and "Presbyterian College Team has 26 Straight Victories," "O.P.C. Cardinals Meet Dallas Shoe Girls Here Tuesday," and "Durant Six Closes with 27th in Row."

Chapter 13

I gathered information from several sources to re-create the atmosphere surrounding the national tournament in Shreveport. These include the Women's National AAU Basketball Tournament promotional publication, March 1932 (from scrapbooks); a photograph of the Louisiana State Fair Coliseum, https://www.flickr.com/photos/98728033@N08/10313557735/; (accessed July 12, 2014); "Abandoned Rails of Shreveport Union Station," http://www.abandonedrails.com/Shreveport_Union_Station Downtown (accessed July 10, 2014); "Shreveport: Our History in Pictures," http://downtownshreveport.com/history/our-history-in-pics/ (accessed July 10, 2014).

Some of the following newspaper articles were found in scrapbooks and did not contain any publication information; some did contain dates. Glancing around with Flint Dupre [sports column], *Shreveport (LA) Times*, March 1932; "National Cage Meet Opens Monday: Six Games Will Be Played First Day in Girls' Tournament"; Otis Harris, As We Were Saying [sports column]; Bill Parker, "Girl Loopers Open Tourney: Lopsided Scores Feature Start of Nat'l Meet at Shreveport," *Abilene (TX) Reporter-News*, March 22, 1932, 2. The reproduction of the AAU letter from Grover C. Thames was copied from the one that came from Doll's scrapbook.

I attended the tournament each day aided by the following sources (most articles were pasted in Doll's scrapbook without a masthead): T. Raymond Sage, "Cage Champions of Dallas Score Easy Win; Louisiana Representatives Defeated," *Shreveport (LA) Times*; "Houston Girls Again Victors in U.S. Meet"; Bill Parker, "Durant, Tulsa Girls Victors in U.S. Meet: Two State Teams Forge to A.A.U. Quarterfinals at Shreveport," *Oklahoman* (Oklahoma City), March 23, 1932, 12; "Cardinals Swamp Kansas Sextet to Go into Quarter Finals," *Durant (OK)*

Daily Democrat; Louis Cox, "Cyclones to Clash with Randolph Six in Wednesday Melee," Down the Amateur Alley [column], publication unknown; Cotton McCoy, "4 Leaders Survive at Coliseum," *Shreveport (LA) Journal*; "Durant Girls Reach Semifinal Round in Fast Play at Shreveport: Favorites Go through Tests as Scheduled," publication unknown; Bill Parker, "Girls' Basket Meet Near End: National A.A.U. Semi-Finalists Almost Same as Last Year," *Miami (OK) Daily News-Record*, March 24, 1932, 5; Bill Parker, "Durant Lassies Defeat Wichita," *Daily Ardmoreite* (Ardmore, OK), March 25, 1932.

My description of the beauty contest came from personal stories from the players and Cotton McCoy, "Shreveport Will Have 5 Entrants: Play in A.A.U. Tournament Advanced to Quarter-Finals," *Shreveport (LA) Journal*, March 23, 1932, 10; "Don't Crowd Us Men! Beauty Reigns Today in Big Cage Tourney," publication unknown; "Miss Lockett Named Beauty Queen," *Shreveport (LA) Times*, March 24, 1932, 9; "Girls in Athletics," publication unknown; "Brunette Beauty Queen," *Corsicana (TX) Semi-Weekly Light*, March 28, 1930, 2. Gossip about sports writers describing female players' bodies was in "Sports Slant," *The Hutchinson News*, February 5, 1929, 7; Susan K. Cahn, *Coming on Strong: Gender and Sexuality in Twentieth-Century Women's Sport* (Cambridge, MA: Harvard University Press, 1994), 95; and Susan E. Cayleff, *Babe: The Life and Legend of Babe Didrikson Zaharias* (Champaign: University of Illinois Press, 1995), 91.

Events at the free-throw contest were drawn from "Kansas Girl Leads in Free-Throwing Contest," *Shreveport (LA) Times*, March 24, 1932, 10; Helen Carney, "Girl Who Leads in Goal Shooting Castor Product," *Shreveport (LA) Times*, March 24, 1932, 9; "Shreveport Girl Crowned Queen of Goal Makers," *Shreveport (LA) Times*, March 24, 1932, 11; and "Shreveport Girls Sets Free Throw Record," *Shreveport (LA) Journal*, March 23, 1932, 10.

Vick told me about her run-in with Babb in our telephone interview, and I don't think she ever forgave him.

My depiction of Henderson's KWKH interview with the Cardinals was constructed from personal stories and other sources, including "O.P.C. Court Stars Speak over Radio," publication unknown; Victor Murdock, "Victor Murdock Learns How Babb Can Direct Winning Cage Team," *Wichita (KS) Eagle*.

Margery Land May, "Hello-World Henderson," *Independent Record* (Helena, MT), April 7, 1929, 19; "Henderson Asks for More Power," *Harrisburg (PA) Telegraph*, April 8, 1930, 2; "'Hello-World' Henderson Has Broadcast Way to Popularity with Many Thousands," *Tipton (IN) Tribune*, February 8, 1930, 7; Faded Signals: A Celebration of Broadcast History in Pictures and Sounds, http://fadedsignals.com/post/38588182990/kwkh-signed-on-the-air-in-1926-from -shreveport (accessed June 19, 2014); and Clifford J. Doerksen, "Chapter 5: That Doggone Radio Man," excerpt from *American Babel: Rogue Radio Broadcasters of the Jazz Age*, American Radioworks: Hearing America, A Century of Music on the Radio, http://americanradioworks.publicradio.org/features/radio/e1.html (accessed June 19, 2014).

The OPC school song was found in Lucille's "Oklahoma Presbyterian College for Girls" school booklet.

Chapter 14

I gleaned the conversation in the opening scene from my interviews, scrapbooks, and Lucille's personal writings. The quote about Babe came from Helen Carney, "Coach Who Brought Babe Didrikson to Front as Athlete Gives All Credit to Great Girl: Girl Developed on Given Chance in Various Sports," *Shreveport (LA) Times*, March 25, 1932, 11. Additional information came from T. Raymond Sage, "Dallas, Oklahoma Cagers Fight Way to Championship Round of National Tourney," *Shreveport (LA) Times*, March 25, 1932, 11; "Durant Seeks 33rd Win in National Title," *Durant (OK) Daily Democrat*, March 25, 1932, page unknown; and Bill Parker, "A.A.U. Title Honors to be Game's Stake," publication unknown.

Lucille's writings and personal interviews, plus the following sources, helped me construct the play-by-play between the Cardinals and the Cyclones. T. Raymond Sage, "Oklahoma Presbyterian College Girls Win National . . . : Dallas Squad Dethroned in Great Contest Decided by Margin of Three Points," *Shreveport (LA) Times*, March 26, 1932, 13–14; Bill Parker for the Associated Press, "Oklahoma Lassies Win National Cage Title Shreveport: First Time in Five Years Dallas Teams Have Not Held the Honors," *Corsicana (TX) Daily Sun*, March 26, 1932, 9; "Valliant O.P.C. Girls Come from behind Twice to Defeat Champs 35 to 33," *Durant (OK) Daily Democrat*, March 1932. "1,000 Calls Received on Cardinal Game," *Durant (OK) Daily Democrat*; and Cotton McCoy, "Oklahomans End Texas Monopoly," *Shreveport (LA) Journal*, March 26, 1932, 13.

Chapter 15

I wouldn't have been able to write about the final celebration without Vetrus Hampton, "The Cardinals Bring Home the Bacon," *Harlow's Weekly: A Journal of Comments and Current Events (Oklahoma City, OK)*, April 16, 1932, 8–9. In addition, I consulted "Durant Honors A.A.U. Champs," *Miami (OK) Daily News-Record*, March 27, 1932, 4; "Durant's National Champs Compiled 31 Straight Wins," *Durant (OK) Daily Democrat*; "Royal Welcome Is Given Girl Cage Title-holders," *Durant (OK) Daily Democrat*; and "Cardinals Close Victorious Season," *Polished Pebbles*, 1932, 4.

Doll's scrapbook prominently displayed the Associated Press article "Doll Harris New Queen of Country's Girl Basketball Players . . . ," April 1, 1932; and the scrapbook also contained the memorabilia and letter I quoted in this chapter. An account of Babb's marriage was in "Member of O.P.C. Faculty Marries at Ardmore," *Polished Pebbles*, 1932, 2.

Descriptions of the beginning of the next season came from personal interviews and "Doll Harris and Basket Team Seek New Victims," *Hutchinson (KS) News*, January 24, 1933, 2. During my interviews with players, I uncovered the story about Babe Didrikson's visit to OPC the fall of 1932. The final quote came from Lloyd Gregory, "Just a Bunch of Country Girls Who Won the National Basket Ball Championship," Looking 'Em Over, *Houston Post-Dispatch*.

Epilogue

My family and I attended the Sports Hall of Fame ceremony in 2003, and my mother accepted the award for Uncle Sam. Generous stories from friends and relatives along with local obituaries provided details about how the players lived out their lives. The final quote from Lucille Thurman Berry came from her unpublished autobiography, "The Way the Ball Bounces! Or Swish Went the Net! Or My Name Is in the Hall of Fame."

DUST BOWL GIRLS

★ ★ ★

Kicking Up More Dust:
Dust Bowl Girls and the Epic Battle
for Women's Right to Be Athletic Badasses

Questions for Discussion

Kicking Up More Dust
Dust Bowl Girls and the Epic Battle
for Women's Right to Be Athletic Badasses

by Lydia Reeder

When I was nine or ten, I would sit for hours watching men's basketball (women's basketball had yet to debut on TV). I even told Mom, who loved the game, too, that I wanted muscular legs just like those male athletes. She looked at me as if I had announced that I was from another planet.

"Girls aren't supposed to look like that," she said.

"Why not?" I asked.

"It's just not ladylike."

We've come a long way since that conversation with my mother: women's sports have grown more competitive and popular. Interest in the 2015 Women's World Cup rose 121 percent over 2011. The six matches that featured the U.S. team averaged 5.3 million viewers; the final game, the United States against Japan, drew more than 20 million viewers. According to a study sponsored by the USC Center for Feminist Research, 294,000 high school girls played interscholastic sports in 1971. Today, 3.1 million play, much closer to the 4.4 million boys participating in high school sports.

Title IX prohibits discrimination on the basis of sex in any federally funded education program or activity. And yet, even today, top athletes like Serena Williams and Simone Biles are disparaged for their looks. According to the Tucker Center for Research on Girls and Women in Sports, female athletes are much more likely than male athletes to be portrayed in sexually provocative poses. It's heartbreaking and infuriating and not all that different from what women experienced decades ago.

I've spent the last several years researching the Oklahoma Presbyterian College (OPC) Cardinals, a women's basketball team from the 1930s, for my book *Dust Bowl Girls*. So when I read about Williams being mocked as too masculine, I thought of how Babe Didrikson, one of America's greatest athletes and the OPC Cardinals' toughest opponent back in 1932, was described as boyish-looking, with the manners of a rancher's hired hand. And it wasn't just sportswriters who criticized her for her appearance. School teachers did, too.

Back when the OPC Cardinals were winning games, top female athletes had to put aside their own fears about being publicly ridiculed to pursue excellence in the sports they loved. These athletes were pioneers exploring new territory that had been claimed by only men. And, they had powerful enemies.

Instead of being passionate mentors for young athletes, women who were influential physical educators fought to outlaw women's competitive sports altogether. They launched a national campaign that resembled a religious revival aimed at eliminating aggressive team sports and saving the feminine souls of American girls. Their leader was Lou Henry Hoover, First Lady of the United States of America.

According to Hoover, young women should repress any desires to be star athletes because they were not "pioneers enough to discover their own possibilities." In other words, a girl shouldn't work too hard to get good at anything, because by her very nature she didn't have, and would never develop, the courage, power, and self-knowledge to succeed. Hoover labeled the general tendency to copy boys' athletics with an emphasis on setting records and having championships "a cancer that must be killed."

This dark philosophy, that girls and women can't be trusted to be in charge of their own bodies and lives, continues today. *It* has become the cancer that makes girls hate how they look or question their own abilities.

Even though millions of girls and women play sports every day, with tens of thousands competing in college and professional athletics, television coverage of women's sports is sparse: media coverage of women's sports in 2014 was only 2 to 3 percent. Hollywood has consistently overlooked stories about epic female athletes like Babe Didrikson, Jackie Joyner-Kersee, or the United States' phenomenal 1999 Women's World Cup Soccer champs. Compared to the barrage of information about male athletes, news about women's accomplishments, past and present, is vague and distorted.

We must do better.

We must embrace the emerging cultural norm about women athletes that buries outdated ideas about femininity. We need to know more about the champion swimmers; track stars; basketball, softball, soccer, and hockey teams; dogsled racers, golfers, and the myriad others who have plainly established that women are winners. Historic champions like the OPC Cardinals and current badasses like the Williams sisters, Ali Krieger, Simone Biles, Ali Raisman, and Sue Bird should be celebrated, not for their hairstyles, clothing, or makeup, but for their pioneering spirit, perseverance, and athletic prowess. By inspiring young girls to strive for greatness, they are winning that epic battle, started years ago, for the right to have strong bodies and even stronger spirits.

Reprinted with permission from *Bustle*

QUESTIONS FOR DISCUSSION

1. Before reading *Dust Bowl Girls*, did you know that women played highly competitive basketball in the 1930s? What aspects of the game surprised you the most compared to women's basketball today?

2. Sam Babb had a disability that he had lived with since he was a teenager. How do you think that affected his personality? Do you think it contributed to his becoming a psychology professor or even a basketball coach? Why or why not?

3. After Title IX passed in 1972, women gained equal rights to educational programs, including athletics. How do you think sports, including basketball, have changed for women since 1972? If Title IX had been in existence in 1931, how would the Cardinals' circumstances have changed?

4. "Covering the court like a red plague, the Oklahoma Presbyterian Cardinals completely annihilated Houston's home team," Toka Lee Fields read to her beaming teammates (page 129) from an article that appeared in the *Houston Post-Dispatch* sports section. Sportswriters seemed to fall in love with the young team. Were you surprised by the level of coverage women's basketball received? How did the sportswriters depict the women athletes on teams, particularly when it came to femininity? Did Babe Didrikson

receive the same type of publicity as the Cardinal players? How was she different?

5. Didrikson's team, the national-champion Dallas Golden Cyclones, was sponsored by Employers Casualty, a successful insurance company. The underdog Cardinals beat the Golden Cyclones twice during regular season play, with Doll Harris scoring a phenomenal twenty-seven points in one game. Why were the Cardinals able to beat the Golden Cyclones? How did the "gift of teamwork" (page 171) help Doll and the Cardinals win? Or what do you think gave them the edge?

6. Doll Harris is described as having "Bull-dog tenacity" by her high school coach (page 55). What characteristics made her a good leader and which aspects of her personality do you think caused problems for the Cardinals?

7. Coach Babb had a strict set of rules that the team had to follow during the season. Were Babb's rules—including a policy against sweets and a 10 p.m. curfew—over the top? How do you think they compare to today's standards for college athletes?

8. All of the Cardinal players kept scrapbooks full of clipped newspaper articles and keepsakes like ticket stubs, tournament brochures, and personal letters. What role do primary and secondary sources play in telling this story?

9. At the end of *Dust Bowl Girls*, Sam Babb is being interviewed by the sports editor of the *Houston Post-Dispatch*, who describes the Cardinals as "pretty and attractive," adding that "their speed and grace is amazing" (page 255). In turn, Babb describes his players as "just a bunch of country girls who like to play basketball." Why would Babb downplay the Cardinals' exceptional athletic abilities and emphasize their ordinariness? Was it strategic? Do you think that's how he really felt?

ANDY NEWBURG

For LYDIA REEDER, this is a family story: Coach Sam Babb is her great-uncle. A former associate editor at *Whole Life Times* in Los Angeles and *Delicious Magazine* in Boulder, Colorado, she lives in Denver with her husband.